# ~ *Comments from People Like You* ~

**The following are a few comments from some of the many people who applied what they learned from these instructions and teachings. They were able to rapidly experience how to command their world with exactness and even put a date on it!**

"This knowledge is contagious and easy to implement in all areas of my life. The simple, precise and personal directions have empowered me to overcome difficult circumstances. I have become a goal setting, budget busting, award-winning employee."
—**Sandra Adragna**, *Senior Accounts Exec. Entertainment Publications, Tucson, AZ*

"These are lessons we were born knowing to be true. So, I will say this: These little reminders rocked my world and dramatically changed how I view life and how I travel through it. I am happier than I have ever been."
—**Kevin DeCook**, *Sales Person, Model, College Student, Happy Individual, Tucson, AZ*

"As a young girl I was moved by the song 'Let There be Peace on Earth and Let it Begin with Me.' Through applying Pamela Ann's teachings, I now know how to let it begin with me. Scriptures and things I have studied finally make sense."
—**Leslie Whitman**, *Hair Stylist, Tucson, AZ*

"If you really do desire a change, you have to ask for it with your heart and feel it deep inside. Thank you for all that you've done to help me understand how to ask for better things. And thank you

for being so awesome. I've been blessed to have met you."
—**Juan Rauda**, *PC Repair & Service Specialist, Juarez, Chihuahua, Mexico*

"The stories and lessons have blessed my life and brought me joy as I incorporate the simple principles taught."
—**Jennifer Barney**, Married, *Mother of 7 children, Gilbert, AZ*

"Through Pamela Ann's teachings, I now see my world and those around me through new eyes. I am more understanding and aware of other's actions and choices. Now, even when something may initially appear negative, I can consistently see the deeper value of the experience and view it in a positive light."
—**Shama Thathi,** *College Law Student, Tucson, AZ*

"I feel most people on this planet are unaware of their true potential to create and manifest. It is very rare we have the opportunity and pleasure of understanding our own connection with source energy. I feel this information is invaluable to humanity. If it is understood and applied, it will activate the heart love space we all deserve."
—**Mark Sanders (William),** *Owner of A Five Star Co. HVAC Contracting, Rockland, CA*

"Pamela Ann is an example of transforming life's challenges into learning experiences…It is such a joy to see her doing what she does best—inspiring others to be the best they can be."
—**Helene Gaudard-Castillo**, *Craniosacral and Licensed Massage Therapist, Tucson, AZ*

"I have had so many amazing changes happen in my life by applying the things I learn. I've also seen many other lives change for the better. Thank you Pamela Ann for all that you've taught me and continue to teach me. I Love you!"
—**Mandy Richardson,** *Nanny, Hairdresser, Oahu, HI*

"Anytime I feel like life starts to get chaotic or stressful, I always stop myself and think, 'What has Pamela Ann taught me?' and 'How can I apply it in my life NOW?' I now know I can quickly and easily command my world! It's amazing! I can honestly say it has changed my view on life. I'm so completely happy and I love it! I am grateful for the teachings Pamela Ann has shared with me."
—**Shauna Trejo**, *College student, Gilbert, AZ*

"Pamela has helped me to realize my abilities and given me the courage to enjoy them…she enables me to see all the good that this world holds for me."
—**Jerry Menichini**, *President of Best Legal Services, Inc., Philadelphia, PA*

"Without Pamela's guidance and instructions I would not have known how I could develop a personal relationship with those who created me. She also taught me that while I am united with them, I can activate eternal laws and powers so I can create the life I prefer to live. I know I never would have been able to heal this rapidly without this active faith. It would have taken me years had I continued with a therapist or counselor."
—**Claudia Artz**, *Real Estate Agent, Phoenix, AZ*

"After my first session with Pamela Ann, I was left feeling totally at peace and excited for all of the beautiful blessings life has to offer. She is a wonderful example of what you can attain no matter where you come from or what your current beliefs are. Her kind and nurturing spirit is infectious and I now feel inspired to pay it forward to others in my life. I absolutely love her and look forward to what the future holds!"
—**Michelle Miron,** *Host of BlogTalkRadio show* Love Your Life with Michelle, *Winnipeg, Manitoba, Canada*

"My deepest and most heartfelt thanks for the blessings you share…I was touched to my core…You are a most special lady, and angel for me, and I am grateful to God for bringing you into my life. I believe the blessings are from Him, but you are the most amazing spokesperson I know. Love, peace and happiness to you, amazing Lady."
—**Lanny Henderson**, *Kangan Water Distributor for AZ*

"Pamela Ann Ezell adds value and peace to others through reawaking the mind, body and spirit to their true vision and purpose. I have seen firsthand the abilities and lessons she shares for all to learn."
—**Susan Grantham**, *CEO,* Saguaro Business Associates, LLC, Saguaro Business Conferences, *Mother of 3, AZ*

"I applied for my dream job as a RN. I hadn't heard anything for 6 months and figured they had written me off. Then I was reading Pam's book and decided that I would like to get together with my 'Team' and get my perfect job. The day after I started reading her book I got a call from the hospital to interview for that perfect position that very day. I just knew they were going to love me and hire me. Two hours after the interview, they hired me! My 'Team' and I created the perfect world for me!! :)"
—**Trisha Chism**, Registered Nurse, Pediatric Hematology/ Oncology unit, Mesa, AZ

"I love the way Pamela Ann teaches us about how to deal with our trials in a positive way and looking at those as life changing experiences. She truly inspires me to be that better person and to go after what I truly desire. I am so grateful to her for the inspiration she has given to my daughter who is only in the 8th grade. I am so grateful to her for taking the time to write this book and share her feelings and experiences with the world. Thank you."
—**Shannon Bangerter**, *Married, Mother of 5, Gilbert, AZ*

"I have been continually amazed by Pamela Ann's ability to maintain an eternal perspective. Her confident, fearless attitude is, I believe, the fruits of her complete certainty in her connection to Heaven. It is inspiring. She is a seeker of truth and joy. She teaches those who will hear how to live with confidence and gratitude in the truth of their own divine connection. I have watched miracles happen as she guides troubled hearts into the light and vision that shines from that truth."
—**Janet Nelson**, *Homemaker and Community Leader (plus on call Mother, Grandmother, Neighbor and Friend!), Sandy, UT*

"We recently went through one of the most difficult challenges we've ever faced as a couple and as a family. Pam's positive counsel and energy, her insight, encouragement, and love helped us through that time. We now have a greater love for each other, and a greater understanding of the power of our thoughts and words - we have learned to create our own joy and how to work with our "Team" to make positive changes in our lives and in the lives of our children."
—**Mel & Liz Claridge**, *Tucson, AZ*

"Now that I am learning these teachings I feel I can trust again. I can also love others unconditionally. I no longer feel alone and afraid because I am in partnership with my true creator. I feel reborn…like I have been resuscitated…alive after 60 years on this earth. It is joyful, miraculous and exhilarating! It is like Pamela Ann is the love that helped me build my bridge back to God. I'm eternally grateful to her!"
—**Debbie Waters,** *Elder Caregiver, Devoted Mother and Grandmother, Salt Lake City, UT*

"Pamela Ann Ezell has been a dear friend of my family since I was young. I have witnessed her living what she teaches and it is truly amazing! I am inspired by her example and teachings and am in the process of creating a life filled with love and happiness!

I am 29 years old. I am a wife and stay at home mother to 2 darling children! Thank you Pamela Ann for your positive influence in my life! I love you so much!"
—**Kayla Eggleston**, *Homemaker, Queen Creek, AZ*

"I have known Pamela Ann since I was 6 years old. Her inspired teachings and ability to know just what you need, when you need it is truly a miracle. After working with her over the last several years I realized that I too could apply what she taught and miracles would show up in my life as well. I will forever be indebted to her for showing me the path that would help me overcome a 15-year drug addiction. That was in 1997 and my life has never been the same since."
—**Jashin Howell,** *Entrepreneur & Internet Marketer, Mesa, AZ*

"Through listening and reading some of Pamela's teachings, I have found that being and staying positive through negative situations have proven to work in my favor. I have told myself the way something will happen, I have envisioned the way something will happen, and I have witnessed that exact thing happen. It is an amazing phenomenon to realize you have a power inside of you that can influence the way your lunch break, your day or your week can play out. I have also found a sense of peace during stressful times while reading some of Pamela's stories. I find her and her message very soothing."
—**Clair Scull**, *Administrative Assistant, Portland, OR*

"I would recommend this book for people of all ages, but perhaps (as a woman in her twenties) even more for young adults and those of us who have just started trying to figure out our place in the world. It's an invaluable resource for learning how to not only think and achieve what you want your life to be like, but also in teaching you how to create your own positive energy and surround yourself with it. With all the turmoil of peer pressure in high school, and the stress of a society that encourages competition in school, work, and everyday life from a young age, this book helps look past that to creating your own happiness and positive energy. "

—**Rebecca Lane**, *Freelance Editor/Writer, Tucson, AZ*

"Even though I am only thirteen I have been deeply moved by what Pamela Ann writes, and by the topics she has spoken about. I have read some of Pamela Ann's stories and I have really grown fond of them. They have changed my life or that is, helped me change my life for the better. :) After reading and listening to Pamela Ann I have had a natural desire to follow in her footsteps and to become a motivational speaker. Pamela Ann has helped many people, including me, find answers and find our inner selves. Thank you."

—**Samantha**, *Junior High School Student*

"I came to the United States in 2009 as a refuge (from Iraq) escaping from all the violence and persecution I faced there. My life was all about studying and education. I thought the arts were a waste of time that could be used for something better. I never sang or danced before and never imagined myself doing it. But deep in my mind, I really wanted to do that.

"I had the chance to see the performance of Up With People while they were in Tucson, AZ. It is an international educational organization that travels all around the world to spread the message of peace through music and community service. I dreamed about joining them but never believed that I could be part of that. In one crazy moment I decided to apply, although I couldn't afford the tuition fee.

"Then I met Pamela at a party. We had a really uplifting conversation that cured a lot of my unhealed wounds. I discovered a lot of things about me as a person. I also learned there is a huge difference between *I want* and *I hope*."

"After my visit with Pamela, I had the confidence of making this decision; not only making the decision, but believing in it. The very next day I received a grant to join the group. Now, I know that everything is achievable if you believe in it.

"I am the first Iraqi and refugee in Up With People from the time it founded in 1965. I also sing a solo song in the show and dance and sing with the cast for the rest of the songs. I am now a person who believes that music is the best way to send the message of peace, respect, and love to all over the world.

"I would like to express my gratitude and thankfulness for my amazing friend and spiritual coach. Thank you Pamela for inspiring me."
—**Fady Sarkees**, *Dentist, Up With People Iraqi Cast Representative, from Baghdad, Iraq*

"All my life I have been told I am a child of God and I am a princess in the kingdom of God with the potential to be a queen. Listening and learning from Pam has helped me truly understand what that means. I have learned that I can create now the life and world that I desire to have. Ever since Pam has shared with me I am constantly hearing or reading talks from the leaders of the church that reinforce everything she is saying. This is proof to me that what she is saying is true. I have seen a change in my life and in the lives of my family. We have had miracles happen, and a more positive outlook on life. Thank you from the bottom of my heart Pam for opening up my eyes to a wonderful world of possibilities. Love you!"
—**Missy Carter**, *Community Leader, Mother of 8, Tucson, AZ*

# Mindset

## of

# Miracles

# Mindset of Miracles

## Create the Life You Prefer

**Instructions and Personal Stories of
How You Can Command Your Daily World
With Exactness and Even Put a Date on It!**

*Pamela Ann Ezell*

**EZ Lightning Books**               **Amazon Publishing**

EZ Lightning Books
PO Box 87052
Tucson, AZ 85754
(520) 333-6015
www.PamelaAnnEzell.com
PamelaAnn@ezlightning.com

Pamela Ann encourages the sharing of this powerful, uplifting information with others and welcomes your inquiries to do so. Please feel free to contact her so she can provide the permission you seek.

The information contained in this book is intended to be educational and not for diagnosis, prescription, or treatment of any health disorder whatsoever. This information should not replace consultation with a competent healthcare professional. The content of the book is intended to be used as an adjunct to a rational and responsible healthcare program prescribed by a healthcare practitioner. The author and publisher are in no way liable for any misuse of the material.

EZ Lightning Books is a trademark owned by EZ Lightning Enterprises Limited Liability Company.

Published through Amazon Books

Book Cover Design: Michael Claridge
Book Photography: Michael Lane
Book Layout Design: Autumn Topping
Print Ready Setup: Michael Claridge

For more information about special discounts for bulk purchases please contact EZ Lightning Enterprises Limited Liability Company.

The mission of Pamela Ann Ezell and EZ Lightning LLC is to teach others how to command their world with exactness and even put a date on it!

Remember your eternal birthright.

Awaken and activate your power
and ability to command your world
with exactness by connecting with the
Divine Beings who created you.

~ Pamela Ann ~

# ~ *Dedication* ~

This book is dedicated to the Divine Beings who created me. Because of the exquisite opportunity to experience this life, I was able to rediscover my Eternal Birthright to form with exactness the world I desire. I now have the immense joy of being able to mutually uplift and share with others our ability to purposefully live the lives we prefer through connecting to those beings.

This book is also dedicated to my husband, children, grandchildren, friends and acquaintances. These individuals have all provided rich opportunities for me to learn and grow because they were willing to come into my life and create with me.

Lastly, this book is dedicated to you. Join with me now and learn these simple eternal laws and principles. Allow yourself to easily and quickly apply them in your everyday life. Claim your Eternal Birthright and begin creating the world and the miracles you desire. Go within and connect to the Power that created you.

# ~ *Thank You* ~

To Ronnie, the love of my life…Thank you for being the magnificent man that you are as well as my eternal companion. I truly love and adore you.

You are the perfect expression of the promise I was given by the Divine when I was a lonely, heartbroken little girl, "…We will give you everything your heart desires, but especially a husband that loves you!"

If I could take all the playful, romantic and courageous novels, movies, fairy tales, poems and psalms expressing the vast, deep and abiding feelings two souls can have for each other, they would pale in comparison to what we share together.

There really is a "Happily Ever After."

# ~ *Contents* ~

## *Foreword*

## *Preface*

## Part I. Developing Your *Mindset of Miracles*

CHAPTER ONE   1

## *Steps to Prepare Your Vessel*

You Are Becoming Sleepy.................................................3
Personally Creating While Reading this Book.........................4
Some Thoughts About the Divine.....................................5

CHAPTER TWO   7

## *The Team, The Power and The Divine*

Introducing the Core Group...............................................8
Our Team Members Are Perfect in Every Way........................9
We Are All Vital to the Whole.........................................10
What Is the Divine?.....................................................10
"What If I Don't Believe In the Divine?"..............................11
They Continue To Love Us ............................................12

Additional Sources of Information......................................13
TAKE ACTION!..............................................................14

CHAPTER THREE    15

## My Quest for the
## Mindset of Miracles

Meeting My Master, My Master Teacher.........................16
Further From or Closer To the "Light".........................18
That's Your Master Teacher!.....................................20
The Perfect Plan Includes Imperfect Parents................21
TAKE ACTION! ..............................................................23

CHAPTER FOUR    25

## Feeling Alone?

The Best Kind of Flu You Can Catch...........................27
How Is This Rapid Change Possible?..........................30
Creating, Destroying or Repeating ............................31
TAKE ACTION! ..............................................................32

CHAPTER FIVE    35

## Childhood Songs

Profound Truths by Simple Means...............................35
Creating a Place for More.........................................37
Toss Out the Oars and Float!.....................................37
Which Direction Are You Steering Your Boat?............39
TAKE ACTION! ..............................................................40

CHAPTER SIX    41

# Staying Centered In Your Hurricane

A Hurricane that Responds to Our Requests .............................41
Distractions and Drama.............................................................42
Thrown Out to Greet the Chaos.................................................43
Why Those Tactics Were Never Successful................................45
I Am With The Great I Am!.......................................................45
Returning to the Center of the Hurricane.................................46
TAKE ACTION! ........................................................................47


CHAPTER SEVEN    49

# Reconnecting to Your Team

Preparing for a Long Journey....................................................50
Creating Your Road Map for Life..............................................52
The Meaning of Enthusiasm .....................................................55
Remember to Always Give Thanks ...........................................56
TAKE ACTION! ........................................................................57


CHAPTER EIGHT    59

# Four-Letter Words

What I'm Really Talking About..................................................59
The Candidate............................................................................60
Sir Galahad................................................................................63
Ten Bananas or Nine Bananas...................................................66
Self Re-Indoctrination...............................................................68
Hunkering Down or Opening Up...............................................69
"COURAGE Pamela Ann, COURAGE!".....................................70

Staying the Course..................................................71
My Eternal Truth..................................................73
It's a Conscious Decision!..................................74
TAKE ACTION! ..................................................74

CHAPTER NINE   75

# Creating Only Harmonious Relationships

OK, Go Ahead and Give It a Try..................................76
Keep the BIG Picture Perspective..............................78
Practicing What I Teach..................................81
A Shift in My Soul..................................83
TAKE ACTION! ..................................................84

CHAPTER TEN   87

# Still Have a Hitch in Your Giddy Up?

A Plan of Action to Restore Our Lives..................................87
Restoring My Personal Joy..................................89
Forgiving Ourselves and All Others..................................90
The Misery of Living the Lie..................................91
Restoring Others..................................93
Recommit to Keeping Your Personal Honor..................94
The Basic Steps to Restoring Your Personal Joy..................95
Every Experience Is Ultimately For Our Good..................95
TAKE ACTION! ..................................................96

# Part II: Personal Stories of Applying Our Mindset of Miracles

# It's Only Slightly Breezy Now

Only Win-Win Situations.................................................100
Promises to Keep and Mouths to Feed..........................101
The Reawakening...........................................................102
Keep That Good Feeling................................................103
"Go Help Chef Mickey Set Up!"....................................104
I Have a Wonderful Feeling...........................................106
Creating the Same World Over and Over.......................107
Activating the Plan to Shift Someday into *Now*!............109
Your Treasure Trove of Truth........................................111
TAKE ACTION! ............................................................112

# The Watch, The Washer and The Window

"What am I to Learn From These Experiences?"..............114
Discord and Disharmony...............................................115
The Gift.......................................................................116
Feeling Sleepy and Irritated.........................................118
The Perfect Ending to an Amazing Weekend.................124
Thumbs Up..................................................................125
TAKE ACTION #1! .......................................................126
TAKE ACTION #2! .......................................................126

# Do You Have a New Kitten?

Sharing a Plan for Our Increased Happiness..................127
Is It a "He" or a "She?".................................................130

Creating Precisely What We Prefer.................................132
TAKE ACTION!.................................................133

CHAPTER FOURTEEN    135

## Skittles and Emma

Feelings of Contention........................................136
Undaunted, She Persisted......................................137
TAKE ACTION!.................................................138

CHAPTER FIFTEEN    139

## "¿Qué Prefiere...12c o 3d?"

Following My Impressions......................................140
Averting a Volcanic Eruption..................................141
Creating the Winning Plan We Preferred........................142
Seeing and Feeling the Plan Materialize.......................144
It Was More Than a Coincidence................................146
TAKE ACTION! ................................................147

CHAPTER SIXTEEN    149

## A Knock Came to My Door

Pouring Out the Desires of My Heart...........................150
"Do You Think You Can Run This Business?".....................151
The Pure Flood of Intelligence................................152
Voice of the Flesh or Voice of Inspiration....................153
Putting the Business Plan into Action.........................155
Making the Move...............................................157
Oops! No Money Allotted for Furniture.........................157
Time for a Change.............................................158
TAKE ACTION! ................................................161

CHAPTER SEVENTEEN    163

## How to Create a Council Meeting

Praying With Your Whole Soul................................................164
Gifts of the Spirit.................................................................167
You Ask, They Answer.........................................................168
TAKE ACTION! .................................................................169


CHAPTER EIGHTEEN    171

## Picture This Instead

Removing the Wedge, Allowing the Healing...........................171
Food, Glorious Food!...........................................................172
Planning Our Miracle..........................................................174
Picture This for Thanksgiving..............................................175
Let the Festivities Begin!.....................................................176
Giving Thanks and Feeling Thankful.....................................179
Something Extraordinary......................................................181
TAKE ACTION! .................................................................182


CHAPTER NINETEEN    183

## And That Gift Is My Gift

Preparing for the Fun!..........................................................184
"You Didn't Say Bingo!".......................................................187
The Gift Was Not the Present I Was Seeking...........................188
Stay the Course!.................................................................188
TAKE ACTION! .................................................................189

CHAPTER TWENTY   191

## The Box in the Tall Grass

The Plan for Multiplicity....................................191
Searching for Juan............................................192
Juan, Juan, Juan, Juan.......................................193
Hearing the Still Small Voice............................194
Calming Comforting Guidance.........................195
A Persistent Thought.......................................196
Responding to the Words of Inspiration............198
TAKE ACTION! ................................................200

CHAPTER TWENTY-ONE   203

## Reading Stories and Playing Monopoly

"These Stories You Tell Us Are Real!"..............203
Teaching Eternal Laws by Playing Games.........204
Playing Games While Being Connected.............206
A Different Outcome.........................................207
A Winning Attitude in the Game of Life............208
TAKE ACTION! ................................................209

CHAPTER TWENTY-TWO   **211**

## Valley Fever, Bells Palsy and The Still Small Voice

A Happy, Smart Little Mutt..............................212
Something Just Didn't Feel Right......................213
Once Again Hearing that Inspired Voice............215
Grateful for Guidance......................................216
TAKE ACTION! ................................................217

CHAPTER TWENTY-THREE   219

## The Rice Experiment

Being Ignored is Devastating .................................................220
Responsive Elements.............................................................221
Creating Your Own Rice Experiment......................................224
TAKE ACTION! ....................................................................225

CHAPTER TWENTY-FOUR   227

## The Fearful Husband and The Zen Man

"I've Heard About Those Exercises Before!"..........................228
What We Expect is Exactly What We Create...........................231
Simple Solutions, Powerful Results!......................................233
One Soul Speaking to Another Soul.......................................233
"I'm Feeling Afraid!"..............................................................234
The Zen Man.........................................................................235
Allowing the Blessings to Flow In.........................................237
Which One Are You?..............................................................237
TAKE ACTION! ....................................................................238

CHAPTER TWENTY-FIVE   239

## Only Green Lights

The Power to Change Time.....................................................240
"We Love Green Lights!".........................................................240
The Lord's Time ....................................................................241
Prophet's Time......................................................................243
TAKE ACTION! ....................................................................244

CHAPTER TWENTY-SIX    247

## Recognizing and Releasing Personal Fears

Creating a Game to Conquer My Fear.................................248
Moving Forward in My Adventure.....................................249
Feeling My Way Toward My Goal.......................................250
Our Feelings Are Our Perfect Guiding Compass..................251
Magnets in Fowl Size Noggins..........................................251
TAKE ACTION! ................................................................252

CHAPTER TWENTY-SEVEN    253

## Little White Lies

Finding My Perfect Excuse!..............................................253
Pulling Myself Back from the Slippery Slope.......................254
Genuine or Phony?..........................................................255
Your True Genuine Feelings Will Never Fail!......................255
Just In Time!..................................................................257
TAKE ACTION! ...............................................................258

CHAPTER TWENTY-EIGHT    259

## The Prophecies, Song of Joy, Full of Prayer

That's My Knight in Shining Armor?..................................259
An Inspired Knowing.......................................................264
The Daily Odyssey..........................................................265
Her Ordeal.....................................................................266
A Crushing Weight on My Chest.......................................267
Song of Joy, Full of Prayer...............................................269
TAKE ACTION! ...............................................................270

# Releasing Negative Feelings

Be Aware, Be Purpose-Filled, Be Genuine ............................272
Taking It Like a Man?! ............................................................272
Creating the World He Preferred ..........................................274
TAKE ACTION! .......................................................................276

# Some Clarification

Flash Points that Distract .......................................................277
Wealth and Happiness .............................................................278
Keep Your Perspective ............................................................278

# Millions of Dollars

Releasing Distractions ............................................................282
Creating Our Preferences .......................................................283
TAKE ACTION! .......................................................................286

# Green Cars

Someday Forming Into Now .....................................................289
Where Did These Cars Come From? ........................................291
Adding the Bells and Whistles ...............................................292
Creating With Others ..............................................................292
Go Ahead and Think BIG! ......................................................295
Appreciate the Blessings You Now Have ...............................296
TAKE ACTION! .......................................................................297

CHAPTER THIRTY-TWO    299

# *Creating Your Mindset of Miracles*

## Part III: The Conclusion of *Mindset of Miracles*

CHAPTER THIRTY-THREE    303

# *Wrapping It Up*

Creating Your Road Map for Life ....................................304
Turn Off Everything that Sabotages You ........................304
Your Feelings Are Your Perfect Guides ..........................305
Ask, Nothing Wavering, and It Will Be Given .................305
Create What You Prefer NOW! ......................................306
Draw Only Harmonious Relationships ...........................306
Send an Invitation from One Soul to Another ..................307
Release Four Letter Words ............................................308
Become an Honorable Being! .........................................309
MONEY MONEY MONEY! ...........................................310
Your Personal Happiness ...............................................311
You Were Created to Experience Joy! .............................314
TAKE ACTION! ............................................................315

# *Creating Your Roadmap for Life*

# *Acknowledgements*

# *About the Author*

# *Submit Your Story*

# ~ Foreword ~
## By Michael Claridge

Ever since I was a child I have looked up to people who do great things. I'd see a magician do magical feats that left the audience in excited wonder. Then I'd hurry home and pretend I was the Amazing Michael to an audience of one, me in the mirror. The crowd would go wild!

I'd see a famous basketball star outscore everyone else on the court and soon I'd be outside envisioning me making every basket. The crowd would enthusiastically stand up and cheer. I gave countless concerts while lathered up in the shower. I interviewed Presidents, Kings and Queens and other great world leaders in my daydreams as I walked home from school.

When I grew older the boyish fantasies faded but admiration for those who achieve great things did not. I saw remarkable men and women who, against enormous odds and obstacles would create great things and make masterpieces of their lives. I'd often think to myself if they could create great things then certainly I could too.

I read that successful people don't become successful all by themselves; that almost every one of them had at least one very influential mentor in their lives. And so on my quest to create great things I began to search for accomplished mentors from whom I could learn.

I started looking for someone who not only could teach me, but someone who was authentic, who actually walked the talk. Too many times you'll find people who pontificate on this or that as if they understand the subject entirely only to find out later they are worse off than you are.

I am not a big proponent of the adage, "Fake it till you make it." After all, that's exactly what I had been doing in front of the mirror for so many years. For me, faking it wasn't making it. I desired to find a mentor who was actually creating great things, and living in a great way. I concluded that if they were creating great things with their lives then surely they could teach me to do the same with mine.

Back in the late fall of 2004 I became acquainted with Ronnie and Pamela Ann Ezell. We soon became good friends. On more than one occasion they graciously invited me and my family to spend our summer vacation at their penthouse or condos in Puerto Peñasco, Mexico, or on their houseboat on the lake.

We always had so much fun. I was also honored to cater many events (wedding receptions, parties, graduations, political campaign fundraisers, etc.) in their home, which were always well attended and beautifully decorated. All who were at the festivities enjoyed them tremendously.

The more time I spent with them the more I came to see them as remarkable people who create great things. They are down to earth, kind hearted, generous people. I have grown to admire them and appreciate them.

Ronnie is the owner of a very successful messenger service. He's one of the most diligent, dedicated workingmen I know. He always has a kind word, a funny story, or invaluable advice. I am grateful for his leadership, but more importantly I am grateful for his friendship.

Pamela Ann and I were instant friends. It didn't take long torecognize there was a special connection between us. We spoke the same vocabulary, we saw the world through very similar lenses, and both of us had an enthusiasm and gusto for enjoying every single moment in life.

But at that time my life was vastly different than hers. You see, I was a single father of two boys on the backside of my second divorce, I was struggling financially, and I was a very depressed man. I remembered the saying, "When the student is ready the teacher will appear." Well I was definitely ready and then voila... Pamela Ann appeared!

During the first part of 2010 I started experiencing some major shifts in my life. And the more I spoke with Pamela the clearer everything became for me. I very quickly recognized that she was the profoundly influential mentor I was seeking. Literally applying what she teaches has opened within me an ability to allow into my life a constant flow of miraculous experiences and eternal insights plus understanding.

Throughout the first year of training with her I have written, recorded, and performed in front of major audiences five original songs. I have had one miracle after another unfold before my very eyes. I am living proof that what she teaches, when actively applied, actually works. I cannot even begin to express the magnitude of my gratitude to Pamela Ann for how she has helped me, supported me, and championed me. She has been an amazing mentor, and more importantly, a true friend.

It was through her instrumentality that I was able to sing at a Naturalization Ceremony here in Tucson, Arizona—which lead to a standing invitation to sing at every future ceremony. I have also been honored to perform at several of her seminars, which have opened many other doors of opportunity for me.

Recently I was able to perform at a major Presidential Campaign Rally where state Senators and dignitaries were in attendance. I received a standing ovation from an inspired crowd. In fact, these events have been inspirational to all who have attended, and I am grateful and honored I have been able to share my songs with so many people.

Pamela Ann has been an invaluable mentor. Her knowledge is spot on, her influence immense, and her friendship a priceless treasure. My heartfelt gratitude, good wishes, and profound love go out to her.

You hold in your hand a priceless gem. Read it, ponder its message, internalize its meaning, apply and activate its lessons and you will learn the most powerful principles for creating the life you prefer, now. I am a firm believer that nothing happens by accident. This book has come into your life for an important reason. Whether you know it or not you have asked for it, and it has been brought to you.

Think of this book as a seed. If the seed is planted in fertile ground or not, or if the seed is nourished and fed or not is entirely up to you. But I promise you, if you allow yourself to plant this seed in fertile ground, if you continue to nourish it, the seed will grow quickly and easily bear delicious fruit.

Keep remembering to allow yourself to float gently down your stream of life, merrily, merrily, merrily, merrily—because this life is but a dream.

# ~ *Preface* ~

If you are holding this book in your hands, it is because your soul is searching for something—for the touch of the Divine, for joy, for comfort, for hope, for happiness. You are seeking to understand why certain things have occurred in your life. You thirst for true knowledge. You desire to forge a happy life.

If you are holding this book in your hands, it is because you have asked for this knowledge to come to you at this time.

Through the stories presented here, you will receive answers to many questions you have.

I can declare these bold statements because I have continually witnessed an astonishing, extraordinary phenomenon. Shortly after my amazing, motivated clients begin their first training session, they feel an awakening and a shift toward a peaceful relief and awareness; their eyes begin to see their world in a new reality.

They also begin to experience other powerful feelings such as renewed hope, well-being, acceptance, profound love and enlightenment.

That shift can come in a variety of forms, from a gentle "Ah-Ha!" moment to a joyful mind-blowing experience. I am always deeply touched by these moving, mutually uplifting occurrences.

Notice that I describe these individuals as *motivated clients*. They are people who are open and teachable, ready to receive and *activate within* something more deeply meaningful and satisfying in their immediate lives. They are prepared to let go of fearful, sabotaging, distracting stumbling blocks and useless worries that have paralyzed their progress toward the life goals they desire.

These individuals are also prepared to release ego, pride and embarrassment plus indoctrinations, lifestyles or rote habits. They are ready to rid themselves of traditions that no longer serve them or provide value in their daily lives *while still embracing their core beliefs.*

They are the seekers of genuine abiding joy and invigorating happiness undisturbed by any person or situation in this finite world.

Now ask yourself this question:

**"Am I one of those motivated individuals?"**

If your answer is, "Yes!" you too can learn how to purposefully dial in what you would *love* to create in your life, business, health, finances and relationships. These principles are simple eternal laws that can be applied to any situation you encounter.

This knowledge is written for people of all ages, backgrounds and walks of life. It offers an avenue for you to happily create your world as you prefer to have it. Whether you live in a simple tent or a regal mansion, you were created to experience immense joy in every moment of this life.

I am a living example of how powerful these principles can be. I am an ordinary woman: a wife of over 40 years (married to my high school sweetheart), a mother of four children, a grandmother of many, a gardener, a contributor to my neighborhood and community, a dreamer...

I have also experienced great personal loss and rejection. I have suffered crippling abuse that shattered my childhood innocence. I have felt feelings of profound lack, the gnawing of physical hunger, the grip of utter loneliness, fear and suicidal depression. I was homeless in high school. At one point, I even lost my health and was bedridden for over 10 years (my husband actually purchased my burial plot and we made my funeral arrangements).

But amazingly, because I opened myself to the Divine, because I permitted an eternal power to channel energy, intelligence, love and joy through me, my life has been suffused with miracles.

Life with the Divine is an adventure: it has guided me so I could learn from, overcome, master and then release *any* obstacle, difficulty or disharmony that would diminish my personal joy.

Gone are the abuse, lack, hunger, loneliness, fear, depression, homelessness and poor health.

Those situations and feelings have been replaced with bedrock, unshakable confidence and truth that I am personally known and loved by those who created me. And to my amazement, I also discovered that I have the power to connect with them and create *anything* my heart desires!

I also have learned about the mighty healing ability of a deep, abiding, eternal love that completely righted my entire soul. That love set my feet on a sure path. It encouraged me to actively move myself in a direction that brings me continuous joy *every day* of my existence.

As soon as I ask for what I desire, those *Divine* beings who created me answer, "YES!" to *every* request I make.

I can feel the *Power* as they speak to my soul. Then, I watch with joy and anticipation as the next stage of my life miraculously unfolds. I eagerly receive the blessings that were prepared for me. Finally, I give genuine thanks and appreciation for the love and support that I am provided each day. I know that all is possible as long as I am open to this presence.

My family, friends, clients and associates who learn about and actively apply these simple laws also enjoy these same miracles and blessings.

For years, many of them have asked me to write about what I revealed to them so they can refer to it and also share this information with their families and friends. So, here I am, writing this book as well as others in response. I know this information will assist them and you in reawakening your ability to fully reconnect to this magnificent Power.

In this book, you will discover step-by-step examples showing you how to invoke this soul-healing Power and have it come alive in you. You will learn how to personally connect to it and create the world you prefer. You will also discover how to allow that Power to flow into every moment of your existence, if that is your desire.

You will learn how to create miraculous occurrences through different stories of real life experiences. The steps taken to deliberately form those miracles are given to you through individual narratives as well as through *Take Action!* suggestions at the end of each chapter.

For easy reference, a chapter toward the end of this book will provide a condensed version of all the principles taught within these pages. This guide will assist you in personally creating similar experiences. At any time, you can start applying these simple steps and usher similar miracles into your own life.

All right, it's time to get going!

Remember, life is a journey and you are always in the driver's seat. It is you who steers the wheel in the direction of your desired destination. You choose how fast or how slow you would like to go. If you recognize dissatisfaction with what you are experiencing, you can immediately turn and head in a different direction!

You are never stuck unless you decide to apply the brakes and come to a complete stop or put your vehicle into park. In fact, doing so is actually beneficial because stopping for periods of time creates an avenue for you to rest and reflect. It is also a valuable way for you to refresh your energies and regain your bearings or sense of direction.

By the way, no matter what your current situation, you can change your life *at any time,* make course adjustments or even embark upon a completely new adventure.

Allow yourself to feel a tickle of hope and excited anticipation for the adventure you are embarking on. Let this change occur in your mind—better yet, in your entire soul so you can receive and develop your

## *Mindset of Miracles*

OK. Here is the key to your vehicle! Turn on your creative engine.

# Part I. Developing Your
## *Mindset of Miracles*

Awaken Your Faculties.
Remember How to Deliberately Create Your World.

# CHAPTER ONE

# ~ *Steps to Prepare Your Vessel* ~

When you are properly prepared, your ability to usher in, internalize and put into action the information you are now receiving will improve. More importantly, you will start to recognize the moments you connect to your own personal Power to begin to create what you prefer.

With those thoughts in mind, allow yourself to fully enjoy this book and receive the most benefit from its treasures. Take a few moments to prepare your vessel, or body, before you continue to read further. This will only take a couple of minutes, but will make a huge difference for you in the long run.

1. **Drink a large glass of water**. If you are able, add some salt, preferably a mineral rich sea salt (I use Redman's Real Salt), so your body can better absorb the water, eliminating the urge to run to the restroom in ten minutes (I pour about ¼ of a teaspoon or less in my hand, toss it into my mouth and wash it down with the water).

2. **If you are hungry, eat a high protein, low carb snack or light meal** to help awaken your mind. Give your body a few minutes to absorb the water first so it can digest your food (too heavy of a meal will cause you to feel sleepy).

3. **Find a quiet place.** Not an option? Get some earplugs!

4. **Close your eyes and take a few deep, cleansing, belly breaths. As you exhale, visualize yourself releasing any tension, stress, distractions or disharmony from your being.** See them all being pulled and lifted right out of your body. Allow them to go out the nearest window or door. They have already served their usefulness. Let them go. May sound hokey, but it really works!

5. **Now FEEL that release from your body.** Allow every cell of your body to let go of all cares quickly and easily.

6. **Take a few deeper belly breaths, but this time draw in warm, soothing feelings of peace, well-being and clarity of mind.** Let those feelings wash throughout your entire body to fill the recent void you just created. Allow yourself to FEEL this uplifting change resonating within you. Believe this experience is yours to have now.

7. **Take a moment to remember some *feel good moments* in your life.** Picture the times you felt happy and eager or excited with anticipation. Remember when you felt great appreciation or thankfulness for someone or something that happened to you. Or, consider a time you felt especially moved in a joy-filled way.

8. **Remember the warm expanding thrill you felt in your body. Allow that *feeling* to come back into you *now* and hold on to that feeling!** These experiences are examples of when you were more fully connected to those who created you and when you were also connected to your personal Power to create miracles in your daily life.Remember to take a few moments to prepare yourself each time before feasting on the words written for you. As you read, allow yourself to picture these stories in your mind. Pay attention to the steps presented in the following chapters. Better yet, visualize and

feel with your whole soul what you are reading, as if you were actually there; as if you were me.

Ponder these stories and allow yourself to identify how you can allow like-situations into your personal life so you, too, can receive the results you desire.

As you read the stories, you will begin to remember similar experiences from your own life. Write your stories down. Little by little, your eyes will open to see the literal miracles already being performed for you on a daily basis. Acknowledge, appreciate and embrace them. And most of all, give thanks for these supportive blessings.

### You Are Becoming Sleepy…

Have you noticed when a baby first comes to earth how rapidly it grows and learns? Have you noticed also how much it sleeps? It is amassing and internalizing a tremendous amount of information, constantly being nourished with perfect eternal love, pure intelligence and clear understanding. During its sleeping moments, it is able to more efficiently *download* these details into every whit of its being. It is able to do this because it is accessing the Divine that knows all things past, present and future. We, too, can receive this knowledge at anytime, but only when we are open to accept it.

While you read, do not be surprised if, at times, you feel sleepy and have a desire to lay the book down and take a nap. This is a healthy and powerful bodily response to what you are learning.

Your inclination should not be resisted. Allow yourself to listen to those feelings and slumber for as long as you feel is necessary.

Something important will take place while you are sleeping.

You will be allowing this valuable information to be woven into the cells of your body and vestiges of your soul. Deep within, you already know all the information I am sharing with you. I'm simply assisting you in reawakening your faculties to the knowledge of these eternal laws.

Your feelings in your body will help you in validating the truths you are reading. The results of your reawakening will help you more rapidly apply the information you receive in your everyday life.

## Personally Creating While Reading this Book

I highly recommend that you first read through the entire book if your intention is to internalize and activate this powerful information and eternal laws. Then I suggest that you begin again and read a chapter a week while applying the TAKE ACTION section at the end of each chapter. Allow a genuine shift to occur within you.

To assist you in this process, this book was printed in a way so that you can take it and personalize it. Notice that all the chapters are arranged to begin on the right page. Because of this there often is some extra space for you to be able to write some of your personal insights and *Ah Ha! moments* down *as soon as you receive them.*

Notice too that the paragraphs are oftentimes short; thus creating space between them for that same reason. Those spaces between the paragraphs also provide some built in breaths for you to enjoy so you can slow down a bit to savor and ponder the material that is being presented to you.

Your personal additional comments will assist you in remembering those insightful moments and will also provide you with a specific place where you can easily find them again.

Refer to this book from time to time, especially if you begin to slide back into exploring situations in your life that you prefer to let go of. Your review of these simple laws and how to activate them will immediately assist you in moving forward with the life you choose to experience.

## Some Explanation

While reading the introduction to this book you may have encountered certain terms or phrases that may have given you pause. This is no accident. I have deliberately released using words such as *want* and *need* and replaced them with words such as *prefer* and *desire*.

In fact, I rarely use *want* and *need* type of words in this book or in my daily speech and I encourage you to do the same. *Want* and *need* are four-letter-type words that diminish your power to create. They are words that come from a place of lack. Words like *now*, *choose* and *prefer* are take action words that encourage you to move forward in your new adventurous life. Allow those words to resonate and take root in your soul.

## Some Thoughts About the Divine

I'm going to be sharing with you some thoughts about the Divine. I can teach you how to rapidly create what you prefer, but only if I include this key element to your success. Otherwise, I will be withholding vital knowledge and you will still be left searching for that valuable piece of information!

As this information is presented to you, let go of thinking it to death…that's a real fun-killer. I actually don't get all hung up on a lot of details; I just allow myself to accept that the Divine exists; then, I simply open up and enjoy the amazing adventures we create together.

It is possible to have continual joy in every moment of your life.
So have fun on this thrilling journey!

# CHAPTER TWO

# ~ *The Team, The Power and The Divine* ~

As I explained earlier in this book, I present *my* experiences in terms that personally resonate with *me*. If the terms I use cause you to close down because they are foreign or unfamiliar, or if you feel disharmony because they are different from your personal expression, feel free to insert whatever words will positively support you and your core beliefs.

Remember: I'm simply laying out the details of what *I have learned and lived* in hopes that you may also understand how to more fully connect to your own creative powers.

Also, remember that this book is written to provide uplift and insight to people from all over the world with diverse backgrounds. Some of them believe in one God. Others believe in multiple Gods. Moreover, lots of people have feelings of fear, anger or unworthiness associated with that topic. (If you activate the teachings in this book you can rapidly receive insight to dispel those discouraging feelings.)

There are those who have no concept of a pre-life or an after-life. Nor do they have any base of background knowledge that they can presently recall of any godly or spiritual beings. In fact even the word God is completely foreign to them.

With that awareness in mind, some background information is pivotal to provide a foundation of understanding of what I am sharing in this book.

I am a respecter of all people and completely love and accept them wherever they may be in their life journey. I am not a representative of any particular form of religion. Again, I am simply sharing my amazing, life transforming personal experiences with you.

## Introducing the Core Group

I have a *Team* who has been assigned to assist me. I believe my personal Team consists of God, ministering angels, spiritual beings, intelligences, my ancestors, the elements… I have always been connected to this Team who provides me pure, eternal love and intelligence.

I am able to reach out and speak with my Team at anytime to receive comfort, guidance, instructions and protection from them.

You have your own specially selected personal Team as well. It is up to you to discover who is on your Team. You are the only one who has the power to ask for this supportive knowledge to personally come to you. Your soul will literally feel and bear witness when your truth is revealed. Allow yourself the time to receive this enlightenment. Look forward to receiving it.

You may already have discovered this information. If so, allow yourself to fully *activate* this powerful knowledge. It is truly worthwhile.

As I was completing the final edit of this chapter, I received a phone call from Jessi, a long time friend and client. She had just completed one of my *Spa and Soul Days* the previous weekend and she shared her reaction to the word Team. That particular word had negative connotations for her, and immediately reduced her feelings of joy and well-being.

From her viewpoint, a significant amount of her family's quality time had been lost because her former husband spent excessive hours watching professional sporting games and events. So the word "team" was a reminder of many sad and discouraging occasions.

However, she soon happily began identifying what she preferred, and recognized the words *God Helpers* or *Helpers* as her personal way to identify with her uplifting group. In the same way, you too will swiftly come to identify your own amazing, encouraging supporters.

### Our Team Members Are Perfect in Every Way

The Team members I have written about are perfect in every way. They are completely free of any pettiness, pride, ego or insecurities.

They truly understand the various steps we take to permit our soul's maturing through the experiences we glean here on earth. They are not easily offended. They see the big picture at all times and are able to maintain a perfect, consistent love. That love is solidly anchored in the eternal relationship they have with us in spite of our temporary, mortal, vacillating thoughts, feelings and actions.

Our individual Teams do not get hung up on the names we call them. They are not going to split hairs if we refer to them by only a couple of the thousand sacred or reverent names by which they have been known throughout time. All of those names refer to the same beings.

## We Are All Vital to the Whole

It is important to remember we are all vital to the whole. We are each a part of our Team and they are a part of us. We are also all connected to one another while we are each creating our worlds.

If we try to exclude or ostracize another person, group or country, because of some discord or difference of opinion, it is as if we are trying to sever an appendage of our own body! We literally would not be able to function as perfectly without that portion of our being. We would not feel our full expression of complete harmony and wholeness with everything that touches our lives.

It is exceedingly important that we allow ourselves to become one with each other so we can become more fully one with the Divine.

## What Is the Divine?

I once visited with a woman over the phone. During the conversation, I referred to a Being in my *Divine* group as a *he.* She quickly corrected my statement by informing me that there is no *he* or *she.*

This was the truth that personally resonated with her.

I appreciated her sharing her beliefs with me, and I took some time to ponder over them. I was thankful I allowed my mind to remain open to what she was sharing with me.

I soon realized that she was describing the *Power* that creates all, which of course has no gender, and I was describing one of my *Team* members that utilizes that *Power*. This Being specifically directs and commands that Power and also teaches me how to purposefully use it.

You can also utilize this same Power when you are connected to your own personal Team.

So what then is the Divine? The Divine simply means *both* the Power *and* the Team that are able to use that Power.

### "What If I Don't Believe In the Divine?"

Our Team members do not get all ruffled up if we don't believe in them for a season, or if we choose to think they don't even exist at all. Nor are they going to rain down some sort of wrath of heaven upon us when we question and search for answers as we develop personal faith and knowledge about mortal and eternal truths.

These beings know they are real and are immovably secure in their state of being. They are free of any desires to take a straw poll to learn if they are still popular, accepted or rejected by others. Those opinions shift as quickly as the wind changes directions. Why would they or any of us expend precious time and energy on that anyway?

Yet, in spite of our sometimes faltering and questioning faith—blaming them for chaos or disasters *we* have created—our Teams still continue to love, bless and encourage us.

We can choose to move further away from or closer to their enlightenment and source of Power at any time. Whether we deny or acknowledge this source of well-being and nourishment, they are still consistently there for us.

They understand we are trying to gain experience. They know we are ultimately seeking harmony in our lives. Often this questioning and searching is part of that process, and so is the stumbling and hesitancy because of the unknown.

A man who was wrestling mightily with a lengthy and challenging divorce and child custody situation once asked this question at a retreat class I was teaching:

"What if I don't even believe in the existence of God?"

What immediately flowed from my lips were these loving, inspired words, which comforted all of us: "That's all right if you don't believe in them for a season because they continue to believe in you!"

Be at peace. Be easy with yourself and with others. This heating, stretching, molding, tempering and cooling is part of our course of action as we examine, learn and grow from the opportunities presented to us.

To better help you understand what I am sharing with you, let's look at this from a slightly different perspective.

## They Continue To Love Us

I am a mother and grandmother. When my posterity goes through their learning and expansion opportunities—sometimes struggling, becoming disillusioned, frustrated or angry—I understand their plight. I too have gone through similar adventures in the course of my own experiences.

I know life is a process. There are many pivotal steps necessary for that progression to take place. During our physical development we first learn how to hold our heads up. Then we roll over, sit up, crawl, stand, walk and finally run. We learn life-skills and eternal laws by similar methods, through specific precepts, step by step, line upon line.

I would not consider it necessary to scold my children or grandchildren if they stumbled during their first tentative steps in learning to walk.

Neither do I consider it necessary to punish or shame them when they are wrestling with becoming one with their soul.

One of my children walked the day he turned nine months old even though he was born a month premature! Others took their sweet time…yet they all eventually learned how to walk. It is the same with learning and mastering our life skills.

We each have plenty of time and more to get these concepts *under our belts.* In fact, we have all eternity!

I continue to love and desire my family members' highest good, even when they are at odds with themselves and everyone around them. I understand they will not remain in this state forever. I know they are here to gain wisdom from the experiences they have purposefully drawn to themselves. I'm confident they will readily release those growth opportunities when they have mastered their desired experiences. Then they will move on to other life adventures.

If I, as a mortal mother, grasp this truth of the reality of what is required during our temporal expansion, how much more perfectly are we understood, loved and adored by our personal Team? I have only known them to treat each of us with tenderness and affection.

## Additional Sources of Information

The Divine will provide you with information from many sources. Allow yourself to believe you are capable of receiving his knowledge.

Inspired people will just walk up to you and give you information you desire to know; or something will pop up on the Internet, TV, and radio or in conversations you have. Sometimes you will feel your Team's uplifting encouragement while reading a book or scripture, or listening to a lesson, talk or presentation.

You will also begin receiving pure *intelligence* that will flow into your mind; not mere mortal words! This is pivotal, because communicating through floods of pure intelligence results in perfect understanding of these treasures of knowledge being revealed to you.

As a result, there are no misunderstandings about the instructions you are receiving and the concepts you are learning.

## TAKE ACTION!

**There are many ways to gather the information and experiences you desire to have. Let yourself recognize that you are able to receive this knowledge from your Team. Start noticing your increased awareness and Ah-Ha! moments that begin to come to you. Find a notepad or journal today and begin recording your experiences! Allow yourself to believe you are worthy to receive this knowledge now.**

**Take the time to genuinely become an honorable, respectful, courageous, virtuous, accepting, happy being in life. That use of your quality time will be worth every minute you spend. Commit to yourself that you will immediately start to incorporate this knowledge into your life.**

# CHAPTER THREE

# ~ My Quest for the Mindset of Miracles ~

As a child, I have only one brief memory of my mother. If it were not for photographs, I would never have known the deep rich color of her hair and eyes or the radiance of her bright smile. I cannot recall the playful sound of her voice, the sweet smell of her skin or the tender touch of her embrace.

And yet, I knew my mother. In fact, I knew her so well my older family members and friends commented on how I have some of her same talents, mannerisms and vocal inflections. I found those observations somehow comforting.

My likeness to my mother was especially noteworthy considering that I was taken away from her when I was only two years old. Because she was ill with cancer, my older brother and I went to live with our fraternal grandmother and maiden aunt. Soon after, my mother passed over to a far better place.

My father was not well either. However, his illness was not of the physical kind. My first memory of my father was of him molesting me when I was 18 months old. During that first attack I glanced over and saw my mother standing by the hinges of the left side of my open bedroom door in her white nightgown.

She had been awakened by my muffled cries. Her eyes were open wide with a look of horror and her mouth was agape as she witnessed what was happening to her baby girl.

As a youth she had come from a tumultuous background. But now that she was a young adult, she thought she had left all the twisted misery behind her. Instead she realized she had married it instead.

A year later, after she developed a rare cancer in her sinus cavity and lost control of her eyes—those same eyes that saw her worst waking nightmare—she was gone.

As a result of these events, I was left without earthly parents to protect and guide me.

The details of those experiences are not part of this book. Yet, I confess those events caused my soul to catapult into a search for comfort, help and enlightenment.

Thankfully, I found what I was searching for. In fact, *I have completely healed from the crippling effects of those early childhood experiences.* As a result of that discovery, I have been able to go forward and enjoy a rich, full, satisfying, happy and adventuresome life.

## Meeting My Master, My Master Teacher

The first times I remember being taught some of this perfect knowledge, was when I was three years old. Someone told me I would be able to see my mother again in *eternity*. I didn't know what that word meant. Yet I felt curious and motivated to understand. As I pondered that word, eternity, I started to see bands of beautiful swirling colors like a dream in my mind that continued into the distance and never ended.

After that wonderful experience, I understood eternity to be a beautiful place. I thought, "When I am with my mommy again, we will always be able to be together."

I felt completely satisfied with the answer I had received. I later realized that even though she had died, we had never been fully separated from one another!

Following that incident, whenever I desired any information, help or protection, a loving being would come to me and assist me. This individual came into my presence in a male form (how perfect for me since I had felt injured by my earthly father!). Furthermore, I had desired to have someone in my life who was nurturing and trustworthy, especially from that gender.

I soon discovered that this kind being knew everything about me and loved me. He even had a great sense of humor.

If I did something wrong, he would never punish or chastise me and he never scolded. Instead, he sorrowed with me for a moment because my personal joy had been diminished.

Afterwards, he patiently and lovingly instructed me on what to do to overcome my unhappy feelings so my joy could be restored. He assured me that I was always worthy to receive that joy.

This individual is the first member of my personal Team. I refer to him as my *Master*, my *Master Teacher*. He was and still is consistently available for me.

I was amazed that, in spite of living in a physically and emotionally abusive environment, I felt somehow shielded from my unhappy home life because of the comforting eternal connection I had firmly re-established with the Divine.

My Team explained to me why the key people in my life were acting and reacting toward me in such a cruel manner. This Team taught me how to see my world through their eyes; eyes that could view my life situation with an eternal perspective.

After that awakened *revelation*, I felt compassion for my family and willingly chose not to exacerbate the situation. My Team helped me to literally and figuratively *lift my burdens* so I could bear them more easily.

As a result, I felt more like an outside observer of what was happening around me and less like an active participant. I was able to detach a large portion of my intellect from that hellhole of an environment and move on to enjoy a happy productive life. Now, as an adult, I actually have many wonderful, joy-filled memories of my childhood because of the consistent, tender, nurturing, uplifting relationship I personally developed with my eternal Team.

The smaller portion of my intelligence, that part which bore the painful darker side of my life and held on to its secrets until I was mature enough to process them, has long ago been reunited with the rest of me and has reintegrated fully into my soul. (There is not sufficient space in this text to adequately share that life-altering miraculous story. I will share that experience with you in another book.)

## Further From or Closer To the "Light"

Sometimes I turned my attentions and actions toward goals that resulted in less than happy outcomes. During those moments, I felt miserable. Any pain I experienced in my life was caused from my moving away from the light, knowledge and comfort that my Master and the rest of my Team provided for me.

When I chose to live life somewhat disconnected from that light by trying to go it alone, I stumbled in darkness and created chaos and discord for myself.

I use the words "somewhat disconnected from the light" since it is impossible for any of us to ever become completely disconnected from it.

We are each individually completely loved and adored by our Team. Because they so enjoy interacting with us, they know how to tenderly touch our souls. They understand how to succor us back into their affectionate embrace whenever we are ready to feel those desires and respond to them.

Thankfully, after recognizing how forlorn I had become, I once again found a way to redirect my energies to come back more fully into my Master Teacher's presence. He and the rest of my Team Members always heartedly welcomed me back. They never abandoned me.

Meanwhile, at home, I had no one to speak to about my special, personal relationship with the Divine. My mother had died of cancer and my father was my molester. Who then could I tell?

Many times, children share these sweet experiences with adults they trust. Unfortunately, often they are told their special companion is just an *imaginary friend*. Not long afterwards, when children understand what the word imaginary means, they close the door to belief and no longer trust that this portal of perfect knowledge, protection, understanding and comfort exists.

I always kept that door to the Divine open, although sometimes more fully than other times.

The truth is that those *friends* are not imaginary. From the moment I met my Master Teacher, I understood he was not an invention in my mind and in fact was much more significant to me than just a loving, understanding and highly intelligent instructor. But I was not yet ready to admit to others that he was the magnificent being I recognized him to actually be.

I felt this way not because I was ashamed or embarrassed about our relationship, but because I was not a braggart. I also did not desire to initiate feelings in others that would cause them to suspect I was elevated or more important than they were. Even at three years old, I understood each person is highly valued and worthy of the utmost respect and care.

And lastly, I knew that this amazing, heavenly companion was such a holy being that out of reverence, I was not to speak his name lightly or treat it as commonplace.

It was not until I was an adult that I revealed to others the true name of my beloved companion and Master Teacher, or spoke of the many stories I had experienced because of my personal relationship with him. Then, one day I could no longer contain this amazing good news and my personal truth. I began relating some of this information along with some of my adventures with others.

Now, with this book, I am sharing a portion of it with you.

## That's Your Master Teacher!

My Master Teacher's name is Jesus Christ, the Son of God. He is my Elder Brother and Savior who adores me and I adore him. Yes, I have a personal amazing relationship with him for which I will be forever grateful. Yes, I know I am loved and cherished by my Savior. And yes, we have created many miracles together.

He also introduced me to the other members of my Team. I soon understood that I literally had a personal relationship with those who created me. Isn't that what we at some level are all

seeking? That is precisely the crux or bottom line of this book…
to develop a personal relationship with the Divine and then begin
purposefully creating with them!

Our ability to create chaos and misery or joy and well-being
reflects directly on how united we are with one another as well
as with our Team.

My Master Teacher shared with me early on in my training that
I am not above or below anyone else. He taught me I could do
anything my heart desired, "As long as it did not impinge upon
the rights and freedoms of others." Yep, that was the word he
used, *impinge.*

I now understand I cannot encroach upon another's space or
freedoms unless they at some level invite me to do so. In fact,
just my desiring to impose or invade another's personal domain
would trigger a catalyst of discord within me. Simply thinking
about striving to control another would begin the process of
diminishing my personal joy. This shrinking of happiness would
occur long before I could ever try to affect someone else.

In other words, my loving Master Teacher taught me this valuable
truth so I could more perfectly maintain my individual bliss.

Another lesson he taught me was about the real plan for parents
from an eternal perspective.

### The Perfect Plan Includes Imperfect Parents

As a child, my Master Teacher, as well as the rest of my Team,
taught me treasured knowledge. Sometimes, adults in my life
would question one another about eternal subjects to which they
did not know the answers. I marveled that they did not understand
such seemingly basic principles that my Master Teacher had

previously taught me. From those experiences, I realized at an early age that adults don't always have the answers to life's questions.

Thankfully, I have come to recognize as an adult, that this is part of the perfect plan. If parents, teachers and leaders always had the right answers, then they in essence would become the sole bridge between the Divine and us. Eventually they would pass away and we would lose what we thought was our only source for all wisdom and support.

Pretty scary place to be stuck!

Thankfully, most of us figure out that the adults in our lives haven't cornered the market in perfect knowledge. That is why we often start questioning and searching for answers long before we leave home.

However, if this is the action you have taken in the past, consistently going to other people for your guidance and instruction, perhaps it would be beneficial to focus your attention on the following actions:

- **Take the time** to become keenly aware of your thoughts and feelings.

- **Open your soul** so you can completely connect with the Divine.

- **Permit yourself** to develop a personal relationship with your Team.

- **Learn how to recognize and discern** their voices when they are communicating with you. You can do this. Trust that you have this ability and are able to *hear* them.

- **Ask, receive, then fully open yourself to allow** in and receive the informative directions and gifts from your Team.

- **Remember to thank them** for those blessings.

- **Actively apply** this knowledge in your daily life.

These applied actions are worth any energy you expend because your union with the Divine is pivotal to your being able to create amazing adventures. While united with them you'll gain confidence in your ability to choose experiences in this world that are personally satisfying and worthwhile to you.

Over the years I have searched for, found and developed my *Mindset of Miracles.* You, too, have this ability to usher in this literally miraculous way of daily living.

I am forever grateful I desired to know more. I'm thankful I asked for understanding of the word *eternity* at the tender age of three. I am also profoundly appreciative that the answer to my question was immediately given to me.

Because of these experiences, I knew I had found the way to open the door to my specific desires. I then happily flung that door *wide open*!

Begin to enjoy the full measure of your soul's potential with those who personally created you and adore you. Take hold and swiftly open your door *now*!

### TAKE ACTION!

**Print or copy the bullet points at the end of this chapter. Place them where you can easily read them before you go to bed and**

when you awake in the morning. Refer to them throughout your day. Keep pondering those points and begin to excitedly look forward to the evidence of these great desires as they quickly form and are presented to you. Write down your experiences or record them on your phone. Have fun!

# CHAPTER FOUR

# ~ *Feeling Alone?* ~

- Do you sometimes feel lonely in the middle of a crowd?

- Do you wish you had a soul companion even though you are married?

- Have you ever felt like you just don't feel completely at home even in your own house?

- When you hear about someone who has recently passed over, do you sometimes secretly think: "You are the lucky one. You get to leave and go back to the place where you dwelled in eternity, before this existence, happy without a care in your world?"

- Have you ever noticed you sometimes feel like you are tentatively sitting on the fence post in this world, but leaning more in that opposite direction, longing to go back to that safe, loving, peaceful, heavenly home?

It's a wanderlust of sorts, this longing and searching for a more deeply satisfying relationship with someone or something you have known before. If you have been experiencing those thoughts and feelings, go ahead and admit it—you're just plain ol' homesick from not being fully united with the Divine.

Whether we recognize it or not, sometimes we feel the desire to be more fully reconnected to our family and Team members that are already *Home.*

Not long ago I had breakfast with one of my clients and a friend of hers. It was the first time I had met this friend, who happened to be a well-known entertainment personality in our city. After a brief introduction, we ordered our breakfast and began to visit.

The friend, an exuberant, charismatic person, was usually engaged in a whirl of activities and surrounded by adoring people, yet I could feel a deep loneliness and sorrow within this person's inner soul. Suddenly, I found myself asking many of the same questions that I mentioned at the beginning of this chapter.

Within moments, tears sprang forth and started spilling down the cheeks of this powerful individual, their loneliness was so profound.

You see, it isn't personally satisfying to go through life wearing a confident, upbeat external mask or shell when deep within our core we feel an empty loneliness. That dark feeling of melancholy saps our energies and distracts us from fully enjoying life.

If you have felt such feelings of loneliness, lack and separation, you are not completely showing up to experience this life and the beautiful world created for your pleasure and enjoyment!

No worries. You will learn how to resolve all the above longings and actually happily participate in each and every day while being completely present. You won't feel lonely again or homesick either if you apply what you are being taught!

At times, during my busy life, I too would lose my bearings and begin feeling that loneliness, usually when I was trying to do everything on my own, forcing my way through life. Those are the times I took life way too seriously. I forgot to remain childlike; teachable, quick to forgive and filled with appreciation and amazement. I'd allow myself to get sidetracked or distracted from utilizing my perfect resource.

That is when I would let the door to the Divine slide almost completely shut. During those periods, only a small crack of light showed through.

After a while, I grew weary of the hardship and mess I created and I actively took the simple steps of turning back and feeling my increased connection with my Master Teacher and the rest of my Team.

Thankfully, that is exactly what my amazing client's friend decided to do; while more fully connecting to the Divine, loneliness was released and balance was regained.

## The Best Kind of Flu You Can Catch

Over the years I have had many experiences while living and playing with my Team. I have often shared my stories with family, friends, acquaintances and even with the people I have had the pleasure of meeting while traveling or doing my daily errands.

When I tell my experiences to others, something always occurs. I feel a warm, peaceful joy or thrill inside me that begins flowing in and enlarging in my chest, then quickly spreads throughout my body. It is my indication I am completely connected to the Divine, my Team and that Power. Shortly after that, the people I speak with also allow themselves to feel that connection. It is wonderfully contagious, the best kind of flu you could ever catch.

This feeling spreads quickly and is filled with that Power of unconditional eternal love and acceptance.

This phenomenon is an experience beyond mere mortal words.

It is one soul speaking to another.

Our bodies and spirits simultaneously share with one another as we are speaking, and the communication becomes more pure and easily understood. No longer confined to the clumsiness and inadequacies of base mortal language, we can literally feel he validation, clarity and truth of the words being spoken through these additional resources.

Most of the time, the individuals I teach see the world changing right before their eyes. During the first hour of their initial training sessions, many of them exclaim: "This stuff really works!"

A student related a story to me that happened on her way home from her first *introductory group class*. Before she even reached the first stoplight, she started feeling, experiencing and seeing the evidence of that Power to create come alive in her. She listened to an inspired thought and turned around to go back and pick up her purse that she had left behind.

Only moments after this occurred, I found the unfamiliar purse, picked it up and immediately walked to the gate to give it to the person that had forgotten it. I felt an assured feeling that someone would be appearing shortly to retrieve their belongings and I acted upon that feeling. To our delight, we met each other simultaneously at the gate!

She didn't call on the phone to let me know she was coming and I didn't even take the time to look inside the purse to discover its owner. We just both acted upon what we *felt impressed* to do.

One Saturday toward the end of a *Spa and Soul Day*, at the *EZ Lightning Training Center,* a recovering alcoholic announced to his other classmates that he was no longer a victim of his circumstances. He activated that belief in his body that evening and has since shared with me several amazing stories of how he let go of anger, frustration, blame, judgment, unworthiness and shame. His life now reflects that freeing transformation.

This last December, I provided *private training* to a couple during the most profoundly shocking and trying time of their personal, family and married lives. It felt like the perfect storm yet they too experienced this life altering shift the first time we met.

On their third and last visit, the wife shared with me, "You don't know this but I have been on antidepressants for twenty-five years and have been unable to wean off of them."

She then turned to her husband and told him, "And I would like you to know that after our first session with Pamela Ann, I was able to stop taking my medications!"

A businesswoman who had been very concerned about all the problems her mother was creating and suffering from suddenly *got it* while I was training her about receiving the peace, assurance and restoration that is available to all of us.

Because she happened to be a Christian woman I trained her in a manner that she could easily understand. I shared a vision in my mind that I had recently experienced that week while driving home from Mexico. I saw the Savior on the cross with his arms opened wide, giving his all for our personal eternal happiness and joy. He had already paid the price for any sorrow, illness, loss, heartache or mistake anyone has ever or will ever experience.

I then assured her that within a blink of an eye we can each be released of those paralyzing difficulties if we will also fully open our arms and accept his gift of these atoning powers.

I explained to her that her mom had a Savior and she (the daughter) was not that being. I encouraged her to believe and have faith that those blessings are always available for her mother whenever she (the mother) is willing to accept them.

As soon as this woman internalized this truth, she allowed those healing powers to enter her soul and instantly released months of heavy burdens of worry about her mother. Her entire body felt the shift of relief. Her radiant countenance and words of happiness bore witness of what she was feeling.

She now shares this information with all her friends, just like the rest of the students who are awakening to their creative abilities.

## How Is This Rapid Change Possible?

How was this possible for these people? This rapid change was achievable because they learned how to genuinely connect to something greater than themselves. They then activated a power that had the ability to overcome all the things that distracted, blocked or sabotaged their progressive forward movements in life.

They were each able to do this because they allowed themselves to open up, trust and receive their desires while being fully connected to the Divine.

They also learned how to apply eternal laws and simple life-skills, which provided them with remarkable results.

That is why those who have been on medications, alcohol drugs and tobacco are able to stop using those substances to comfort themselves from their unbearable circumstances.

They are able to allow this change because this reawakening and transformational change  provides them with effective life-skills. With their connection to the Divine, they are literally able to shift their body chemistry and heal their lives; drawing to them what they prefer instead!

The Power that formed this world is based on and generated by *Eternal Love*. This is the Power that will stop your *internal wrestling*. It can aright what you perceive as the wounded, broken parts of your being. This is the love that can unite our world. It is by this Power that we are now individually creating our own world.

### Creating, Destroying or Repeating

However, if we are not aware of how to tap into this Power and purposefully utilize it, with deliberate intent, we can destroy our world or create the same world over and over. That bears repeating:

*We are individually creating our world, destroying our world, or creating the same world over and over.*

*What are you doing with your world right now?*

This is precisely why it is imperative we become one with each other, genuinely allowing ourselves to develop deep feelings of love and best wishes for *everyone*. If we feel less than accepting, appreciative or we do not desire good toward all, we simply are sabotaging our personal joy along with our ability to fully connect with the Divine.

All feelings that are less than uplifting will only prove to be distractions and energy wasters. They are diversions away from our preferred path of well-being.

It is your Divine birthright to be able to connect with your Team and create your world. This is the most joy-filled, exhilarating way to exist in this life that I am aware of.

Remember to keep it simple and enjoy this process. If you begin to feel like this adventure is work, you are trying too hard to make it happen and you have slid off course. If that is where you find yourself, it's okay too. I'll show you how to quickly get back on track. Your Team will be there to assist you as well.

> **NOTE:** You too are a person that has the ability to receive visions on a regular basis. How do I know this? Because you are able to have visions or dreams when you sleep. Science can record those activities even if you do not remember each one of them. You can have visions when you ponder and meditate. You can also have visions while your eyes are open, because you know how to *daydream*. That is a form of being able to *envision* something or in other words have a *vision!* Allow yourself to develop this gift. Believe it is possible.

You have the power to ask to see what you desire to know and it will be shown to you!

## TAKE ACTION!

**Now is the time to discover what you would really love to experience in your life. Look over the points on the following list and begin actively applying them in your life today!**

- **Have fun as you ponder and meditate about what you would like to create. Let those ideas form and come into your soul.**

- Ask for what you specifically desire while completely believing in your entire being, nothing wavering, that you have already received that desire. Recognize in your thoughts, visions, feelings and words that your preference at some level has already arrived (it first is created in a spiritual dimension).

- Allow yourself to fully receive what you have asked for; embrace and accept it.

- Give thanks for all that has been and is now being provided for you. Feel that genuine gratitude for what you now have so you will be open to receive more.

- Look forward to the many blessings swiftly coming to you now. Feel your increased excitement.

- Hold on to those feelings. They drive your blessings and miracles from the spiritual realm into your physical world!

- Recognize those blessings as they appear and who assisted you in creating them. Acknowledge where those gifts came from; appreciate them.

- Give thanks AGAIN!

# Chapter Five

# ~ *Childhood Songs* ~

Many years ago, when life seemed especially disconnected and upside down, a familiar childhood song entered my mind. I began to sing:

**Row, row, row your boat,**
**Gently down the stream.**
**Merrily, merrily, merrily, merrily,**
**Life is but a dream.**

Suddenly that simple song indicated to me how I was to live my life! I am to send my boat or body *down* the stream. And not just down, but *gently down* the stream of life. I am also to be *merry* or joy-filled as I'm doing it. How is it possible to maintain that *merry* attitude? Because… "This life is but a dream." It is not the main reality!

I took a deep breath and heartily bellowed out that song several times. As I sang, I released all my concerns, worries and fears, allowing a calm, peaceful feeling to flood the newly formed space inside my soul.

## Profound Truths by Simple Means

Over time, as I better understood this simple, powerful song, I learned how to apply its message to my daily life. Whenever I tried to use oars, invariably I would start heading *upstream* and madly row against the current while feeling very alone. Sometimes I even tried to strap an engine on that sucker and attempted to fire it up, unsuccessfully yanking over and over on the starter cord! I was determined to force that boat upstream no matter what it took!

After much effort, I would eventually become angry or frustrated and then discouraged: "How in tarnation was I supposed feel a Sally-Sunshine merry attitude with this blankety-blank miserable situation I was stuck in? Surely there was someone around that I could blame for this screw up if I just looked hard enough!"

I would then search for someone I could blame for my miserable feelings. Actually, if I simply glanced into the water and gazed at my own reflection I would have quickly discovered who had squarely landed me in the middle of this particular snafu.

I would also realize that I was completely worn out. And after a while, sometimes a *long* while, I would let go of the struggle. I'd stop rowing with the oars or pulling that engine starter cord and sprawl out from sheer exhaustion. I just didn't have any more fight left.

Sound familiar?

Because I was so completely worn out, I discovered I would begin to relax; I was just too pooped to do anything else. I'd then allow myself to begin flowing along with life again. Surprisingly, and to my relief, I started floating *down* stream. Soon my merry attitude would surface intact.

I now recognize the times that I struggled were the times that I personally created chaos and discord in my own life. In other words, I was destroying my world.

## Creating a Place for More

One morning as I read some Scriptures, I came across a verse that spoke to my soul. It said that if someone had only a desire to improve in their life, all they had to do was just allow that desire to work within their soul until they could create a place for more of God's words to come into them.

I had been feeling quite ill and was bedridden for years because of very low blood pressure. In fact, my blood pressure was so low the machines the doctor and the nurses were using at the hospital could not record it when they were conducting my Tilt Table Test. They could not understand how I was still alive, let alone conscious and still speaking to them!

I was so worn down at the time from an overwhelming lack of oxygen in my body that I didn't even have a full portion of a desire to improve my circumstances. But I did have a sliver of a desire to let a desire work a place into my heart where it could grow. So I planted that tiny spec of a seed and started to feel a slight glimmer of hope as it began to grow into something bigger.

That seed did in fact sprout and grow. And soon, it began to bear good fruits. I continue to enjoy those same delicious fruits even to this day.

## Toss Out the Oars and Float!

I have long since thrown away the oars to my boat. I now *float, float, float* gently down the stream! I now *get it!* Finally, I have let go of the fight and submitted to the fact that on my own, I had no Power or ability to move forward. I also rediscovered how that stream moves and why it is so important for me to fully release any wishes to row against it.

The stream of life is moved by the Divine. These beings and intelligences move our personal streams as quickly or as slowly as we each individually request our *waters* to flow.

Sometimes we get an exhilarated rush when we go really fast over rapids and waterfalls. Other times, we just desire to move at a slower pace and feel the stream gently caress and refresh us as we languidly float along, enjoying the sun as it dapples our skin with its light through the leaves of the trees sheltering our stream.

There are also segments in our lives when we may sometimes slip over to the side of that flowing stream, allowing ourselves to go round and round in an eddy as we create our world over and over.

The water may become a bit stagnant and fetid because fresh waters are not renewing and replenishing that area. But this is not a permanent trap! We do not have to stay stuck there forever. Why?

Because an eddy is usually just a small gentle whirlpool; at *anytime* we can easily and quickly make a course adjustment, kick or paddle a little and be back flowing down the main stream of our life again!

Since we are the ones directing how fast or slow we would like our stream to flow, we can send out our desires and make requests for the twists and turns we prefer to experience. Our Team responds to those desires. I am certain of this fact. We have always been the ones and always will be the ones sending out the requests for how our lives will unfold.

Our individual Team is attentive and quickly responds to our wishes. They unite with us as they assist in bringing to us information and experiences *we* have asked for. We have the individual agency to decide how we will live and experience our lives.

Our personal Team will never take away our ability to choose and nothing is ever forced upon us. They eagerly await our requests and quickly respond to our desires.

This truth is quite evident in the following clear statements:

***Ask and it is given. Seek and you will find. Knock and the door will be opened.***

Nowhere in those statements does it say, "Ask, seek and knock and in a few years, perhaps a decade or two, we will provide for you." Really look at those bold words. The members of your Team are prepared to give you your requests *now*!

We are the ones doing the asking, receiving, seeking, finding and knocking. We even open the door! And it is always unlocked! So what are you asking, seeking and knocking for? What are you creating now? Is it what you purposefully desire? What are you requesting of your Team?

## Which Direction Are You Steering Your Boat?

Sometimes when I realize I'm out of kilter or in a funk I simply ask myself, "Am I steering my boat upstream or downstream?" The answer readily becomes apparent and helps me recognize if I've been floating my boat downstream, paddling upstream or stagnating in an eddy. With that renewed awareness, I can then quickly make a slight course adjustment and head off into a better feeling direction.

***Remember that childlike tune and those carefree lyrics. They can help you keep your eternal perspective.***

## TAKE ACTION!

While you are moving through each day, go ahead and sing that simple childhood song, remembering to go gently down the stream of life with a merry attitude. From time to time also ask yourself this question, "Am I paddling my boat upstream or floating it downstream?" Allow yourself to quickly turn in a better feeling direction if you recognize you have slid off course.

# CHAPTER SIX

# ~ *Staying Centered In Your Hurricane* ~

When I was a child, my Master Teacher taught me about the importance of staying in the center of *my personal hurricane* because, in the center of this hurricane, there is peace, love, light and clarity of thought.

## A Hurricane that Responds to Our Requests

The hurricane I am referring to is not the frightening destructive hurricane we see on the weather channels. I am referring to the hurricane of life and experience. That hurricane had tremendous power and the ability to affect my world; but unlike a real hurricane, it responded to my attentions and commands.

On the edges of my hurricane were exciting relationships, rewarding experiences and profound growth opportunities. I called them into creation and they became part of the spinning mix around me whenever I expressed a desire to learn about them.

When I chose to receive some of them into my existence and gave them my full attention, they quickly moved into the center of my world.

As soon as I learned all I wished to learn about the situation I had purposefully drawn to me, I released it and sent it back out into the edges of the hurricane, so that I could bring in another opportunity for expansion.

I could command to me many prospects for my personal growth simultaneously or savor them one by one. I could study and understand something in five minutes, fifty years or a lifetime. It was entirely up to me how fast or slow I learned from my experiences.

There were times, when I stood in the center of that cyclonic mixture, that I felt a sure balance and a firm confidence. I could easily and quickly walk my way through any situation, reaching a successful outcome while remaining unscathed from any turmoil. I felt a calm well-being.

## Distractions and Drama

Within that swirling mix, however, I could also allow myself to get distracted and caught up in the drama of life beyond the edges of my hurricane's calm center. These experiences were filled with the gossip, judgments and negativity that others were experimenting with in their hurricanes.

I discovered I could quickly become a part of the discord I was viewing, speaking about, feeling passion for, or listening to.

If I gave my attention to those negative issues, they would instantly become part of my swirling mix of choices. Simply because I focused my attention on others' misery and chaos, I ultimately drew that turmoil into my own reality and into the lives of those I interacted with. It seemed to me that it would happen in a blink of an eye; I would be thrown out of my center and tossed toward the rough outer edges of my hurricane because I unwittingly allowed that action!

While I was out there, I felt as if I was being *knocked around* and *beaten down* or *buffeted* as I stumbled in the darkness. I tried to regain control of the situation by forcing others to do my will. They would bristle, angrily rage against me and become abusive. I would try to work harder and apply sheer willpower to overcome my misery, but I felt like I only became more and more befuddled.

I was filled with anxiety, doubt, worry, fear and loneliness. I had difficulty eating and sleeping; I was gripped twenty-four/seven by the vice of constant, unrelenting stress. I became exhausted and lost all energy, sinking into feelings of discouragement; unable to function at times. I became depressed and ill. My very soul felt like it was dying.

It seemed as though there was no place of peace or rest for me, no way to return to the clear, sane, calm center of the storm.

## Thrown Out to Greet the Chaos

I finally recognized that every time I had those experiences, I had not been deliberately living my life fully connected to my Team. I had not consciously directed my *thoughts* and *feelings* toward that which would bring me continual happiness. By abdicating that awareness, that I was personally directing my life, I gave my attention to the discord of others and their world. In doing so I drew into my surroundings the very opposite of my individual peace. I was thrown out of my calm center—out to greet the chaos.

When I suffered and struggled in this darkness I also learned valuable information that ultimately helped me grow and expand in numerous ways. These experiences sharpened my awareness of how I conducted my life, helping me identify and chisel out with exactness what I preferred to release from my life and precisely dial in what I would love to draw into my world instead.

I learned that even these experiences had merit and value for me (or I would not have given my attentions to them). Those teaching opportunities also helped me increase my desire to be more attentive to and aware of what I thought, envisioned, felt, spoke and heard within my soul.

I began to realize there were also moments when I tried to give others my personal Power. Sometimes it was because I simply didn't choose to take the time to think through what I actually desired to experience. I just went along with what the *crowd* was doing or what I assumed *society expected* from me. At times, I even I jumped on the *bandwagon* and did the things that were most *popular.*

Those experiences were short lived because I soon realized that it was not personally satisfying to mimic others when I could spend my life creating my passions.

Other times, I recognized that I allowed myself to feel like a victim when I abdicated my ability to actively and purposefully direct my life. If I let myself be affected by the whims and desires of those I associated with, I noticed that feelings of bitterness and hopelessness soon grew within me.

> **NOTE:** How often do you hear people blaming others for *making* them do something?

I even caught myself trying to please people to win their approval and fit in. Sometimes I'd ask their opinion on how I should live my life—never a winning game plan! Even well-meaning individuals, at times, wanted to direct my choices and actions.

Thankfully, I soon awoke from my slumber and swiftly arighted my situation.

## Why Those Tactics Were Never Successful

I now clearly understand why those tactics were never successful. Most people don't know how the heck to live their own lives with consistent happiness and joy. How can they possibly know how to run my life? Why would I ever willingly desire to have them make my decisions for me?

Occasionally, I recognized others wished to control and relegate me into a neat little box. I definitely knew I did not desire that!

Not even God will take away our ability to choose what we create in our lives. Certainly no mortal could have that Power to take away our agency to direct our lives.

For the record, it is impossible to give someone else your Power; it just doesn't work that way.

More importantly, why would any of us ever try to give up creating the life we prefer to go along with others? They are not aware of the eternal big picture that we would delight in experiencing while here on this earth. My truth and your truth is:

*I AM in charge of my personal happiness or unhappiness.*

*I AM directing my life situations at EVERY moment.*

*I AM able to create changes in my world at ANY TIME.*

### I Am With The Great I Am!

These are profound thoughts, especially when we remember "*I am*" represents the person making those statements…*me!* I also recognize *I AM* represents the name of Deity as well. So in essence, *The Great I AM* is actually Teaming with me while *I am* identifying and defining what I prefer to experience in my life.

Now that's an absolutely winning combination for creating a knock-out-of-the-ballpark, amazing life (especially when we consider that the Divine knows all things past, present and future). A council meeting with this group is pretty powerful and a huge confidence builder. When we allow ourselves to join together with the Divine to create our individual world, all doubts can be cast aside! (I will teach you how to form that meeting in the chapter, *How to Create a Council Meeting.*)

## Returning to the Center of the Hurricane

Thankfully, this realization was the key to my restored well-being. I let those truths resonate throughout my soul and decided to remember them whenever I found myself in a miserable predicament. I changed my viewpoint on how I saw everything in life.

Now, when an opportunity (that seemingly appears as a *challenge)* presents itself, I realize I actually have asked to draw forth this situation so I can learn from it and master it.

Instead of avoiding or running from the *problem,* which always seems to increase the stress, size and fervor of the turmoil, I take the necessary steps to more fully connect to the Divine. Then, while I am united with them, I start facing these opportunities for growth and expansion when they first arrive in my life.

I also form questions in my mind, receive the answers to them and act upon those responses.

The following are some of the questions I ask when I realize I have lost my balance:

- **"Am I centered in my hurricane right now;** feeling peace, well-being and clarity of mind?"

- **"What am I to learn from this situation?"**

- **"How can I become more enlightened** and aware because of this experience?"

- **"What adjustment can I make in my life** that will allow a change to take place within me so I can once again feel the calm center of my hurricane?"

## TAKE ACTION!

**Whenever you first feel out of sync within your soul and discombobulated, simply answer these four questions. Then, take action and reconnect with your Team. Next, follow through with the insight, inspiration and information you receive. Finally, keep your focus on *your* personal goals and get your creative *mojo* back!**

# CHAPTER SEVEN

# ~ *Reconnecting to Your Team* ~

Still wondering how you can more fully connect to your personal Team? Sometimes we forget how to feel that union. It is a weird and disconcerting experience when our bond is weakened.

Think back to a time just before an important event, holiday or birthday. Did you feel excited and full of happy anticipation? Perhaps at times, as a youth, you felt carefree, giddy abandon when you ran, laughed and played with your favorite friends.

***If you have felt these sensations in the past, then you know how it felt when you were united with your Team!***

Do you recall a time when you felt sheer bliss and all was right in your world for that moment? Perhaps it was on a perfect, clear spring day early in the morning when the dew still lingered on the leaves. Or the first time you ever saw snow falling, hushed upon the earth as it turned into a magical, winter kingdom. You may have felt the wonder of it all as you saw your world from a different, refreshing perspective. Maybe it was while you enjoyed a beautiful, lingering sunset. As the colors gently flowed into their magnificent crescendo perhaps you felt peaceful and deep satisfaction. How about when you read something inspiring, moving or uplifting? Have you ever felt some great *Ah-Ha!* moments?

During those times in my life I felt a tickle and a warm, wonderful feeling inside that began in my heart. Shortly thereafter my chest expanded with an amazing, increased feeling of well-being and happiness. Those feelings soon radiated throughout my entire body. Sometimes I was so moved I cried tears of joy while I experienced deep feelings of gratitude and appreciation. Other times, I felt overwhelming love and complete acceptance for others, as well as for myself. At those times, all seemed right with me and my world.

I'm sharing these details with you so you can reflect back and better identify the times when you also have had similar experiences and sensations. Open up your awareness and remember those moments. This reawakening to your good feelings is important for your progress in rapidly creating the world you prefer.

These are specific examples of when your soul indicated to you that you were connected to the Divine. During this time, you were literally partnered with your Team, becoming one in purpose with them and the Power that creates all that has been and ever will be.

In other words, we have the ability to experience a living Atonement or *At-One-Ment* with those who have created us!

We can keep those wonderful, uplifting, healing, united feelings every moment of our day if that is our desire. *We allow* this union to take place. But, how exactly do we recreate that unified relationship if we are not feeling one with our Team now?

**Preparing for a Long Journey**

Picture yourself preparing to go on a long journey you have never taken before to another country across the sea; a trip that begins in another city several hours away and lasts for a couple of months. Would you just wake up one day, jump in the car and head out in the general direction of wherever you think your final destination might be?

Instead of haphazardly beginning, wouldn't you carefully plan your trip and then stick to that plan, referring to it often?

Certainly you would service and fuel your vehicle, pack up some clothes and personal items, arrange cash for food and incidentals, activate a couple of credit cards, bring your passport, change your cell phone to an international plan or get a phone card, set up hotel arrangements, purchase tickets, gather maps and plot your course and activities!

Yet how many people just wake up every day and *wing it* when it comes to living their life? How many people feel insecure, uncertain and frightened as they are tossed to and fro like an insignificant little cork by huge waves in the ocean of this mortal experience?

No wonder many of us are so miserable, confused and frustrated. No wonder we do not feel like we are reaching our full potential as we meander about each day.

Sure, we have our basic responsibilities that we manage to handle regularly, but what about the passionate exciting dreams and goals that we would love to reach? Are we deliberately moving in a direction that will result in our achieving those dreams and goals so we can experience a more vitally alive and satisfying existence?

Remember that at any moment we can release those impotent feelings and deliberately take charge of where we are heading!

Just as the forming of a well-planned journey is essential for a successful vacation or trip, so too is a roadmap for life pivotal to our continuous progression. This important preparation will assist you in discovering your *Life Mission* (you know, the main reason you came here to this earth; what you would love to accomplish and contribute while here), so you can confidently and excitedly move forward and experience it.

## Creating Your Road Map for Life

If you have not yet taken hold of this opportunity to form your life desires, take some time now to write out your *Road Map for Life.* Clearly decide your preferred route while keeping your final destination in mind. You will be amazed how simple, quick and enjoyable this valuable exercise is.

**First, get three sheets of paper and something to write with. Go ahead and do it NOW!** (By the way, there just happens to be three pages toward the end of this book in chapter 34, **"Creating Your Road Map For Life"**).

Not at home? Don't have a pencil or pen? No problem! Let go of feeling shy. Start activating what you are learning. Venture out of your comfort zone and borrow it from someone. Remember, ask and it is given. Allow yourself to start asking now while believing and feeling you will easily and quickly receive what you desire. It really is that simple.

**HANDWRITE on your first piece of paper all the situations or moments that come to your mind when you were thankful, joy filled or experiencing gratitude.** Take a few moments to allow yourself to think of the times you felt thankful for something in your life. The example could be as simple as the purr of a kitten, the song of a bird, a full moon sparkling over the ocean at night, the fresh smell of the earth after a summer rain, or it could be something bigger.

**Shift your body to feel how you felt at that time when you were thankful. Allow that feeling to grow within you.**

Go ahead and fill up the entire page. You can easily and quickly open up and do this. Then look over the page and read it aloud with *feeling*. Let your body resonate the appreciation you felt during those times. The things you have written are specific moments when your Team has been with you and blessed you with opportunities to feel a warm pleasant feeling of love, joy and well-being within yourself and also with others.

Continue this activity. Then say with genuine feeling:

**"More experiences like these in my life now, please. Thank you!"**

Those feelings help you to open your soul to receive more fully that connection to the source that created you. It helps to prepare your vessel or body to expand and begin the creative process you desire. Those genuine uplifted feelings help form your desires so they can swiftly come into your present moment instead of remaining in a nebulous *someday* spiritual dimension.

**On the second page, write down the names of the people who have been there for you.** Think of those people who fully accept and appreciate you. Some of them were free of any judgment, while others were complete strangers who expressed understanding or kindness to you. Include the people that you admire and respect. List their attributes, strengths, talents, qualities and characteristics that you also feel would be valuable in your life.

Everyone, including me, has a Jekyll and Hyde inside of them. So, remember when the best part of the people in your life showed up for you, then clearly picture and write down those preferred moments.

Let go of any other feelings that may pop up which are contrary to your preferred desires. Specifically acknowledge those distractions as they arise instead of shoving them back down where they brood and fester. As soon as you notice negative thoughts, completely allow yourself to release them from your soul. Especially let go of jealousy, envy or lack. Those feelings push you further away from the Divine.

Genuinely allow yourself to feel happy for other individuals when they have wonderful things happen to them. Be grateful they have provided you with examples of possibilities and opportunities that can come into your life. Be thankful they helped you to more clearly define what you would enjoy experiencing. Now say with feeling:

**"More people and experiences like this in my life now, please; more of this in all of our lives now. Thank you!"**

These feelings help you to form more harmonious relationships and assist you in becoming one with others and your world. In turn you are better able to connect with your creative source.

On the third page, write down what you would love to see happen **while releasing any concerns about how your dreams will be accomplished**. Set aside any distractions that may pop up. Instead, focus your attentions on what you feel passionate about creating.

Start adding the details about what you prefer. Feel excited about the opportunities now swiftly coming into your life. The more details the better. Those details will help you recognize your blessings as they come to you. Reach out, grasp hold of and receive those gifts fully into your life.

Be bold. Put a date on it. Be brave. Let go of any hesitation or wavering. Say it out loud. You can even tell others about your preferences. Plant the seed of your dreams in them and allow them to create with you.

Lastly, say with excited feelings and deliberate intent:

***"I would love to allow this into my life now, please. Thank you!"***

Or create your own personal statement that invokes an Enthusiasm within you about what you would like to currently experience.

### The Meaning of Enthusiasm

The Greeks constructed the word Enthusiasm from three smaller words: en+Theos+im, which translates to *in God me* or *God inspiring within* or *God in me*.

Simply put, the word Enthusiasm perfectly describes how you feel when you are connected to your Team and are using the Power of love to create your world. It is an action word that helps you to live not in the past or the future but in the present!

So ***hold on to your Enthusiastic feelings***! These feelings validate and activate your Powers to create, literally unleashing your ability to command into your life the exact desires of your soul.

Remember, as soon as you think, picture and speak about your preferences, they begin to be formed in a spiritual dimension. You can call them into your present world when you fuel those dreams and desires with your wonderful feelings of Enthusiasm, while releasing any wavering doubt.

However, if you say, "Someday this will happen," or "It's going to happen soon," it will remain in your future.

Notice that it is profoundly important our desires are stated in the *now* form. Such as:

**"I would love to have this opportunity in my life now!"**

That is why the *N* word is pivotal in our creative process and success.

## Remember to Always Give Thanks

Remember to always give thanks whenever you discover evidence of the many tender mercies, blessings and love being extended to you daily. Start looking for them. You will be amazed at how much good is continuously prepared on your personal behalf and freely showered upon you.

The action of giving thanks is twofold. First, it shows your respect and appreciation. And second, it expands your soul to more fully unite with your personal Team and others. In short, it causes everyone participating to feel good!

These exercises may initially seem too simple to have profound, long-lasting effects. I can assure you they have great Power and are even more potent when you add your well-defined intentions and motivations. Include them with your desire to create something wondrous in your life.

Then add all the above with your excited feelings and believe it is possible for you to receive the passions of your soul.

These three pages will assist you in forming a clearer view of where you are headed. They can help you release the stumbling blocks of fear, doubt and indecisiveness while increasing your *Fun Factor* on your journey! Relax and enjoy this process. You are already on your path.

*"Nothing great was ever achieved without enthusiasm."*
~Ralph Waldo Emerson

## TAKE ACTION!

Stop whatever you are doing and actually begin putting together your **THREE-PAGE ROAD MAP FOR LIFE**. Promise yourself that you will complete this map this evening or early in the morning when you are fresh, before your day begins. You are worth taking that quality time! Allow yourself to feel lighthearted and playful as you quickly write this information while being connected to your Team.

# CHAPTER EIGHT

# ~ Four-Letter Words ~

**@#$%!**

We've all heard these four-letter words before. Even fine, upstanding, humble people use them… including your tea-toting auntie or Sabbath day teacher.

These expressions don't usually bring out the best feelings in us. If we are not experiencing upbeat feelings, we usually will not be creating the world we desire. In fact, when we think, speak, listen to, and then feel how these words resonate inside our bodies, we often unwittingly push ourselves away from our Team and connection to our Power.

### What I'm Really Talking About

The four-letter words I am referring to are not the expressions you might be imagining. What I am alluding to are terms such as: *work, task, hard, fear, help, make, dumb, pain, need, want, hate…*

There are other words that feel like four-letter words. For example: *try, force, rescue, sacrifice, doubt, discouragement, should, worry and long-suffering…*

Remember that *words have great power!* Let's consider the word *work* for an example. As soon as we begin to think, speak or hear this word, and then feel how it resonates in our body, we can start to lose the strength of our Power if we identify *work* with difficulty, hardship, sweat, etc.

In reality, *work* can be a perfectly fine word. It depends on the thoughts and feelings we attach to the words that determine if they truly are *four-letter words* to our souls.

*Play* can even be a four-letter word if we equate it with laziness, misuse of time or guilt.

We sometimes have a knee jerk reaction to the word *make* that will resonate within us. It feels like we are forcing something to happen. That word definitely forms diminished feelings inside your being instead of *allowing* your blessings to easily and quickly flow into your life.

### The Candidate

How often do we hear the word *hard?*

During the preparations for the last political election, I had the opportunity to meet and train with some of the individuals who were running for political offices. They would represent the state of Arizona in Washington, DC. I also trained personal staff members. Some of them were Democrats and others were Republicans.

Yes, these laws can be applied by everyone.

One of the candidates shared with me some of the usual operational concerns that most individuals in his shoes would experience. One of those concerns was getting people to volunteer and work in the campaign. During our conversation, he said to me, "It's just so hard to find people that will volunteer."

I immediately responded, "You are right. And it will continue to be *hard* as long as you think, feel and act like it is *hard* to find those people. Those are the words you are literally sending out with the passion you are feeling about the situation. In doing so, you have been creating what you believe, which is: **'It is *hard* to find people to volunteer!'**

"But," I told him, "if the results of those situations are less than satisfying to you, you can at any time shift your thoughts, feelings and actions to a new reality.

**"Remember a belief is just a thought you repeatedly keep thinking. Also, what you think and give your attention to is what you create.**

"So if you continually think that something is hard or difficult, it will indeed remain hard and difficult."

I shared with the political candidate that everyone has the opportunity to change their scenario into one they prefer. He could let go of his previous thoughts and feelings about volunteers. Instead, he could think about people eagerly walking through the headquarter doors, asking if they could work with his campaign group.

I further pointed out that the more he could visualize the details he preferred to have, the better. I recommended that he get excited and see this happening *now* and notice how great the synergy felt.

With that thought in mind, we started to think about, visualize and speak about this positive change as though it was currently forming. The details of my instructions to him went something like this:

"See the people as they come with their excited Enthusiasm and genuine desire to contribute. Notice that all of these people are harmonious and enjoy interacting with one another. They look forward each day to creating with the group that has been formed to turn this goal into reality. Observe their good works as they participate in the office or interact with people in the community. Picture them doing a great job of representing and supporting you in your desire to better serve the individuals and families of our state. Allow yourself to feel an excitement and thrill every time you think about those who are currently participating with you in your campaign."

I shared other ideas to assist him in more precisely creating what he would prefer. The following are some of those key points that I shared with him. As you read them, notice how they could apply in your life:

- **Feel thankful and grateful for all those who are presently volunteering and supporting you.** Notice the fine qualities about them and the other people in your life and say, "More of these qualities for all of us and those that are joining us *now*, please. Thank you!"

- **Flood your soul with great anticipation and appreciation for those supportive individuals who are swiftly and easily coming to join your support group.** Recognize that your eternal Team stands shoulder to shoulder with you; they and all these amazing volunteers are mutually creating together. Then relax and enjoy the process while allowing these actions to come into your world.

- **Be sure to properly prepare your body each day prior to speaking or acting with others.** Rest, refresh, feed and replenish yourself. Meditate and exercise. Be fully present, well-prepared and *connected to the Divine.* So that, when you speak, people will better understand, hear and embrace what you desire to do to support their best interests. In turn, they will feel your sincere intentions and develop trust in you.

Notice how the steps of purposefully creating something you prefer can be applied to any assemblage of people, be it a political party, business endeavor, social group, or even a family gathering.

## Sir Galahad

*Rescue* is a word that can feel like a four letter word. *Allow* yourself to release the desire to *rescue* or *save* others. Be comforted in remembering that each of us individually has a personal Team that is perfectly positioned to attend to our every desire. I sometimes share the following statement with individuals who are connected to a Savior-based faith that feel the *need* to save someone (we'll refer to this person who is perceived to be in *need* of rescue as Jane Doe):

"Jane Doe has a Savior that personally knows and loves her and you are not that Redeemer." That pretty well clears up the picture for them (remember the story in an earlier chapter about the woman that was worried about her mother). By the way, many religions and people around the world, not just Christians, embrace the belief in a Savior.

Rescuing usually activates the triangle of victim, rescuer, and persecutor into perpetual motion. It also often sets up an internal shift that one individual is superior over another…never a great scenario.

The *Knight in Shining Armor* usually feels better, stronger, more intelligent or capable than the one he or she is rescuing…usually at the other person's expense.

Sir Galahad sees someone that is perceived as being in *need* and comes to save the damsel in distress from the hardship that in reality *she* has purposefully created, so *she* can gain that experience.

Initially, the person doing the rescuing usually feels pretty great about being able to perform such a feat, but not long afterwards he begins to experience an internal discord. The original gracious feelings often change into irritability, resentment, disdain and even anger.

I have played the role of Sir Galahad, trying to rescue the prince in distress. I soon realized I was making a huge mess of things. I was interfering with what that individual was creating. When I repeatedly tried to remove the boulders from his life's path, he just recreated them.

Except each time he reformed his situation, the problems became magnified and morphed into even more challenging opportunities for growth than before!

Having *win-win* relationships is where consistent well-being can be found. Releasing judgment and allowing complete acceptance moves those relationships swiftly forward.

We can all still participate in being supportive of others in a healthy, *mutually uplifting* manner when we adjust our attitudes and continually recognize that *everyone* has supernal value and is of infinite worth no matter their station or situation in life. We are each continually gathering experience so we can learn from those growth opportunities and master them. These activities are vitally important for our personal expansion.

Well-meaning parents and friends often find themselves in these *rescuing* positions with those they love or feel responsible for.

**If you are a parent or friend of someone that YOU feel needs rescuing…LET GO of that feeling NOW!**

Instead of sending out to others the feelings that you don't believe they are capable of overcoming their challenges, *change your paradigm*! Deeply allow yourself to embrace the truth that they have the ability to swiftly learn from and master the life lessons they have created.

In fact, each of us has the capacity to overcome all things. Hold on to those reassuring feelings. Your sincere belief and encouragement will support the positive shift in the dynamics of the situation they are creating. This can only happen if you sincerely believe this truth.

*Sacrifice* comes hand in glove with *rescuing*. Whoa! Who would ever really choose to create a place in their soul for the feeling of *sacrifice?* Is that an exciting uplifting situation to experience? Where is the blessing for anyone with that feeling? Now before someone jumps all over those last several statements, please read on to better understand where I am coming from.

When each of our children became engaged I shared with them that it was important for them to immediately form their *couplehood.* If I invited them to a family dinner and they already had something else planned that they preferred to attend, they were not to change their plans to accommodate me. I was not interested in having them come to our home if they felt they were sacrificing something else.

This was because the occasion would basically turn into a body count. Their bodies would be there but their Enthusiastic spirits would not be participating. In other words:

**Whatever you decide to do or act upon, do so because you <u>desire</u> to do it. Otherwise, take no action until you've adjusted your soul to feel that desire.**

When we do something with the feeling of drudgery or *sacrifice* while performing a service, the gift is defiled and of no value. But in a moment, the attitude can be shifted to a willing desire. That changed sensation restores the action or service to a blessing for all.

## Ten Bananas or Nine Bananas

I was recently conducting a weekend training session with a husband and wife. The wife asked for me to share with her husband why tithing was such an important principle.

I immediately felt the word *sacrifice* being tied to the word tithing. So I decided to relate a story that had been personally told to me many years ago by a man I knew. The story was about an experience this man had as a young missionary while he was serving in Brazil for a couple of years.

The missionary was responsible for teaching a family six lessons as they were preparing to be baptized into the young man's church. The people were very receptive students and had embraced all the principles that had been presented to them. They eagerly looked forward to their last lesson. That lesson was about tithing, or giving ten percent of what they received to the Lord, to show appreciation for all that was being provided for them by their creator.

The family was crestfallen. They were profoundly poor and did not know how they could possibly live that law. The young man tried to comfort the family by sharing a promise in the scriptures that is given to those who pay an honest tithe. The promise is that the windows of heaven will open and pour out a blessing that cannot be contained.

Shortly after the tithing lesson, the missionary was transferred to another part of the country. He did not know what happened to the family because he was unable to keep in touch with them, so he often wondered how they were and what they decided to do with their concerns.

Then one day, as the missionary was walking down a road, he heard his name being called. He turned to see a car driving toward him on the same road. What was more startling was that the car was filled with people whose arms were waving out the windows. Exuberant smiling faces were also leaning out of the windows while they yelled his name.

When the vehicle came to a stop beside him, he recognized that the people in the car were the same family members he had taught in the previous town.

It was rare to see a car in that area of the country. So the curious young man asked the family, "Whose car are you driving?" The father replied that it was *their* car. Amazing!

Astonished by the answer, the missionary inquired how they were able to afford such an expensive purchase in such a short amount of time.

Then the father shared their story. After the missionary left their home they were very discouraged about their situation. But then they reasoned that they could live on ten bananas and try to figure out life on their own or, "We could live on nine bananas with the Lord's help!" They decided to live on nine bananas with assistance from their creator and that made all the difference.

When the family was first being taught the lesson of tithing, they felt a heavy burden with the *sacrifice* that was being asked of them. They experienced great *lack* in their situation…another four-letter word. But they soon released those thoughts and accompanying feelings and opened up their vision and trust to connect to something far greater than this finite world.

Stepping away from their place of *lack,* this family eagerly chose to connect to the Divine and create with them in that great abundant place where they reside.

### Self Re-Indoctrination

When we slide down into *lack, want, need, can't, won't*—all four-letter words—we have walked away from creating with our resource of wealth. We shut down our floodgates to a mere trickle.

Notice how those feelings literally drive out your empowering feelings of gratitude, thankfulness and appreciation. In fact, being filled with *want* becomes insatiable. Every time you receive one of your wants you soon afterwards want something else.

A man I had been training was amazed at how he, without thinking, continued to re-indoctrinate himself with negative four letter words. Early in his life he formed this habit, probably because he was indoctrinated with these words while he was learning how to communicate with others.

When he visited with me he consistently expressed to me what he *wanted* and *needed.* I shared with him that he would continue to want and need those things and situations.

> **NOTE:** Actually most of the initial conversations that everyone has with me are often liberally filled with these two words until they awaken to what they are creating. At

times even I can slide back into using them because their use is so prevalent in our world.

He then realized that to really unleash his Powers and ability to create, it was imperative that he willingly release those negative thoughts and replace the statements with other more Powerful words such as:

> I *desire* to receive.
> I *prefer* to create.
> I *choose* to allow.
> I would *love* to see.
> I would *like* this.

He soon began rapidly creating the desires of his soul. Yes, he did falter in his ability to consistently let go of those couple of four-letter words and in their place say and think the words he preferred instead. But happily, he was always able to swiftly restore those feel-good flowing energies at any time by applying the simple laws he had learned.

## Hunkering Down or Opening Up

*Fear* and *doubt* are also words that cause us to shrink back or hunker down in an effort to protect ourselves. Beware of that response! As soon as we make that contraction in our souls we swiftly reduce our connection to the Divine.

We can literally try to surround ourselves with bodyguards and still not feel safe. However, we can be shielded with the love and protection that only the union with the Divine can create in us. When we allow our full connection to them, we are completely protected and feel that peace and assurance of their sheltering comfort. It literally feels like we are placed in a different realm or dimension where only well-being and harmonious relationships can enter. All else is confounded and eventually departs.

Once, I willingly allowed myself to plunge into an extremely challenging situation which arose from a work project I had undertaken. The situation was serious: my life was being threatened. In fact, the situation was so serious that I was provided with bodyguards and escorts throughout this tumultuous time.

But in reality, my personal safety and the peace in my soul was never provided by those men. After all, how could they possibly protect me or give me assurance and comfort every moment of the day and night?

While I did appreciate these individuals' efforts and friendship, my protection was literally provided by the unwavering shielding that I received from my Team. I had a sure trust that I was being watched over, directed and protected This was my cornerstone of truth. In fact, I was absolutely certain that this blessing of protection and well-being extended to the entire organization, its investors, owners and employees.

I understood that I was being given the opportunity to learn about courage and that I should not run or shrink back from this experience. I knew that at some level this was important to me now and would serve me later in life.

### "COURAGE Pamela Ann, COURAGE!"

It was during this time that my girlfriend Sandee gave me a simple bracelet that really helped me to stay the course. She had seemingly given it to me *from out of the blue* and had no idea how powerful her gift would become to me.

**NOTE:** Actually, the words *from out of the blue* take on a whole new meaning when you recognize the loving, attentive protective hand your Team has in your life to consistently support your personal happiness and success!

As soon as I saw it I knew that she had been inspired to provide me with this specific, pivotal reminder of my Divine assurance and help. On the bracelet there was written the words to the Serenity Prayer; the one that is used by those who embrace the Alcoholics and Narcotics Anonymous Programs. It said:

> God grant me the serenity to accept the things I cannot change; *Courage* to change the things I can, and wisdom to know the difference.

*Courage* was the largest word written on the bracelet. It was squarely positioned in the center of the poem so that I could easily and plainly see it whenever I glanced at it. I looked at that bracelet often. I would say to myself, "Courage, Pamela Ann, courage!" and then allow the feeling of that word to enlarge and expand within me.

### Staying the Course

At times, I became distracted by the threats to my personal safety, by the bullying antics of some and by the continuous sabotage of others who were trying to prevent me from reforming the organization for which I was responsible.

Fear, loneliness, confusion and doubt started to creep into my soul. My ability to perform my duties began to weaken.

Whenever I recognized the slightest diversion from my preferred course, however, I would immediately refocus my attention upon maintaining my courage, stewardship and the desires of my heart.

I chose to steadfastly move toward protecting the best interest, financial investment and property of those I represented. Each time I regrouped, I quickly released and cleansed myself of all unnecessary feelings.

Next, I flooded my soul with thankfulness and appreciation for all the blessings I had received in my life. I continued the replenishing of my soul by expanding it with the excitement of the many people and opportunities that were swiftly coming now to assist me in stabilizing the organization I was working for and supporting. In my mind and body I could clearly see and feel that encouraging change as though it had already physically happened!

Finally, I allowed my full connection with the Divine to come into me.

Once again the feelings of peace, love, and well-being returned as did my ability to purposefully create what I preferred. I was then able to use my Powers to succeed in reaching every goal to which I had committed during my term of responsibility.

A key element of my being able to restore my happy feelings and Power was when I genuinely came to a place where I could completely love and accept the individuals that had tried to sabotage me so I could redirect my energies and return to my plan to create a healthy resolution to the organizational concerns.

In the next chapter, *Creating Only Harmonious Relationships,* we will discuss examples of how we can draw to us harmonious relationships in all areas of our lives, even those areas which were originally discordant.

## My Eternal Truth

Several months after I had completed my commitments, I was visiting with the wife of the bodyguard that stayed with me at night during the most challenging time. She told me that her husband did not understand how I could continue to remain so happy and peaceful amid such an intense and chaotic period. I revealed to her the source of my comforting feelings. I openly admitted this eternal truth:

***One person profoundly connected to their Divine source of energy is more powerful than a million individuals who are not connected.***

There are other four letter words that can trip us up if we allow them to take root in our souls. Some of those words are *hate,* and *vice (or any form of contention).* Those words create discord or wedges between us and the other people in our lives. The feelings that are generated from those words drain and misuse our energies. Those feelings will implode our world.

> **NOTE:** More examples of how to release passionate negative feelings will be shared in the next chapter, *Creating Only Harmonious Relationships.*

Remember the eternal law:

***When we are one with each other, we can be one with the Divine.***

Because the Divine love and adore all of us, it is imperative we release any disabling, divisive feelings.

Also release any vestiges of envy or jealousy. They expand your feelings of lack.

Remember the second page of "**Your Road Map for Life**." Be thankful others have provided examples of what you prefer to have or experience in your life. Start seeing the same wonderful opportunities coming to you. Ask for these valuable blessings and realized dreams that you have observed in other people's lives, to come quickly into your own life *now*. And ask for more of those wonderful situations to occur for the people who provided those examples for you.

*"More of this in our lives NOW, please. Thank you!"*

### It's a Conscious Decision!

Consciously make the decision to release all the four-letter-words easily and quickly from your being. Those words only sabotage and distract you from your personal happiness. Allow uplifting thoughts and feelings to fill the void that was created when you cleansed out those other expressions and sensations.

Purposefully draw into your daily life words such as: *fun, joy, well-being, trust, faith,* **Enthusiasim,** *honor, peace, genuineness, playfulness, forgiveness, happiness, abundance, humor, hope* and *love.*

By the way, even though *hope* and *love* are four-letter words, I encourage you to hang on to them. They are definitely keepers!

### TAKE ACTION!

**Begin now to release all four-letter words from your life and choose to replace them with encouraging words that have a positive powerful effect in the situations you are creating. I have discovered that finding someone who is willing to partner with you in this mutually uplifting activity is very helpful.**

# CHAPTER NINE

# ~ Creating Only Harmonious Relationships ~

If you are still feeling like you are not fully connected to the Divine, perhaps the next step is to ask yourself if you are *one* with the *other* people in your life. Previously, I mentioned that it is important we first become one with each other if we are to fully become one with the Divine. In this chapter, I'm going to teach you how to do just that.

If you have any beef with anyone, this is the perfect time for you to willingly gather up all those feelings, along with their origins, and release them. You can have greater personal joy and an ability to create what you prefer by letting go of those negative feelings and energy wasters!

I personally know what I am sharing with you actually works. Well over a decade ago, I created a very miserable relationship with an individual that taught me I was capable of experiencing genuine feelings of hatred. I confess that I had actually never felt that profoundly unsettling feeling before. Moreover, I was not the only one that felt that response with this individual. In fact, most of the people in this person's life also felt that same passionate feeling.

However, thankfully, I soon began to learn I had the ability to completely release this response and totally heal the cankering, poisonous, raw feelings that were associated with this connection.

Today, we both delight in a happy, healthy, mutually respectful, supportive relationship. I am so very grateful we both allowed ourselves to create such a profound change of heart for one another! I now enjoy an unwavering eternal love and affection for this magnificent soul and friend. Through this experience, I now clearly understand how to absolutely command and receive my exact preferences in relationships.

## OK, Go Ahead and Give It a Try

Identify a person you feel a disagreement with, a discomfort with, or have a negative reaction towards. Let yourself genuinely recognize traits or attributes you admire in this individual. Acknowledge you have allowed this person to come and participate in your life because you have chosen to learn something from the opportunity that has arisen through the relationship you've formed. Take a moment to think:

What if this individual agreed to take the time to come into your life for the sole purpose of interacting with you so you both could be strengthened through activating this powerful knowledge?

At first, it may seem difficult to find something you respect or admire about that person, but it is definitely possible to do this if you consistently inch your way toward your goal. Allow yourself to let go of judgment and view him, or her, through new eyes: eternal eyes.

When you are with this person and his family or friends, perhaps you notice how he delights in his little daughter, son or grandchild. Observe him laughing or see his pleased smile when he is with his loved ones. Feel how relaxed and how easily he acts around the people he appreciates and values. Then say to yourself, and be sure to include a genuine *feeling* of desire for this to be activated within you:

*"More of this in our lives NOW, please. Thank you!"*

By this time, you may have these words tattooed across your mind. Well, what can I say? These words truly have the Power to change your world when you sincerely say them with real intent and feeling.

Pull out the stops and get on a roll. Rapidly flood your thoughts with what you admire in someone you would like to improve your relationship with and notice how quickly your feelings are lifted concerning her. It can be simple things such as she is always on time and consistent. Or she has a quick wit. Maybe she is kind to animals. Perhaps she volunteers for the community. Does she have a beautiful smile? Is she a wonderful dancer? Notice if she has skills and talents you would like to cultivate.

Add some humor and fun to this experience if you are able. Lighten up, release any tensions and allow some joy to seep into this activity.

Focus, think and feel excited about these positive behaviors or abilities whenever that person enters your mind. You don't even have to be physically with him to picture the both of you enjoying quality time together. Also, notice other relationships you appreciate as a further example of what you would like to see in your life with this particular person. Continue to ask for more of those positive situations or qualities to be present in your relationship with him now.

Sometimes it is helpful to detach from your physical self along with any discordant emotions that may arise when you think of each of these individuals. Let your spirit become an impartial observer.

Imagine yourself sitting about eight to ten feet higher than everyone else on a comfortable corner shelf near the ceiling of the room or even in the tree branches if you are outside. Then with a relaxed attitude, just quietly scan over the situation that you are viewing; start seeing and feeling a relationship you prefer.

If you speak about this person to others, only relate the uplifting things you see in her. Readily release any dialogue or comments that could draw you away from your own elevating, progressive goal. If the other person proceeds to continue in the direction from which you have purposefully turned away, by speaking gossip, for example, change the subject or excuse yourself from the conversation! Remember this law:

***I create more of whatever I think about, visualize, speak of, feel strongly about and focus my attentions on or observe.***

Remember, you will only create more of those unhappy situations for you and the people involved in these activities if you continue. This is an eternal law that is very real and filled with Power. If you value others and yourself, consistently and consciously choose outcomes you prefer. Then watch the uplifting, mutually rewarding, enjoyable changes that you have purposefully asked for to start forming and swiftly multiply!

## Keep the BIG Picture Perspective

Continue with your goal and allow yourself to see this individual for who he (or she) truly is: an eternal spiritual brother (or sister... you get the picture) who is journeying on his own adventures while gathering in experience as he lives in a mortal body. He, too, is learning how to harmonize his life with everything in his existence, just as you are learning how to harmonize with others.

Besides, we can only practice mastering these skills if there is someone willing to participate with us.

Stay the course of what you desire. *Believe, BELIEVE* and ***BELIEVE*** that this shift in your relationship *is indeed possible!* Get a little thrill when you think about the change that is now beginning to take shape. Start looking for the evidence of this change and trust it is your truth. Enjoy your ability to become one with everyone in your life as you also genuinely wish the best to come into their lives.

It doesn't matter if this other individual ever changes. What matters is that you have allowed yourself to make an adjustment to such a degree that you recognize this person has never actually impacted your personal well-being in a negative way. You have simply let yourself become drawn to them (and they were drawn to you, as well!), so you could both learn something that was mutually significant.

You may even realize the entire relationship was just a distraction from pursuing a specific goal you currently desire to create because you are hesitant, lack confidence or are fearful of striking out into new territory.

Sometimes we choose to stay busy by creating distractions, drama or chaos so we can stall our forward movements. Lots of people live *Soap Opera* lives.

What kind of life are you presently living? Feeling *offended* by others' antics or *blaming* another person for your unhappy situation can be some of those tactics we create. If this is a reflection of what you are experiencing, just remember you have the ability to choose not to be offended by them or anyone else ever again! That decision is quite freeing.

## I'm Done!

You can come to a place where you recognize that you have completed gathering what you were supposed to glean from interacting with an individual, but that person may choose to continue learning about discord in their lives. You have the ability to completely let go of any desire to judge them or expend any energy trying to understand their motives. You can just let them be.

Allow yourself to completely accept each individual just the way they are. It is a relief to know you don't have to fix them, change them, rescue them, or even enlighten them. Be comforted in knowing that you can continue your relationship if it is mutually valuable or you can readily release them and move on to something new.

Stay open and aware. A way will be provided for you to create the necessary adjustments so you can embark on a new life adventure.

If you do recognize it is time to release people from your presence, do it with the highest feelings of best wishes and genuine love and affection. Wish them well on their continued journey.

If you do this, you soon will discover that you are free of the shackles of negativity, which if kept, would have interfered with your ability to more fully enjoy your life. When you let go of discordant relationships in a positive manner, your ability to draw into your life only harmonious relationships increases.

**NOTE: Remember, unless you feel your life is in danger, do not leave a relationship until you have completed what you desire to learn from the connection with that person.** If you run from it or allow yourself to feel rescued temporarily by someone else, you will just create the same basic scenario again except next time it will usually be bigger and more intense! Release each relationship correctly, with the best intentions for the person's involvement in that particular experience.

***Allow yourself to master a situation the first time around.***

But no worries, if you haven't gleaned what you desire the first time, the opportunity will return for your further enlightenment until you are ready to let it go. Multiple relationships with the same type of personality is a great example of this repeating scenario. Multiple scrapes with the law is another. These situations often get more exacerbated with every personal relationship or legal *bump in the road.*

## Practicing What I Teach

As I mentioned before, I have had plenty of opportunities to practice what I teach to others and have learned that these exercises are valuable, effective tools when put into effect.

There came a time in my life, when I worked as a member of a board, that I desired to learn about creating more harmonious relationships. To my amazement, I drew to myself much disharmony. Ouch! This definitely was not an enjoyable situation for any of the participants.

I was very involved in thinking, feeling and speaking to others about what I disliked concerning the situation. My actions only poured fuel on the blazing fire. I continued to magnify the intensity of the situation because of my misplaced focus. The individuals that were interacting around me definitely did not have positive feelings toward me.

It became apparent that one man in particular had been given skewed information about me prior to his ever joining the group, and that information had influenced his opinion of me in a negative way. Furthermore, he hadn't checked out the facts or verified the information he had been given. Instead, he trusted his source. The man was hostile, inflamed and angry when he came to our meetings. I felt frustrated and misjudged...it was not a pleasant experience.

Then I remembered this simple powerful eternal law:

**What You Give Your Attention To Is What You Create**

Thankfully, I *awoke* and realized that I was the one who had been creating this entire situation. I now clearly understood that I actually had the power to immediately change my circumstances at any time!

I also realized that it was my responsibility, my *opportunity* to adjust how I acted or reacted to this entire situation. I remembered that my personal happiness or unhappiness was solely in my own hands...not in the hands of someone who didn't even know me.

I then purposefully chose not to replay the negative interactions that had taken place during our meetings in my mind because those activities consistently produced more of what I disliked.

Because I knew absolutely nothing about this individual, it was initially difficult to picture him with his friends or family—to be able to find his positive attributes. So I chose to see this man as a young boy, before he became hardened and jaded. I saw him as a cute little tow-headed child with a mop of straight hair and beautiful, crystal-clear blue eyes. I pictured him playing with his friends as he ran around, enjoying the carefree days of his youth.

Warm feelings of affection for him began to swell inside me, as if he were my brother (because in reality he was my eternal brother).

Every time I thought of this man, I envisioned this scene.

### A Shift in My Soul

Because of this shift in my soul, I was able to maintain those genuine, tender feelings even at our meetings. No longer did I feel friction with this man. Instead, I held onto my peaceful sense of calm and well-being. I was then able to use my energies to remain focused on the business at hand. After the meetings, I no longer felt drained, I felt renewed.

As a result of this major shift, a sense of peace was solidly anchored within me once again.

I literally came to the place where I felt deeply thankful for him and for the other individuals who had created such disharmony with me; they helped me recognize what I no longer desired to participate in.

Because of their willingness to spend a significant amount of quality time interacting with me, I rapidly identified what I preferred instead. Within a few months, I gleaned heaps of experience in these powerful skills that would continue to be of great benefit to me.

At last, I mastered my ability to allow what I specifically requested to come quickly and easily into my life. Instead of learning how to create harmonious relationships out of disharmony, I learned a great truth through this experience. That truth is:

*We can draw to ourselves only harmonious relationships continually for the rest of our lives if that is our desire.*

It is literally possible to draw out only the best from others as well as ourselves! Even though this situation initially felt hopeless and overwhelming, it soon helped me to remember that when we integrate with our Team, all things are possible. That sure knowledge is especially encouraging when we realize our life's purpose. Simply put:

***The purpose of our life is to be able to gain experience and learn how to harmonize our life with others.***

*Others* is not limited to people. *Others* includes the elements, plants, moving creatures, our finances, bodies and so forth. Everything in this world, the world itself and beyond—all that is throughout time—is part of this group we have the opportunity and pleasure to harmonize with. Play with these ideas:

• Have fun with learning how to enjoy your entire world.

• Awaken to the opportunities constantly surrounding you.

• Stay focused on your goals.

• Unite with your Team. Feel that shift in your body.

When your soul is focused on your preferred goals while united with your Team, everything else begins to be released from your life. Your deliberate attention upon what you prefer to create makes all the difference in your capacity to succeed and consistently obtain the harmonious relationships you desire.

## TAKE ACTION!

**Begin identifying any people with whom you feel you are experiencing some separation or conflict. Start employing the information you learned in this chapter. See them through**

your eternal eyes as literal brothers and sisters who have come to help you learn and master experiences that are important to you. Start seeing them as your blessing. Continue this process until you genuinely feel complete love and acceptance for yourself and all others.

# CHAPTER TEN

# ~ *Still Have a Hitch in Your Giddy Up?* ~

Are you an onion that has a few more layers to peel away before you will allow yourself to enjoy that amazing connection you are seeking? Have you made decisions that have diminished your personal joy? Do you sometimes feel unworthy of receiving great opportunities or relationships and blessings? Maybe you feel God is just a way creepy guy, gal or *it;* a tough being that abandoned you and the people you care about? Are you feeling hopeless because you've recognized there is a wedge between you and the dreams you would love to have come into your life? Or do you just feel you've completely screwed everything up?

If you answered, "yes" to any of the above questions, the following may assist you in your desires to continue your forward movement.

## A Plan of Action to Restore Our Lives

Sometimes, we would just like to learn how to straighten out the kinks in our lives when we feel off-kilter. I usually tell my clients that if what they are doing is deeply satisfying, continue those activities. But, if what they are doing has lost its value and is no longer providing them what they enjoy, then do something different!

There is a plan of action we can unleash to create a change if we feel we have flubbed up and are unhappy about where our life is headed. Many people want to avoid this restorative shift. They don't want to stop and take a close look at their lives and examine how their daily dealings and blunders have been affecting them and others. The last thing they want to do is bring some eternal being into the mix. (Hmmm, notice all the *want* words popping up?)

If they happen to believe God is an angry, punishing being who will carve out a pound or two of their flesh while they submit to this transformational process, that reaction makes perfect sense. In fact, it sounds pretty painful.

Who would willingly choose to experience that? Talk about agony! Most of us would run away in the opposite direction as fast as our feet could carry us!

With those thoughts in mind, I can understand why some prefer to keep as much distance as possible between themselves and God, avoiding that whole situation.

However, from my personal experience of over sixty years, I have never encountered an angry, jealous, judgmental, punishing God or Celestial being. This concept is completely foreign to me.

While yes, I have heard of the statement that we are to *fear God,* inside my soul (and because of my personal relationship with my Master Teacher) I have always understood the full meaning of the word *fear* to be deep respect and reverence for God while holding these beings in the highest esteem. That always has felt reasonable to me because this is how they treat each of us, as well.

I'm not going to digress into a lot of explanations of the details of this process. However, I'm going to cut to the chase and share the simple steps I take with my Team to restore my personal joy when

I temporarily lose it. It always proves to be a relieving, renewing, enlightening experience for me.

## Restoring My Personal Joy

When I made a choice that resulted in unhappiness, I oftentimes would feel absolutely miserable. It seemed like everyone and everything was at odds with me. Whatever I said or did just assisted in digging myself into a deeper hole. I would become so enmeshed in my befuddled mess that I was oblivious to the fact that my escape and assistance for my rescue was just waiting for my asking.

Whether I noticed them or not, my Team would always be poised and readied for me with tender feelings of love, understanding and compassion.

Eventually, I would realize and acknowledge I was headed in a direction that was diverting me from my intended goal of bliss and well-being. I'd recognize my choices and actions were affecting me as well as others in a negative way. I would desire to create a change. I'd then reach out to my Team and ask for their support.

My heart would feel broken and contrite; broken and contrite means that I humbly opened it up to the healing experience that only the Divine could provide. I willingly and completely submitted my soul so my loving Team could fully connect with me and reach into the core of my being.

While there, my Team thoughtfully taught, caringly guided and instructed me as they assisted in restoring my personal joy.

There was no fear, misery, worry, punishment, judgment or pain during this healing process. (However, fear, misery, worry and pain were the distressing feelings I experienced in my being when I put off and procrastinated allowing in this miraculous soul healing transformation.)

Thankfully, I was able to be totally restored *after* I stopped the running, procrastinating, denying and avoiding. In addition, I completely overcame my concerns and mastered what I was to learn from those experiences.

Throughout this restoritive process I felt my Team's kindly affection and acceptance, much to my personal relief.

I am assured all of us are worthy of this response from the Divine no matter what we are doing or creating in our worlds.

In fact, sometimes, when we have made a decision that has temporarily diminished our happiness, we actually are more open to listening to their guidance and redirection. Those are often our times of greatest growth and expansion. Each experience has prepared us for more eternal development; each experience was actually for our own good.

## Forgiving Ourselves and All Others

At times, when we recognize we have created a situation that has affected our ability to feel joy, it seems like we are often harder on ourselves than we would ever be with anyone else.

Before you continue this chapter, if by chance you are feeling less than happy about your life decisions, it is important you allow yourself to let the following words resonate their truth within your entire soul:

*There is NOTHING you have ever thought, said or done that has lessened your Team's personal love and affection for you. They value you. They champion you. They adore you and believe in you and your greatness. You are their joy. You are always worthy and able to call upon them for their light, knowledge, comfort and companionship.*

Read the above words a few times out loud. Let your truth resonate throughout you entire body. This is your truth. This is your reality. Allow your whole body to believe it…simply BELIEVE!

## The Misery of Living the Lie

One client of mine shared his feelings of personal disgust, fear, shame and deep sorrow for some life decisions he had made. He no longer respected or trusted himself. As a result, his personal honor (the ability and Power to rapidly create with his Team) and fullness of joy was greatly diminished.

This person's life had become a lie. He had his public and family life, but he also lived a secret life that was constantly invading his thoughts and focus to the point that even when he was at work or with his family, his energies were continually turning toward that personally destroying distraction. His body was drained, he felt depressed, and he suffered from anxiety plus sleep disturbances. In essence, this man's soul was withering.

Although my client had not verbally disclosed his covert actions to his spouse or close friends and business associates, somehow those key people became aware of this person's betrayal and deceit.

One day, early on in this person's training, I explained that even when the specific words of our actions are not audibly spoken, our souls are clearly communicating what we are thinking, feeling and doing to the souls of others. If we are feeling discord in our beings, we are also sending that feeling out to those around us and it is reflected back to us.

In this case, that lack of trust and respect was some of what this client felt from those that were closest to him.

I instructed my client that it was imperative that he first allowed himself to come to a place of complete forgiveness, love and acceptance for himself. His personal Team would assist him in this process. I continued to instruct him. This is what I said:

- **The reason your personal forgiveness is so important** is that until you learn what this experience feels like, you cannot know how to feel those healing, supportive emotions of complete love and acceptance from and for the Divine or anyone else.

- **And if you are not sending out those genuine feelings for yourself as well as all others,** how can those feelings be reflected back to you?

- **You actually are being blessed continually with tender kindness** from your Team and others. But until you fully allow those authentic feelings of self-forgiveness, love and acceptance to blossom within your soul, you will not be able to fully allow yourself to receive those sweet satisfying relationships because of your own feelings of unworthiness.

- **If you perceive you have wronged someone else,** how can you expect them to forgive you if you will not even allow yourself to forgive you?

    **Note: The word perceive is used here** because, the *others* in our lives are also actively creating their own world with their Teams and have drawn themselves into this learning adventure for a specific reason as well. At any time they can choose to turn to a better feeling place. There really aren't any victims here.

The actions of completely forgiving, loving and accepting ourselves as an individual first can actually rapidly assist us in healing our life conflicts. Those actions also help us consciously choose more uplifting loving decisions that consistently increase our personal happiness.

A friend had a history of creating disharmony by living in abusive relationships and making choices that were not loving or respectful of her best interests. She compounded those problems with addictions to food and the computer that temporarily numbed her private pain.

Again, I instructed her in coming to the place of complete love and acceptance of herself while making life decisions that would reflect those uplifting changes. In fact, to help her remember that commitment, I encouraged her to either write or tattoo a tiny little heart somewhere on her person. That little heart was an external constant reminder to be loving and true to her best eternal interests while daily living that internal personal vow.

These commitments and actions are worthwhile because by better understanding and allowing ourselves to personally develop our individual well-being, we will be more able to understand and allow ourselves to love and accept the Divine and all others.

## Restoring Others

After completing my own awakening and initial healing, I sometimes realized that my actions had also affected others and I understood it was necessary for me to ask for their forgiveness.

It was pivotal for our complete restoration and opened the door for our mutual uplift. This action greatly assisted my healing and reuniting with others that had previously been at odds with me.

Many years ago a significant person in my life passed on gossip to a number of other people who were important to me. None of these *stories* were based on any truth about me. I was aware of what was being said and did not respond to the slanderous conversations. Instead, I forgave her and went on living my amazing life.

Years later she realized what she had done and apologized to me. She also restored me and set the record straight. She went to the other individuals she had previously spoken to and told them the truth. I felt deeply appreciative of her actions on my behalf.

Today we have a mutually loving, supportive relationship. She now openly champions me in all I am doing and is genuinely there for me.

So, if along the way you recognize you've seemingly injured another person, make amends for what you have done. This sincere activity helps you to more perfectly develop your oneness with others and your oneness with the Divine. It also stops the distracting nagging feelings and thoughts that you have unfinished business, which usually turns out to be another energy waster.

In other words, while you are allowing these changes, take care of all the loose ends so you can then move forward unencumbered. Allow your honest, honorable life to be restored. The truth really does set you free.

## Recommit to Keeping Your Personal Honor

By the way, once you have dusted yourself off and gotten back on course, and you are headed in the direction that you prefer, do yourself a favor and willingly decide to let go of creating that choice again. That vital awareness helps you steer past those eddies in your life so you can maintain your personal joy. This activated personal promise also helps you let go of creating the same world over and over.

### The Basic Steps to Restoring Your Personal Joy

- **Recognize you made a decision that diminished your happiness**.

- **Ask for help and guidance from your Team.** Connect to them. Willingly open your heart so they can teach and minister to you and help you restore your joy and honor.

- **Feel their love and affection. Follow their counsel and put it into action.**

- **Forgive yourself** and allow yourself to feel increased loving, accepting feelings for yourself.

- **If what you have done has affected others, go to them *while connected to the Divine*** and let that contagious healing process begin. Restore them. For example, if you have damaged their property or taken something from them, replace it and ask their forgiveness.

- **Commit to let go of that unhappy choice and not repeat it in the future.**

### Every Experience Is Ultimately For Our Good

Every experience has value; even the ones we feel are painful. They still are important to us or we would not have drawn them into our world in the first place.

Years ago I learned nothing is intended for our destruction or discouragement. All of our life experiences can be for our growth and expansion.

With this truth in mind, it is a comfort to know that *it is literally impossible to fail* because all our life, every facet of it, has value for us. In other words, every experience is ultimately for our good.

Ponder the following thought:

*So, if everything we experience is ultimately for our good...do we ever actually make mistakes?*

### TAKE ACTION!

**What is your answer to this question? The answer lies in the comforting words before it. Let those words sink deeply into your soul and feel the relief they bring.**

# Part II: Personal Stories of Applying Our *Mindset of Miracles*

Now that you have been properly prepared to receive your personal *Mindset of Miracles*, we are going to toss out any uncertainty; no gently tip-toeing into the water. Instead, we are going to dive in headfirst and commence this adventure with a BIG SPLASH!

Go ahead and place yourself within these stories as a way to assist you in creating miracles in your own life. Allow yourself to shift within, awaken and activate your ability to create your exact desires.

**Remember:** These stories have been written for people of all ages. Some stories even relate examples of miracles and awakenings that children have experienced. Stay open to their simple applications for powerful results that can be applied in all the areas of your daily life.

These laws are simple. When life becomes difficult and complicated, it is when we are trying to make and force things to happen while we are less connected to the Divine.

Okay, it's time for you to jump into the following true stories and actual examples of how the Divine can actively participate with you in this life now.

# CHAPTER ELEVEN

# ~ It's Only Slightly Breezy Now ~

The first evening I met Chef Mickey, I thought he was a strikingly handsome man in his white uniform jacket. He was well over six feet tall and extremely fit from working in the kitchen. He had beautiful bronze skin and his long, shiny, black curly hair was slicked back into a ponytail. He had high, chiseled cheek bones, flaring nostrils and beautiful full lips, together with gentle ebony eyes and dark lashes—the perfect combination to send many girls' hearts aflutter. To top it all off, he was a man of great passion who loved to cook. His creations were both magnificent to the eye and delicious to the pallet.

Earlier that day, I had become the President of the Homeowner's Association at a resort in Mexico, so some of the owners took me out to celebrate at a fine Mexican restaurant. While there, the chef came out and introduced himself to us.

I found him to be soft-spoken and not boastful, yet he had a powerful commanding charismatic presence as he briefly visited with the other people at our table. Although we never exchanged a word, he definitely left a lasting impression. I felt it was important for me to take note and remember this man because I clearly knew from the feeling I received that this chef was part of an amazing plan and experience that was being formed.

## Only Win-Win Situations

Meanwhile, we were having some problems with our restaurant at the resort; business was not flourishing. As a result, I began to think about what options would be available for us if it shut down.

About four months after meeting Chef Mickey, an owner from the resort approached me and gave me Chef Mickey's business card. I had been so busy with other matters; I hadn't given him much thought. By late spring, the original proprietor of the resort restaurant had sold out to another individual and they were trying to make a go of the business.

In August, while having a business lunch at a café, I once again crossed paths with Chef Mickey. I reminded him of our brief encounter earlier in the year, and informed him that I worked at the resort.

With surprising candor, he immediately responded by telling me he felt he was supposed to cook for us at the resort. I quickly replied that I also knew this was so. I disclosed to him that I already had his card and would be getting in touch with him in the near future.

Now, I believe in mutually beneficial situations. Early on, I had already decided I would never take this chef away from another restaurant so he could work for us. Nor would I ever deliberately undermine the success of our resort restaurant.

With that in mind, I thought when the time came for this chef to team with us, his commitment to the restaurant he worked for would have already come to a close. Moreover, his involvement at the resort would be free of any interference with the well-being of our existing restaurant. I felt an assured calm feeling with that thought and moved on with my day.

## Promises to Keep and Mouths to Feed

Six months flew by from the last HOA meeting and I found myself preparing for the next one in September. I told the homeowners, in their newsletter, we would provide them with a full breakfast buffet. I was also working and negotiating with our rental company about some real estate classes that were being planned at the resort (which would also require catering).

On Tuesday, before our Saturday meeting, I visited with the woman coordinating the real estate classes. I had to admit that my attentions were somewhat distracted during that meeting because just prior to it I was informed that the resort's restaurant had closed down. We had no one to cook our owners' breakfast! And we had no one to cater all the food for the classes scheduled for the following week!

At this point, I knew it was too late to notify the owners of this change so they could bring down their own provisions. I also calculated the attendees would not have sufficient time to go out for breakfast prior to the morning meeting.

Somehow, I felt a certain assurance that a way would be provided for us to have the owners' buffet we had promised. A little thrill ran through my body when that thought entered my mind. I refocused my attentions to what I'd like to see happen on that Saturday morning and gave no energy to the details of how this breakfast would be created. I just kept that assured feeling whenever I thought about the buffet and then moved on to my other responsibilities.

During my meeting with the event coordinator, the woman suddenly blurted out that a certain café had just closed. Lo and behold, it was the same restaurant in which Chef Mickey worked!

An excited feeling rushed into my body. Here was the exact solution I had asked for. I stopped the meeting for a moment, excused myself and walked immediately over to my desk to retrieve the chef's business card. Then I picked up the phone and started dialing.

Within a moment, Chef Mickey was at the other end of the line, telling me he was available to work for us. We set up an appointment for the following day to begin the planning process.

## The Reawakening

The next day, I excitedly welcomed the chef to our appointment and felt an absolute assurance all was well. We quickly exchanged greetings and spent a little time telling one another about our individual backgrounds.

During this time, he shared with me information about a deep, personal loss. He felt great sorrow and didn't know how to overcome his difficulties. I saw how strongly those experiences had affected his Powers and ability to rapidly create what he would prefer to have happen in his life.

I immediately began training him about connecting to his source of creative Power as well as to his Team so he could start receiving what he purposefully would love to experience in his life now. I taught him how to reawaken himself to his ability to turn toward a better feeling place. I prompted him to let his heart swell with feelings of joy and gratitude. I encouraged him to remember when he felt feelings of Enthusiasm.

I suggested that he now allow those feelings to well up inside of him. I pointed out that when he let himself feel those feelings he was more perfectly connected to the Divine and his ability to create.

I could see his countenance change and a light start coming out of him. I asked how he felt in the center of his chest. He told me he felt good. Within moments, his discouragement had been replaced with feelings of well-being and hope.

After this experience, we eagerly moved on to plan the owners' buffet. With the chef's suggestions, I wrote down the menu and made a grocery list. Then we brainstormed about what we would require to complete the event and I jotted down all the details. The chef also suggested that he create some appetizers for the Monitoring Committee's Friday evening meeting. I thought that would be a great idea too, so we included it in the plans we were forming.

I made a couple of calls to my husband and family to relate to them what we would like them to bring from the list. They, along with some of our employees in our business in the States, started pulling together the items so my husband Ron could drive everything down to Mexico early Friday morning.

When Friday evening came, Chef Mickey, along with his two assistants, were fired up and ready to present the succulent dishes.

## Keep That Good Feeling

While we all enjoyed the savory morsels, Chef Mickey took me aside and told me he didn't have a place to cook the owners' breakfast. He had contacted other restaurants he previously worked for and they all refused to let him use their kitchens. I asked, "Chef Mickey, you lost your good feeling, didn't you?" He admitted that he had. I urged him to try and get it back again.

Then I asked him where he would like to cook the breakfast. He responded that he would like to cook it at a specific grill near our resort. He mentioned the husband of the couple that owned the restaurant was out of town and he didn't think the wife would give permission to use their kitchen. I swiftly curbed that conversation and requested he quickly allow himself to release those thoughts.

Then I told Chef Mickey I had a great feeling and my feeling was that he would be able to work in the kitchen of his choice. In fact, the owner of the grill would be happy to allow this to happen. I asked the chef if he also had a good feeling and he said, "Yes!"

I turned to the committee and asked if they could assist us. I explained what the chef was experiencing and I requested they take a moment to picture the chef and his assistants eagerly working in the kitchen at the grill. Then I invited them to envision seeing, smelling and tasting the food as they prepared it for us.

Next, I asked them to visualize the owners' buffet tomorrow morning with everyone enjoying their breakfast. Finally, I asked each person to allow in a feeling of excitement about what was being prepared for us tomorrow. I waited for a short moment and thanked the committee.

Then, I turned to the chef and said, "Now keep that good feeling inside of you and go ask the owner if you can use her kitchen. She will say, 'Yes' to your request."

Off he went into the night.

### "Go Help Chef Mickey Set Up!"

By the time the committee members left my home and I had cleaned up the dishes and put everything back in order, it was midnight. It felt wonderful to lay my head on my comfortable pillow and pull up the warm covers over my body. I couldn't help but feel giddy with anticipation to see what would unfold for all of us the next morning. I kept picturing the chef and his helpers busily cooking away in the kitchen at the grill. As a smile came to my lips, I drifted off to sleep.

Later, I awoke with a thought in my mind, "Go help Chef Mickey set up the breakfast!" It was still dark outside. I glanced at my watch and pushed the button that lit up its face. It had been broken a few days earlier and now was working perfectly (how the watch was quickly repaired will be discussed in the next chapter). I was thankful I could check the time without having to crawl out from the comfort of my bed.

The hands of the watch indicated it was only 5:00 AM. I groaned and nestled more deeply into my covers. I felt like I had just gone to bed and I desired to sleep longer so I could be better rested to conduct the owners' meeting.

Again, the words came to my mind, "Go help Chef Mickey set up the breakfast!" I bolted right out of bed and quickly changed my entire attitude and feelings. Of course I would help him! I felt delighted to have the opportunity. I quickly slipped on some clothes and headed toward the door.

As I stepped outside, I immediately noticed the strong wind that had formed while I was sleeping. The wind blew so hard it briskly pushed me down the open corridor toward the elevators. I entered one of them and rode down to the ground floor and hurried to the main plaza where the breakfast buffet was being set up. I turned the corner to the plaza and saw tablecloths blowing around, sterno fuel flaming out and a forlorn chef along with his crew wrestling with the unruly situation.

At first, I tried to help by suggesting we move the tables in between pillars to try and protect them from the blustery wind. A funny picture then entered my thoughts. I envisioned us as a few ants desperately moving a leaf around to protect it from the blasts of a jet engine. I started to laugh.

We were trying to do it alone without being fully connected to our Team!

Chef Mickey came to me and said, "Miss Pamela, we *have to* have the breakfast inside the restaurant."

I glanced inside the restaurant and saw all the chairs carefully lined up and organized for the meeting. I instantly saw in my mind's eye the owners trying to balance their plates and utensils on their laps as they ate their breakfast while straining to listen to the information being presented to them. I realized it would be very awkward for them and the noise created would be such a distraction that the meeting would not be productive.

## I Have a Wonderful Feeling

Then, that sweet familiar feeling of calm and perfect assurance came over me. I confidently told the chef the meeting would be inside the restaurant and breakfast would be on the patio, as we had planned. I went on to ask the chef where he cooked breakfast that morning. He smiled and said he cooked it at the nearby grill.

"So you kept your good feeling?" I asked, and he told me he had.

Next, I told him I had a wonderful feeling inside of me: we had the ability to command the elements to change, if that was our desire. I told Chef Mickey I felt it was only slightly breezy now. "But how do you feel?" I asked the Chef. He said he had a wonderful feeling, as well. I asked him if he would be willing to join me and say out loud, "It's only slightly breezy now!" He responded, "Yes!"

Together, with grins of delight and feelings of excited anticipation, nothing wavering, we said in unison, "It's only slightly breezy now!"

We waited for a moment. Afterwards, I asked Chef Mickey, "Now tell me, how is it?"

His eyes got big, his smile enlarged and he exclaimed, "Why Miss Pamela, it's only slightly breezy *now*!"

I then told him he could set up the tables anyway he liked. It was only slightly breezy for the rest of the day, which was perfect for the warm late September weekend.

The owners enjoyed the meal, completely unaware of the events that transpired. I was so thankful that I awoke and chose to respond to that prompting. Together, Chef Mickey and I were able to share in the miracle of commanding the elements to be calmed, and we instantly witnessed the joining of our desires with the Divine to create our world…our miracle.

### Creating the Same World Over and Over

In October, not long after the breakfast, Chef Mickey was hired to provide the meals for the real estate classes. While Chef Mickey visited with me about what he could provide for our resort, he also took the time to share with me a personal dream he had. His real heart's desire was to own his own restaurant.

He'd worked in Vegas for twenty-five years. Then, for many years after, he worked for top successful restaurants in this Mexican resort town. He set up their menus and created their favorite dishes in hopes of one day being able to have some ownership. He went from restaurant to restaurant. To his dismay, ownership had not materialized. Each restaurant proprietor told him, "No."

He was creating his same world over and over again!

I listened to him speak of other personal losses and I could see and feel his despair. I stopped his conversation not long after he began his woeful tale and told him he had the Power to change his world now.

I didn't stop his story because I didn't have the time or because I was not interested. Rather, I stopped him because of how much I cared about this man and his personal happiness—and mine, as well. I knew whatever we focused our attention on was exactly what we would create.

Once more, if we added our negative, passionate feelings to what he had experienced, only more negative outcomes would come rushing into his life as well as mine. So, of course I was not willing to listen to all the details of his lack and loss! I did not desire to create more lack and loss for either one of us.

Once again, I trained him in how he could unleash his Powers to create what he preferred instead. I shared some examples of how I had been able to use this Power in my life by being connected to the Divine. As I spoke words of encouragement and truth, I could feel the connection to my Team increase within me. It felt wonderful. I could see that Chef Mickey also started to feel uplifted and connected, as well.

He had been saying that someday he would have his own restaurant. Well, he had been receiving exactly what he asked for. He asked for a restaurant someday and that is where it would always remain…in his future, not in his present.

I instructed the chef that it was important for him to set aside all frustration, disappointment and sadness. Then, I suggested he clearly focus and envision what he desired to have happen in his life. It was important that he saw his dreams in detail and that he asked for those details to start forming *now.*

"What do you really desire to experience in your life?" I asked him. Without any hesitation he replied that he would love to have a restaurant of his own and name the restaurant "Chef Mickey's Place!"

### Activating the Plan to Shift Someday into *Now*!

I suggested he imagine where the restaurant would be along with any other important details.

"First," I said, "picture the location of where you would like your restaurant. See the details as it is being formed. Visualize the color of the walls as they are being painted and the art you are hanging on them. Observe how the kitchen looks while it is being constructed and organized, along with the bar and seating areas. Notice the furniture you are purchasing and moving into its place as well as the linens, dishes and utensils. Now, see yourself hiring people who love the restaurant business and enjoy working with you in a harmonious way.

"Next," I said, "view yourself going out and purchasing fresh, high-quality food. Then, see, smell and taste your amazing dishes as you prepare them. Picture yourself in every aspect of his creation and see it happening *now*! "

I also told Chef Mickey that he was not to be concerned about how this would all happen. He was to believe it was absolutely possible and to trust that this was his truth. Somehow it would materialize when he was ready to receive it into his life.

I explained to him that everything is first created in a spiritual dimension and then it comes into our physical presence. As soon as we make our requests, by speaking or thinking about them, they start to be organized and are created in that realm, like drawing the blueprints for a home. I went on to share that any form of wavering or vacillating slows, paralyzes or pushes away that forming process.

When we let go of any distractions, fear or doubt and start feeling excited and passionate about our desires, they begin to come into our physical world. We have the ability to purposefully decide when we would like to receive our requests and even put a date and time on those desires... a few years, a month, later this week, *now.*

The final key component to our realizing our wishes is when we open up, believe and trust, with every cell in our being, that this goal is possible through our connection with the Divine. When we are connected to the Divine those requests can rapidly flow into our lives.

I then told him to let an excited feeling well up inside of him because those dreams were now being created. Those feelings literally validated his connection and were driving his desire forward into his reality.

I visited with the chef a handful of times that autumn and then focused my attention on completing my responsibilities at the resort.

Chef Mickey kept his good feelings. A little more than six months after the owners' breakfast and the initial beginning of his training, he called me to invite me to the opening of his new restaurant. He named it "Chef Mickey's Place."

He didn't even have to save up the money. An acquaintance provided all of the funding!

Chef Mickey turned out to be a powerful and rapid creator who accomplished his goal in a short amount of time. But, he shared with me a very important fact about his ability to finally create what he preferred. Somehow, at first, he didn't fully comprehend that when he was utilizing his Power to create he was literally connecting to a creative source that was greater and more powerful than himself. He had united and become one with deity and the restorative Power of the *Living Atonement*…an *At-One-Ment* with God and the rest of his Team.

It wasn't until a friendly priest reminded him of this pivotal fact that the chef was finally able to allow himself to fully internalize what I had taught him about the Divine.

He then applied the simple steps from his training and unleashed the ability to fully create. After struggling for years while seeking ownership of his own restaurant with zero positive results, he was able to quickly experience the joy of his dreams within a few months!

***This is precisely why I share the details of how you, too, can rapidly create whatever your heart desires. And this is why I boldly speak of the Divine and the miracles they would love to create with you.***

### Your Treasure Trove of Truth

You will also easily and quickly draw to you experiences like this one. Take some consistent quality time and apply this knowledge. Sharpen your awareness of what you are thinking and feeling. Let that Team become one with you. With that awareness and connection, the words you are reading will evolve into something more valuable than a bunch of entertaining stories. They will become a treasure trove of information for you to learn how to connect with the Divine and play with them each day of your life. Permit these truths to deeply resonate within you.

## TAKE ACTION!

**Get a piece of paper now and identify a situation or goal you would love to see come easily and quickly to you NOW. Write it down. Add the details as you picture it forming clearly in your mind. Put a date on it. Allow yourself to feel eager anticipation and genuine excitement concerning this goal.**

**Boldly tell others, free of any wavering, about what you desire to create while HOLDING ONTO THOSE GREAT FEELINGS (remember the board meeting).**

**Take no concern if sometimes people respond to what you tell them with puzzled expressions or less than supportive feedback. Just rev up those feelings every time you happen to think about your plan. Refer to that paper as often as you would like to keep that vision fresh and clearly defined in your soul. FEEL and observe the shift in your body and world as your goal begins to form and come to you!**

# CHAPTER TWELVE

# ~ *The Watch, The Washer and The Window* ~

The rich beat of Latin Music pulsed throughout our colorful beachfront home. My body was dancing with delight as I worked up a sweat while scrubbing and polishing in preparation for the upcoming festivities. I usually clean after a party, but the recent winds had caused the sifting sand to seep inside the house. So I enjoyed the music, continuing my rhythmic motions while I washed away the piles of gritty sediment.

It was the Thursday before the September homeowners' meeting and the breakfast buffet at the resort in Mexico. I was preparing for at least thirty people to stay with us in our home.

This group was a lively group of delightful, positive and energetic salsa dancers whose ages ranged from their teens into their sixties (some were bringing their children as well). One of the couples was my beautiful blonde, blue-eyed Swiss daughter Hélène, her handsome and charming, Mexican-American husband and their sweet, cherub-faced, dark tousled-haired, four-year-old son.

I met Hélène over fifteen years ago before she became an American citizen. We soon developed a close friendship. Because of our age difference, I became her American mom and I considered her to be my Swiss daughter.

Hélène and her son were coming that day, while the rest of the dancers were trickling in on Friday and Saturday for their performance Saturday evening. So, I was motivated to breeze through my housework. If I was able to finish my tasks quickly, I would have more time to play with them after they arrived.

A soft-spoken, kind Mexican woman named Trinidad, or Trini as I call her, assisted me as we hurriedly arranged our surroundings to make everything ready for the group's arrival. We happily busied ourselves washing windows, sweeping patios, mopping floors, dusting furniture, cleaning bathrooms and changing linens for the beds.

The washer and dryer were also running in high gear.

### "What am I to Learn From These Experiences?"

After a few hours, Trini came to me with the news that the washer was no longer working. She tried to get it to start, but it would not respond. I then tried several times to start it myself, but it refused to go. Finally after numerous attempts, I picked up the phone and called the resort's maintenance man, Lalo, and asked for help.

Shortly afterwards, I stopped and pondered the situation and took note of how I felt. I recalled that recently, my car window had also stopped working.

When I went through the border crossing, the immigration official had noticed that I opened my door to give him my passport. Curious, the tall, lithe and amiable agent asked me why I opened my door instead of just rolling down the window. I told him the window had stopped working and I would prefer it to remain up for the four-hour trip home to Tucson from Mexico.

After he eyed my Lexus convertible he replied, "Ma'am, that's going to cost you a *lot* of money to get that window fixed!" I remember my immediate inward response at the time was that I preferred to pay nothing to repair the window.

Meanwhile, the night before the washer broke, I realized the light on my watch had stopped working as well. I really enjoyed that simple, waterproof Timex watch with its black leather band. I appreciated the light during the night along with the fact that I could swim with it in the warm ocean by the resort. But I especially treasured the watch because my oldest son had given it to me.

Things were breaking down all around me. The watch, the washer and the window were simply more examples of what were no longer working in harmony with me.

I knew difficult circumstances or activities that appear as obstacles are not brought into my life to discourage me, rather they are opportunities to help me learn and grow. I also recognized that I brought these situations into my life so I could expand my awareness and knowledge.

With that understanding uppermost in my mind, I asked, "What am I to learn from these experiences?"

## Discord and Disharmony

I like to take chunks of time to learn about and master different subjects, ideas and skills that I am interested in. This particular year, I decided I would like to learn about creating more harmonious relationships. The harmony I sought included everything that touched my life.

I had been drawing into my life numerous opportunities to learn about these interactions and connections. I remembered that when we desire to learn about something like harmonious relationships, we sometimes are provided the opposite so we can learn how to purposefully transform our world into a more harmonious place.

I had recently created plenty of discord and disharmony, and anyone that interacted with me during that particular time will attest to this fact.

While I gathered the information on how to create uplifting relationships, I also began to realize that I was now allowing myself to draw to me, understand and apply any form of knowledge I desired.

In fact this was quickly shaping up as one of the most rapid learning times of my life. It felt as though I was gleaning lifetimes of knowledge and experience within a few months. These opportunities were transforming and preparing me for my next adventure. I clearly understood why I was bringing them to me and why they were so important for my strengthening and development. As a result, I was able to quickly master many powerful principles.

With that awareness uppermost in my mind, I completely opened up and submitted to these experiences.

### The Gift

About a month earlier, in August, I met a remarkable couple named Nina and Bracken. I began working with them while they provided marketing services for the resort. They produced a couple of commercials, designed our website and created a thousand DVDs of the resort along with other helpful projects.

As I worked side by side with them, I quickly realized they consciously sought to live a deliberate life focused on drawing to them well-being for themselves and everyone around them. Nina, Bracken and their daughter were a pure delight to work with. They really reached beyond what was required of them.

On Saturday, the week before the owners' meeting, Bracken walked up to me with a book in his hand. He told me he felt I would really like to read it. He informed me it was not available in any bookstore or library. As he handed it to me he told me that the book was a gift from him to me.

I looked down at the book. The book was about creating harmonious relationships in all aspects of life! To my complete amazement, I had in my hand the exact information I requested. I didn't even physically have to go out to find it or buy it!

My body felt a rush of excitement and a flood of immense gratitude. By the feeling my soul expressed, I knew without any doubt this was precisely what I requested. What was more thrilling was that I didn't even have to search for this information. It was handed to me!

I simply asked to be taught this knowledge and knew without any hesitation that the information would somehow be provided. I understood this would absolutely happen for me by the wonderful assured feeling I experienced inside; that feeling of being fully connected to my Team.

Now how difficult was it for me to receive what I desired? I asked and it was literally given to me within a couple of weeks. I am always amazed at how perfectly this Divine interaction and continuous support works.

I appreciated Bracken's courage to hear, feel and follow through with the impression he received to bring the book to me. Instead of second guessing what my response would be, he boldly stepped forward and let me decide whether the material was personally valuable to me.

> **NOTE:** If you feel *impressed* or *inspired* to do something, follow through with it. Often you and the information you share are a literal answer to someone's prayers!

Within moments of receiving this gift, I was grinning and laughing out loud while jumping up and down shouting, "Yes, yes, *yes!*" I gave Bracken a big bear hug and told him I was going to *devour* the book the following day.

### Feeling Sleepy and Irritated

On Sunday, I spent the day in bed or on the couch reading. I ate and drank as I desired. The information in the book was very familiar to me. It was what my Master Teacher had taught me years ago.

Because I had been in the midst of so much turmoil, I had allowed myself to become distracted from the simple laws that would immediately aright my world. The book helped me to remember what I had previously been taught by my inspiring Team. The words proved to be quite comforting to me.

However, it is one thing to be taught something and quite a different situation to be able to consistently apply what you have been taught!

I had just mastered learning how to create harmony out of disharmony. Now I desired to draw to me only harmonious relationships in all aspects of my life. This book helped remind me of what I eternally knew. I also recognized it was important that I learned how to allow a greater shift to happen within my soul so I could fully live the principles I already understood.

Then I noticed a strange thing began to happen to me. I could not stay awake! I kept falling asleep after I read a chapter or two. I would read some more and fall asleep again. This process continued throughout the day until I finally completed the book.

Good thing I got an early start!

At first, I thought it seemed quite odd when my body responded in this manner. It wasn't because I felt disinterested or bored about the subject matter, it was because something else was occurring which allowed the phenomenon to continue.

I finally just relaxed and decided to ponder the situation. I asked why my body responded this way. I was immediately assured it was because I was to go and deeply connect to the Divine that created my physical body so this information could be woven into the very cells of my soul. Through this application I could more fully incorporate what I was being reminded of and readily use the knowledge being provided for me.

I found it interesting that later the same week, my Swiss daughter had the same experience when she listened to the audio version of the book (I had not yet told her what had happened to me while I was reading it).

After a while, the words I read started to become irritating to me.

When I inquired about that feeling, I came to understand it was because I had grasped the treasures of knowledge that had been reawakened within me. My soul understood this information and was itching to apply what I had been reminded of. The intelligence of this Power to harmonize my life with all that surrounds me had come fully alive in my soul.

The following is a very simple example of what I mean:

Picture someone drawing up some house plans and talking about building that home. That experience is very different from when that person actually builds that structure. The first example is more talking about and philosophizing, and the second example is actually activating and physically creating what was spoken about. It's a form of preparing and then activating what you have prepared for, or a time and season kind of thing. In other words:

*There is a time to prepare and study about how to live well during this life and there is a time to fully live and experience life.*

When Thursday arrived I was still allowing myself to understand how to apply what I was currently learning through the examples of the broken watch, the broken washer and the broken window.

Then, like a bolt of lightning the answer struck me. I could feel the truth and Power of the statement form in my soul!

*I had the ability to harmonize my life with all that has been created in this world, even the world itself!*

I am capable of commanding these elements to be restored! The reason I am able to command these elements is because I am an honorable being. It is because of that honor that the elements will respond to my command. It is this same honor that allows gods to create worlds.

When I am allowing myself to think, feel and act in an honorable way, I allow myself to totally connect as one to my Divine Team and those Godly Powers so I can create with them!

I allowed that thought to fully resound in my body. I felt the absolute assurance that this realization was true, because of the ecstatic feeling I received in the core of my soul. That feeling was a witness to the fact that I was now allowing that connection to my Team. I was charged by that pure source of Power that was pouring into me because of that union.

Releasing any hesitation, I quickly pointed to my watch and pronounced in a commanding tone, "The watch works NOW!" I pointed to the washer and said, "The washer works NOW!" Finally, I pointed in the direction of my car and stated, "The window works NOW!"

I was so certain those action statements were completed I didn't even check to see if they worked. I just went forward with my activities of putting my home in order.

About fifteen minutes later, a knock came to my door. When I answered, I saw Lalo the maintenance man. I forgot to call him and tell him I no longer required his help because I absolutely believed the situation had been resolved.

I apologized for not calling him and then showed him the washer now worked. I pushed the button and the machine started right up. I started to laugh with sweet happiness and joy as I witnessed the results to the requests from my soul. I turned the washer off and tried once again. Yep, it worked perfectly. The maid could not believe her eyes! We both were laughing now.

Then, I suddenly realized that if the washer worked, so did the watch and the car window. I excitedly looked at my watch and pushed the button to see if the face would illuminate. Sure enough, it did! I knew the window of my car was working but waited to check it later during the weekend. When I did check the window, it smoothly rolled up and down without any hesitation.

By the way, all three of those items are still working perfectly as I write this book more than two and a half years later!

My whole soul felt a joy-filled exhilaration for what we had all just witnessed. I sent out a prayer and enlarged feelings of thanks and appreciation to my Master Teacher and the rest of my Team for answering my requests.

Shortly after this experience, I filled my entire body with overflowing gratitude for the restoring of these items. I felt as though many loving arms were surrounding me with the jubilation they had all experienced with me. It kind of felt like the huge group hugs and pats on the back after a championship football or basketball game. It seemed like I could hear laughter and congratulations for something well done.

Some of the appreciation they felt was because I had once again acknowledged that my Team existed and I had willingly allowed them to play with me in my daily life. They like having fun and are fun to be with when we are feeling playful and deliberately creative.

Then I received a very clear message from them:

*"The small things that were repaired for you were to give you experience and confidence."*

Also:

*"If we will be there for the little things, we will be there for the big things. REMEMBER THIS!"*

Friday seemed to come and go within a blink of an eye. Saturday and the owners' meeting had finally arrived.

While I was busily setting up for the meeting, Bracken, Nina and their associate approached me with troubled expressions on their faces. They anxiously reported, "Pamela, the internet is not working!"

Now, I understood their words of worry and concern.

They were supposed to show the owners the new website, postcard and first commercial they were in the process of making for the resort in hope that the owners would approve another ten thousand dollars for them to complete the projects. Without the internet, they could not proceed with their presentation. They were dead in the water and understandably frustrated and discouraged.

I remembered it was Bracken who had given me the book about creating harmonious relationships just the Saturday before and I was sure all three of them had read it. I also shared with Nina and Bracken what had just happened with the watch, the washer and the window. Adding to that miraculous fact, I had also just experienced the calming of the winds with the chef earlier that morning. I was certain we were all being watched over and in the tender care of a much bigger force than we could see with our mortal eyes.

So, I calmly looked at them as the light of a familiar, warm assurance expanded in my soul and a wide beam of a smile spread across my lips.

With a raised brow and a twinkle in my eye I said to my three friends, "Well, I've got a wonderful feeling and the feeling is that the internet works perfectly and it works perfectly *now*! But... how do you feel?" They each instantly caught that same feeling and big smiles also appeared upon their faces as they told me that they too had a great feeling!

I then suggested they join me and that we all say that statement together. And that is exactly what we said in unison: "The internet works perfectly and it works perfectly *now!*" Afterwards, I turned and walked up to the front of the room and began conducting the owners' meeting without giving a thought to the internet. I felt absolutely confident everything would be all right.

Halfway through the meeting, the time for the marketing presentation finally came. And guess what? You're right: the internet worked perfectly! The owners were pleased with what they saw and clapped heartily. They then voted to approve another ten thousand dollars for the completion of the twenty thousand dollar plan originally recommended to them.

*"If we will be there for the little things, we will be there for the big things."*

Again that thought ran through my mind as I was filled once more with overwhelming gratitude and humble appreciation at what great works are continually being provided for us.

### The Perfect Ending to an Amazing Weekend

That evening, after a potluck dinner, the salsa group and I enjoyed dancing together by the pool to the lively music. We danced for hours along with the others who were brave enough to join us from the crowd that had gathered to watch the performance.

Afterwards, a big screen movie played on the cool deck of the pool as people enjoyed floating around in the water, relaxing on chaise lounges, lying on beach towels in the grass or sitting on their balconies.

While the people were engaged with the movie, the salsa girls and I, all heated up from hours of dancing, ran down the beach to the ocean, stripped off our clothes and went skinny dipping in the refreshing and gentle, salty surf. The moon sparkled over the water and helped to conceal us under its shimmering liquid cloak.

I felt wonderfully revitalized as we giggled, swam and unwound while we mutually enjoyed the simple pleasure of playing in those warm, soothing swells. What a blessing it was to be in the company of these delightful, kind, supportive and fully alive women after such an eventful few days.

## Thumbs Up

A couple of weeks after the owners' meeting, the same agent at the border, along with two others, noticed my car window was working. When he inquired about it, I rolled it up and down for him several times. Then he asked me how much it cost to fix it.

I replied, "It didn't cost me a thin dime." I told him I got my *mojo* back.

Then, I revealed to the group what really happened. They enjoyed hearing about the story of the watch, the washer and the window. We all felt uplifted and happy as we laughed. I then waved good-bye.

As I drove off into the beautiful Arizona sunset, I called back to them and said, "Let the force be with us!" They jovially responded with an all *thumbs up.*

## TAKE ACTION #1!

**From time to time this week (and for the rest of your life) ask yourself, when you recognize you have drawn to yourself a life learning opportunity, "What am I to learn and master from this experience?"**

## TAKE ACTION #2!

You literally have the ability to command the elements and the world around you. Continue to refine your personal integrity and honorable attributes so your confidence and ability to create with all that touches your life will be strengthened within you. Ask yourself while deeply searching within, "Am I an honorable being in ALL aspects of my life?" Write these words on some sticky notes and post them where you can see them.

Depending on your reply, allow yourself to remain honorable or become more honorable every moment of your life beginning NOW.

# CHAPTER THIRTEEN

# ~ *Do You Have a New Kitten?* ~

It was a Friday morning in the early autumn, just before the air became chilled. Ronnie and I snuggled in our bed under the pineapple-patterned quilt. We visited with each other while we watched the dawning sun as it rose and spread its soothing rays upon the purple mountains. I loved the few extra minutes of time we spent together before we both showered and headed off to work. I was also packing up to leave for the week. We would be separated the entire time and I missed him already.

### Sharing a Plan for Our Increased Happiness

That morning, as we continued to embrace one another in the warm comfort of our bed, I shared with him my excitement about the idea of getting a new kitten for our home.

We already had Rowdy, a twelve-year-old black and grey-striped working cat who was quite the protector of our large gardens and more than a little stuck in his ways. The old man had lived a full productive life but was starting to slow down and become complacent. Heck, he had even survived a nasty fight with a rattlesnake that struck him in the face with a venomous bite. His bloody head looked like a round swollen melon when we discovered him the next day!

"Wouldn't it be nice to have a new kitten in our home?" I asked as I shared my ideas with Ronnie that morning. "It would bring new life to us and perk up Rowdy. He could teach her the ropes as well. We would have fun watching them while they played and tousled with each other. We would also enjoy looking at the world through the little kitten's eyes."

Both my husband and I could picture the idea of the new kitten in our home. We also felt very excited about the possibility of this happening now. Every time I thought about the kitten, my excitement grew.

I imagined and pictured myself driving to the Humane Society or an animal shelter to pick up the kitten. But surprisingly, I also saw myself immediately driving off on my trip that day and I realized I didn't have enough time to search for a new kitten on my own. Yet my excited feelings continued to increase as I got in my car and headed off toward my destination.

We usually choose striped tabby cats when we pick a kitten to join our family...ones preferably without any white on them. We live in a wild part of the desert, nestled in the Tucson Mountains in an area called Deer Ranch. The name fits the spot perfectly because lots of deer run in and around the wash at the base of the sheer rock cliff just a few feet from our garden wall.

It is important that our cats are able to quickly camouflage themselves from the many predators that also call this area home. Mountain lions, wild cats, foxes and hawks patrol those cliffs daily as they look for fresh meals to assuage their hunger. These wild animals would love to devour our feline family members. So, of course white fur was not an option, especially if the cats were prowling around at night for little critters.

Meanwhile, I still thought it would be lots of fun to have a new kitten and I knew I desired to have a female, reasoning it would be a better fit for Rowdy. I enjoyed daydreaming about our future little family member as I continued on my journey that day.

"Brrring Brrring" rang the telephone. Sunday morning my husband called me, all excited with some surprising news. Saturday evening one of the neighbors called and asked him, "Do you have a new little kitten?" His reply was, "No."

Then she told him that she was sure we had a little kitten in one of our protected side yards by the south side of our home. Both the neighbors across the street and the neighbors next door could hear it meowing.

Ronnie knew I hadn't picked out our kitten yet, so he told the friend she was mistaken. The concerned neighbor insisted he look in the area she had described with a flashlight because she was certain she had heard the baby's cries in one of those private gardens.

Grabbing the flashlight, he headed out to search for the little kitten, not only to comfort the neighbors but to also settle his curiosity. He looked carefully around, but found nothing. So he made his way back into the house and went to bed.

The next morning, after my husband returned from meetings, the neighbor called once again. She told him she hoped he didn't mind, but there *was* a baby kitten in our side yard by the Jacuzzi window and she had been feeding him and giving him water!

Our neighbor across the street went on to say that she had checked around the neighborhood and no one was missing any kittens. The neighbors next to us had two darling, grade school-aged children who wanted to keep the little fluff ball, but their dad was allergic to cats. They too were really hoping we'd be willing to keep the kitten. Little did they know our plan was to adopt one as soon as I was able to return home.

Sure enough, when Ronnie went to check, he discovered that a feral mother cat had delivered her little kitten only one day after we had been talking, imagining and feeling excited about adopting a new furry member into our family.

Both Ronnie and I were happily surprised that our desire to receive a new kitten was brought so immediately into being. We didn't even have to go looking for her. Her mother had personally delivered the baby to our home! Nor did we have to search to see if someone had lost her. The neighbors already had checked out the situation for us and even made sure she was cared for until Ronnie returned home.

### Is It a "He" or a "She?"

The kitten looked to be about five weeks old. As it turned out, she was a tiny striped orange tabby cat, just exactly the type we always get, without any white on her. She was joy-filled and completely trusting as she sprinted up into our outstretched hands.

My neighbor corrected me when I referred to the kitten as a *she* and told me it was impossible for the kitten to be female because all orange tabby cats are males and all calico cats are females. I told her I was certain the kitten was a little girl, because we had only thought of a little girl coming to our family.

Statistically speaking, about 80% of orange tabby cats are male. But as it turned out, we received one of the 20% that are female! It was a *she*, just as we imagined! By the way, calico cats can also be male but are unable to reproduce.

The mother looked like a mix of calico with a hint of tabby stripes on her sides and lots of white. She checked on her kitten often but ran away if we came near her. We tried to feed and care for the mother cat, but she didn't trust us and continued to run away. Finally, we took the kitten inside to protect her from the increasingly cold evenings and the wild animals. We were certain that they would soon discover her because of her exuberant meowing.

## Our Timely Precious Gift

One day, a couple of weeks after she brought us her kitten, we discovered that the mother had been killed by a wild animal that had come into our backyard. The beast had left the mother's partially skinned skull behind as a chilling reminder that her life had been snatched away. Had she not given us her baby when she did, the kitten would have also perished.

This little girl is precious in every way and a complete delight to us. Ronnie and I share much laughter and fun together as we watch her skedaddle and scamper about our home.

We named her Skittles.

Her much older brother Rowdy adores her and is very patient. He taught little Skittles how to do many things, including how to drink out of the toilet and jump up on the grand piano. We taught her not to scratch or bite and how to chase ping-pong balls. As a result of our training/interfering, she can play with a grasshopper or mouse for an hour. Later, unscathed and intact, the grasshopper or mouse just flies or runs away. Meanwhile, both cats entertain us as they playfully wrestle with one another in the mornings. Everything has become a toy for her and everyone is her new best friend.

I love it when she curls up on my pillow and purrs us both to sleep at night, or lies near my shoulder on a cushion when I'm using the computer. It is truly amazing to both my husband and me when we realize how fast our world can change.

It never ceases to fill me with appreciation when I realize how we are able to deliberately create our individual world when we purposefully take the steps to use our Powers to connect with the Divine!

## Creating Precisely What We Prefer

First, we thought about, clearly imagined and spoke of the dream we mutually chose to create in our minds. Then we both felt excited about and pictured *in detail* the thoughts of having that dream come true *now*. We continued letting that feeling grow inside us. By the next day, our dream had become our reality because we stayed open to this possibility and allowed this blessing to be ushered in. We received it and then gave thanks.

It is that happy, warm, wonderfully assured feeling part that is the key. It verifies to us we are connected to that which literally creates worlds.

This is a small illustration of what can happen in all of our lives. We are each capable of experiencing these examples daily if we learn about and exercise our Divine birthright to purposefully create our world. It seems like life just could not get any sweeter or more exciting and fun...yet it does.

*"Who would believe such pleasure from a wee ball o' fur?"*

*~Irish saying*

> **Note:** As I scan through this book during the last week of editing it, two years have passed since we were given this sweet little gift we call *Skittles.* Those two years proved to be the happiest years of Rowdy's life. I'm so very thankful I followed my desire to call into our lives someone who would enliven and bless all of us.

Yesterday we said our fond farewells to Rowdy and laid his well-worn body gently to rest in our garden under the apple tree so it could live on while his sprit ran off to play.

## TAKE ACTION!

**You can rapidly create in detail what you would LOVE to see happen in your life. First, think about, clearly imagine and speak of the dream you would like to create. Then feel excited about and picture in detail that dream coming true NOW. Continue letting that feeling grow inside you. Stay open to this possibility and allow this blessing to be ushered in. Receive it and then give thanks. It really is that easy. Remember to have FUN with this adventure!**

# CHAPTER FOURTEEN

# ~ *Skittles and Emma* ~

Our new kitten Skittles grew and flourished as she won all the hearts of those who came to visit our home. But in March, I realized something…or someone was missing. We usually get two kittens at a time when we increase our feline family members. I mentioned this to Ronnie.

Be aware of what you think and speak! Remember, your words have the Power to create!

Soon it came to our attention there was *another* young stray in the neighborhood that had also gone into heat. My neighbor said she would pay to have her fixed so we didn't have more stray kittens popping up, but she didn't have a way of caring for the cat during the two week indoor recovery period the stray required for proper healing.

Now this cat had already survived the cold winter out on her own. I hadn't noticed her because of all the time I was working away from home. My neighbor had thoughtfully put out food to assist the cat during those months. She would have taken her into her home as well but it would not have been a good fit with the animals she had already adopted.

Since she was willing to pay for the surgery, I volunteered to take care of the cat while she healed. Meanwhile, I asked the neighbor if her family would like to pick out a name for her. "Emma" came up as the winning choice.

## Feelings of Contention

As Emma recovered from her surgery, she immediately took to being a house cat. She happily curled up on our bed and clearly announced to Skittles she was unwilling to share that place of honor. In fact, anytime Skittles came near Emma, Emma would soundly thrash the kitten. Then Rowdy would quickly *school* the newcomer. Those behaviors were simply not to be tolerated!

Well, all that strife started producing stress in our home. We were no longer a happy family. Ronnie told me he thought it was time to turn Emma back out into the wild desert or send her to an animal shelter. I then reminded him of the fact that I had also been homeless while I was in high school. I lived in my car or relied on the kindness of others to shelter me during those times. I understood how Emma felt.

I explained Emma's situation to him with a bit more detail. Everything had changed for her. She was recovering from surgery, hormonal changes and adjusting to new surroundings. She also had not yet built feelings of trust for her safety and the new beings in her everyday world. I asked him to be patient for a little longer. I truly felt the situation would soon make a turn for the better. He agreed to let her have a little more time to settle in.

Meanwhile, even though Skittles was consistently rebuffed and rejected by Emma, this resilient, loving little girl continued to be filled with hope that one day she would be able to win over Emma's heart and affection.

## Undaunted, She Persisted

Several times each day, Skittles would approach Emma to test out the situation. It was as though she was saying to her big sister, "Hi. Hello! How are you today? Would you like to play with me?" Each time, Emma angrily hissed, snarled, bit and scratched at Skittles in response.

But undaunted, Skittles persisted and persisted. She held on to who she was and did not let her delightful, playful, lighthearted demeanor change, no matter how rejecting, distrustful and miserable Emma's responses were. Somehow Skittles believed there was hope for her and Emma's relationship, so she continued each day to extend more invitations to that cranky ole girl with an attitude!

Finally, to our amazement and joy, Emma's distrustful hardened heart softened and was completely won over by Skittle's consistent genuine invitations. Now Emma joined the kitten in her happy and adventuresome life. Suddenly these two girls were wrestling and playing all day together. Emma quickly became very attentive to the washing, care and grooming of little Skittles who had lost her mother at such an early age.

The total transformation of their relationship was remarkable and quite heartwarming to both Ronnie and me.

I couldn't help but admire the attitude of this resilient little kitten as she stayed the course of the desires of her heart. She didn't allow anyone to distract her from her goal. She clearly fixed her sights and steadily pursued her plan despite the consistent rejection and negative reactions she encountered. She kept floating down her stream with a merry attitude!

This *little wee ball o' fur* gets it. She didn't waver or falter on her preferred path when distractions from her chosen goal came into her life. As a result of her steadfast unwavering actions she did indeed receive the requests of her little, yet mighty soul!

Ronnie and I had originally pictured that this new kitten we wished for would bring a special positive energy into our home and fill our lives with more love and laughter.

Thankfully, that is exactly what this little blessing has done.

## TAKE ACTION!

**Take no notice of others' rejections or negative reactions. Very often those responses have NOTHING to do with you. They are just reflections of what those individuals are currently experiencing. Perhaps they simply require a *moment* while they regain their bearings. Stay the amazing person that you truly are by keeping your eternal perspective and goals clearly in your sights. Steadily move yourself forward each day toward your desired goals.**

# CHAPTER FIFTEEN

# ~ *"¿Qué Prefiere...12c o 3d?"* ~

It was an early March evening as I lifted out my small carry-on suitcase from the back of the car and rolled it toward the terminal at the Tucson International Airport. I had carefully prepared it earlier that morning while I thought about the fun trip I would be taking with two of our grandchildren.

Ronnie had driven me to the airport where we were almost immediately united with our former son-in-law and his son and daughter. Soon the kids and I would board a plane to fly and see my daughter. She and her new husband were living in Utah while he finished out his commitment just prior to his next job assignment.

Earlier in the day, our family had celebrated the fourth birthday of my youngest grandson at a popular pizza place. It was a pretty festive occasion. As a result of all the family fun, my six-year-old granddaughter and eight-year-old grandson, who were traveling with me, were still quite excited about the party. The birthday cake, vanilla ice cream, root beer soda and pink cotton candy may have contributed to some of their exhilaration. Plus their anticipation and glee about the thought of going on the plane adventure with Nana had been building for days.

We had all been picturing ourselves visiting together, sharing stories, sipping on juices, eating snacks and playing quiet games while flying to our destination.

The time finally arrived for our adventure. We were all packed and ready to go! The children and I kissed and hugged their daddy and papa good-bye numerous times, showed our IDs to security, stripped down, passed through the metal detector, then redressed and gathered up our belongings. Afterwards, we bought something to drink and snack on. Whew! I was ready to chill out for a few minutes.

## Following My Impressions

With that goal in mind, I felt impressed to sit where we would be away from most of the group gathering for the flight. I looked around and finally settled my little brood down on seats in a less populated section of the waiting area so we could catch our breaths and listen for our boarding call.

While sitting there, I noticed two well-dressed young men who obviously, from their good looking yet unique shoes, were not from the United States. They sat directly across from us. I also noticed one of them quietly talking in a foreign language with someone on his phone. It sounded like he spoke one of the romance languages. When he finished his phone conversation and started to visit with his friend sitting next to him, I realized they were speaking Spanish.

I began to feel curious and interested in them. They were relaxed, easygoing and seemed quite likeable. We had time before our flight boarded and I felt even more intrigued about these two young men so I decided to strike up a conversation. I wondered where they were going. "¿A dónde van?" I questioned.

They told me they were traveling to the Moab, Utah area (they worked in construction in the mining industry and had business with one of the open pit mines nearby). I told them I thought it was wonderful they had this opportunity. I also shared with them that my father and some of my other family members used to work in the mines in Arizona and also in some Latin American countries. I then asked where they were from. "Hermosillo, Sonora, Mexico," was their reply.

Hermosillo was a city only a few hours from my beach home.

They also began to ask me questions about what I was doing and why I was flying that early March evening. I told the two gentlemen my nietos, or grandchildren, and I were traveling to see their mom and new dad. I also said my abuelitos, or grandparents, were from Colonia Dublán, Chihuahua, México and that I stayed much of the time in our home at the ocean in Northern Mexico. I invited them to come enjoy the beach and stay at our place sometime. They thought that would be wonderful and gave me one of their business cards.

Meanwhile, the children were enjoying the conversation and listened intently as the rest of us rolled our "R's" and rattled off words in a different language that was unfamiliar to them.

### Averting a Volcanic Eruption

The time passed quickly. Soon we gathered up our carry-on items and prepared to board the plane.

As we stood in line, I glanced at our seat assignments and realized the children and I were not seated next to one another. In fact, we weren't even near each other. I was at the front of the plane while they were at the very back just in front of the restrooms!

I could clearly see the potential of an emotional meltdown from two very excited yet exhausted little people.

They had both played all day without any rest; then added to that, they had consumed a large amount of sugary treats. Plus, it was almost five-thirty in the evening, also known as the *arsenic hour.* To top it all off the children had had excitement building inside for weeks, revving them up with expectations of their trip with their favorite Nana (by the way, I'm their only Nana). I understood the situation could potentially erupt into volcanic explosions of wails and tears in just a few minutes.

I took a brief moment to get my bearings and thought, "Well, this is a perfect opportunity for the children and I to all exercise and use our abilities to create the world we would prefer."

I broke the news to the children as we walked down the ramp to board the plane. Various looks and emotions started welling up on their faces and tears started spilling out. Fear, worry, frustration, disappointment, helplessness were some of the feelings that topped the list.

## Creating the Winning Plan We Preferred

I looked at them and asked them if they would like to join me in using our abilities to create something wonderful for them.

My grandson had already learned a little about remembering how to use his Power from teaching moments I previously shared with him. Plus, he had heard the reports of like experiences from his other cousins when they were with me. He immediately got a twinkle in his eyes and they lit up with eager anticipation. His younger sister was a bit more hesitant.

Without any further delay, I began to tell them a possible game they could play with me if it was their desire to do so. I suggested they easily and quickly release all of their feelings of worry, fear or upset. Then I instructed them to start allowing themselves to get excited in a happy way about what I was now going to share with them. Next, I recommended they allow a wonderful, assuring, warm feeling to start in their chest and go through their entire body.

I went on to explain to them, briefly yet with some detail, that we each have a loving, heavenly kind of Team who know us and enjoy playing with us. They would love to join with us to assist in helping to form the world we would like to live in. In fact, they would enjoy doing that for us right now. But first, I shared, "Let's do our part to connect with them so the Power will be stronger and we can more specifically create what we choose to have happen."

I informed them when we stamp our feet and cry and feel scared or frustrated, we push ourselves away from being able to fully connect to our Team. That's fine if we choose to feel that way and sit far away from each other. We will still be all right and we will still be able to reach our final destination.

However, I went on explaining to them, if we would rather sit *with* each other on this plane, then we can fill our bodies with that great feeling I had taught them earlier and keep that feeling as we pictured what we would really like to have happen instead.

I then described details of the plan and asked the children to visualize it happening to us right *now!*

I told them that first we'd find the location of their seats and I would help them settle in. Then, I would visit with the person assigned to the seat next to them to explain the situation and offer a seat exchange so I could sit with my grandchildren.

The person would notice that my seat was even better than the seat they had been assigned and they would be happy to change with me. That person would not only be very happy with the change but would also feel that uplifting feeling. In the end, everyone would be able to have what they preferred. I told them this is what is called a win-win situation. It is the best way to live life with other people.

## Seeing and Feeling the Plan Materialize

I could feel the warm, exhilarating excitement growing within me and I could see the children were catching onto that feeling as well. Within moments, we were all connected to that Power. My grandchildren's entire countenance shifted and we once again were in the center of our hurricanes with that feeling of peace, calm, well-being and Enthusiastic anticipation.

The three of us eventually made our way to the very back of the plane. We had some difficulty getting the children to their seats because there were suitcases in the aisle. There were people standing near the luggage, blocking our way.

I looked around and realized the baggage belonged to the two young Mexican men I had visited with earlier in the evening. They had never traveled on this smaller type of aircraft and didn't realize their belongings would not fit in the overhead compartments. Because of the language barrier, they didn't understand what they were supposed to do about the situation and were getting concerned.

I quickly instructed them to take their *maletas* to the front of the plane and leave them just outside the door, where they would be placed in the hold underneath the plane. I assured them they would not have any problems getting their suitcases back.

Then, I looked at the empty seat next to my grandchildren. I asked one of the young men if that was his seat. He replied, "Yes." The happy, excited feeling increased within me.

I asked him if he would be interested in an idea I had for him. I indicated that my seat was in the front of the plane where it was quieter than this area near the engines. I also shared that because of the ages of my grandchildren, they would require assistance during the flight. Since he and his friend were not sitting together, I wondered if he would be interested in changing seats with me. I assured him that whatever he decided I would be happy with his decision.

I asked him "¿Qué prefiere: doce c o tres d?" ("What would you prefer: twelve c or three d?")

He briefly weighed the situation and with a grin on his face told me that he preferred sitting in seat three D. With that, he scooped up his luggage and quickly headed to the front of the plane. I patted him on the back and thanked him for his kindness as he walked away.

The children looked at me with wide eyes amazement and smiles of delight. I continued to teach them about the special learning opportunity we had just experienced. I shared with them that it was important that we give thanks and appreciation for all the help we had just received from the Divine. We then each joined together in expressing words of heartfelt gratitude for our blessings.

These caring beings knew exactly what our desires were even before we did. They encouraged us to connect with the young men before we got on that plane. It pays to associate with those who know everything past, present and future!

Everyone walked away feeling like a winner that evening.

## It Was More Than a Coincidence

I never fail to be amazed at the unfolding of such events in my life! I was so thankful I felt inspired to sit in the less crowed portion of the waiting area. I'm glad I released any feelings of timidity and followed through on the impression I received to reach out and visit with these two strangers.

It was more than a coincidence that out of all the people who were going to ride on that plane, that evening, we were drawn to sit and visit with the two kind young men who ended up requiring our help and who also assisted us in turn.

It was a miracle.

Our lives are filled with day-to-day blessings of love and grace whether we take the time to notice them or not. I realize we would have still ended up making it through the trip even without the seating changes. But the important point is that we do not have to just plow through life with miserable feelings and tolerate settling for whatever comes our way. Instead, we can purposefully direct our lives!

*This way of living is the difference between existing in the day to day while trudging through life or living it with wonder and joy every moment if that is our desire.*

On my flight back to Tucson, I noticed that a young mother with her two young children was sitting in the place where my seat was assigned. When I asked her if that was also her seat number, she urgently asked me if I would be willing to change seats. I couldn't help but chortle internally to myself. Without hesitation, I happily told her I would be delighted to do so!

**Note:** Even though this is a story that involves children who are learning how to activate their personal connection to the Divine, it emphasizes the fact that we each can quickly and easily do the same!

## TAKE ACTION!

Today (and for the rest of your life) whenever you begin to notice that events around you are sliding off course, take immediate action and begin reshaping the situation into what you would like to experience instead! Remember to add the details of your preferences and follow through with what you feel impressed to do.

## CHAPTER SIXTEEN

# ~ A Knock Came to My Door ~

After being married for about two years, my husband and I, along with our one-year-old son, moved to a home in the city just three houses away from a bustling street. Within a few years, the two-lane street expanded into six-lanes of rushing traffic. By that time, our small family of three had grown into a family of six with four children going to elementary school.

Sixteen times a day during the school year at least one of my little tikes had to cross that busy street between going to school, playing in sports and attending other community activities.

Sometimes they had a crossing guard to help them. Other times they were on their own.

An uneasy feeling began to grow within me that my children were not safe. It was just a matter of time before one or more of them was going to get seriously injured while crossing that street.

Added to that concern, was the fact that when my eldest son attended his first year of junior high school I noticed that gangs, along with increasing drug problems were forming in our neighborhood. Between the busy street and the gang/drug problems, I started to feel concerned about our situation. I felt it was imperative that we move our family to a different location.

## Pouring Out the Desires of My Heart

Instead of getting all worried and obsessed about these circumstances, I decided to create a solution and plan of action in my mind. I then began to get excited about those possibilities now coming into our family's life.

I went to my source of strength and power. I connected to my Team. Together we formed a *Council Meeting*. As the meeting commenced, we became one in purpose to form the perfect plan to assuage my family's concerns.

While I was on my knees in the middle of that gathering, I shared the specific desires of my heart. I told them about how I would love to be able to sell our home in the city, purchase land in the country, build a home and move my family. I thought it would be wonderful if we could move about six weeks before the end of the school year. That way the children could go to their new school and also develop friendships with the children that lived in and around the neighborhood. Then, all summer they would be able to build on these friendships and start the school year without being the *new kids*.

I also spoke about my wish to help find a way to pay for this change. I preferred to lift this additional financial burden off my husband's shoulders so he could enjoy this adventure with the rest of us. The plan was to create a substantial amount of money in a short amount of time.

Meanwhile, I was also attending college. The emphasis of my studies was in Psychology, Spanish and Writing. Not business. As I spoke in this Team planning session, I acknowledged this fact. I realized I didn't have a piece of paper that would convince others that I was an intelligent person. But I knew that my mind was bright, teachable, and willing to learn.

I made the commitment to release all fear. I would accept anything my Team presented to me. Why? Because I was certain they would prepare an avenue for me to attain this goal. I totally trusted in my Team's ability to give me the skills and knowledge that was required. I also believed I would be able to receive, understand and apply this knowledge when they provided it to me.

Then, I became even more specific in my desire to create with them. My first preference was to be able to work when my children were in school and still have flexibility to spend quality time with them. My next choice was to be able to take a couple of college classes and support my husband by helping in our business. And my last request was to oversee and help build our home because I absolutely loved to build and create things.

As we wrapped up our meeting I had a fabulous feeling all was well. I also felt really excited about discovering and receiving what was being *cooked up* for me to do. Whatever it was, I trusted in what would be provided. I didn't fret and worry at all about how these goals would be accomplished. Rather, I just let go of the details and stayed open to receive whatever came to me.

### "Do You Think You Can Run This Business?"

One Saturday, not long after the *pow-wow* with my special Team, a knock came to the front door of our home. When Ronnie opened the door there stood Judy, our neighbor from across the street. She explained she was the Director of Human Resources for a large national cable TV business that was also in Tucson.

The company preferred to use a subcontractor to do their collections work. She went on to explain that she had been observing us and knew we had fallen on hard times a few years earlier (when Ronnie was working construction and there was a moratorium on building). She noticed we didn't get discouraged or give up.

Instead, we still took good care of our home and our family. Ronnie and I also helped each other pull things together when he decided to form a new business. She saw our entrepreneurial spirit and felt we were the ones to do this collections work.

My husband already had his hands full running our new company. He told the neighbor he didn't have the time to devote to forming another business. And he definitely didn't have the extra energy to run it either. Turning to look at me he asked, "Do you think you can run this business?"

Because of the Team council meeting I had previously had, I was able to respond without any hesitation. Instead of shrinking back with fear or uncertainty, I was able to eagerly reply, "YES!" I knew this was the opportunity I had been looking for. A moment like this is why those meetings are so important!

I had no idea how I was going to accomplish this work, but I did know one thing for sure: the Team I worked with have inspired the most outstanding and motivated people who ever worked in business. If those people could receive that inspiration, so could I!

With that steadfast, supportive thought in mind, I went back to the Divine and humbly asked for the information that would be required to do the job. It was readily given to me.

### The Pure Flood of Intelligence

Suddenly, it seemed like the top of my head was opened up and information just started rushing in! I grabbed a pen and paper and began writing as fast as my hands could move.

When I was finished, I surveyed the details of what I had just received and written on the paper. I was amazed. Before my eyes were the well-organized business plans I required. I was told how to hire the people, how to orient them and what tools they required before I sent them out into the field. The information I recorded even included the list of things I was to purchase to get everything set up and operational.

Next, I was to meet with the company hiring me. I didn't know exactly what to say to guarantee them their company was in good hands, but I did know who had that assurance.

### Voice of the Flesh or Voice of Inspiration

My mind started to fill with questions from the voice of my mortal body. It was the weak, shaky, wavering voice of the flesh:

"Why would this company choose to hire me? I am just a homemaker with four children and I was still attending college. Sure, I have talent and a strong desire to progress and succeed, but I have nothing that would be a big selling point."

> **Remember:** The wavering voice of weakness, lack or fear never comes from the Divine.

I acknowledged that doubting, discouraging and sabotaging monologue in my head. Instead of pushing it back down within me, or shooing it away like a pesky fly, I swiftly, purposefully and completely released it from my soul before it could get a footing in what was being created.

Then, I began *hearing* the sweet, encouraging whisperings of my Team. They shared with me why I was the perfect candidate for this job.

I was self-motivated yet flexible and able to turn on a dime. I could give out assignments and allow others to do their jobs. I was aware and sensitive to what was going on around me and was able make corrections in the course midstream. I could make the hard calls and set healthy boundaries while still encouraging and motivating others. I was well-organized and exact. I didn't give up when things became challenging. In fact, my confidence in learning from the opportunity just strengthened my courage and resolve. I wasn't a quitter. People could count on me to follow through with my commitments.

On my own, I freely acknowledge I am not very capable. But when I unite with the Divine I am absolutely certain of what the outcome of any endeavor will be. It has been and always will be successful. I knew I would be able to glean whatever experience I wished to learn about. I could feel my sure confidence in this forthcoming adventure begin to swell and expand within me as I more fully allowed myself to connect with them.

I continued to allow that shift and confidence to build within me, recognizing and acknowledging that I actually did have lots of strengths. In fact, those who knew me in my community viewed me as a devoted mother, an innovative homemaker as well as a straight-A college student. And, in this newly forming situation, my Team clearly saw me as one heck of an executive!

I wondered how I should physically present myself in the upcoming meeting. I understood that I was to look and act in a professional manner to support the creative changes that were happening within me. My Team clearly instructed me in that goal. All the details of my dress, shoes, hair and makeup were given to me. Even the exact colors of my clothing were included. I later learned they were *power colors*.

Basically, I was told to relax and enjoy this process. My Team would provide all the support I required. Uniting with me in my vessel (body), my Team would allow their flow of confidence and well-being to flow from them, through me and into the people interviewing me. I was transformed into that executive I had envisioned through their inspiration and encouragement. The company hired me on the spot when I went for the initial interview. I drove home giggling out loud with delight about what had transpired thus far.

## Putting the Business Plan into Action

I immediately started hiring, orienting and training people. Right away, we began receiving work orders; routing them in zip codes and sending people out into the field to start collecting money, converter boxes and remotes. If no one was home, they left a door hanger.

I also spot-checked all the areas in the work field by personally going to some of the homes in each zip code area where we had work orders and performing the same duties as the individuals working with me. By doing this, I could better understand what the workers were encountering, and also knew more precisely what the people using the services preferred as well. It helped me stay in touch with the pulse of the situation, and I always had a clear viewpoint about what the customers and the subcontractors I had hired were experiencing.

Often, executives of businesses are so removed from the day-to-day minutia of their business that they actually are quite detached from what is really occurring in the trenches. When this happens, they can become unaware of the demands they have placed on their employees. Their workers start feeling unappreciated and the business fails to thrive because of the negative environment. Instead of feeling like a team player, they begin to feel like slaves. The business then begins to implode.

My oldest daughter once described the situation like this: a team soldier will take the hard slings and arrows for his beloved, caring leader in the heat of battle, but a slave will bend down and let his aloof master receive the onslaught of heavy hits alone. I have always felt a true leader was also a servant to those they led; no one is superior to anyone else. So, that's what I tried to be to my employees: a true leader.

The fledgling business worked well. Amazingly, we were in the **black**, making a profit, the very first month! That is pretty much unheard of with a startup company, but not while playing with this Team!

I ended up hiring over forty people. One weekend out of the month we collected about $40,000 for the company we contracted for (in the early 1980s that money was twice as much as the mortgage of our home). During the rest of the month, we did cleanup collections and posted follow up door hangers. My personal payout was $1,000 a month after taxes and there were substantial bonuses on top of that figure. Not bad considering that our mortgage for our home was only $172 an month.

We also had to haul in a truck-load of equipment to the downtown office for the cable company (actually, what we used was our bronze-colored, family Ford station wagon).

We were really busy! During that same weekend I handled and organized 4,000 work orders that broke out into 16,000 pieces of paper. Without using a computer, I developed a system to quickly locate any one of those papers, and we always balanced to the penny with the monies we collected.

## Making the Move

In the meantime, we were able to purchase four acres of land in the beautiful northeast foothills of Tucson. It felt like things were falling into place because we quickly found the land and received our funds to build our home. We promptly sold off two parcels that were one acre each. The first parcel paid off all the land and the second one gave us a substantial amount to build our house!

We sold our home in the city and moved out to the country six weeks before the children finished their school year. They started in their new schools and quickly began making friends. I continued to work with our other company, attend college and spend quality time with my family while overseeing and helping with the building of our home.

It was exactly what I had requested in the Council Meeting with my Team including the precise date I had asked for to move from the city to the country.

## Oops! No Money Allotted for Furniture

While we were building our new home, we lived in a small trailer. We had one twin bed in one bedroom under which we stuffed our sleeping bags. Ronnie and I slept on a pull out couch/bed in the living room. The only other bedroom was used as an office to run the collection company.

After two years, the project was finally completed and it was time for us to move into our new home. There was just one snag to the plan: we didn't have the money to purchase furniture.

Then one day, Ronnie came home from a business convention in Las Vegas. When I greeted him at the door, he was pale and unshaven. He hadn't slept that weekend and looked tuckered out. I asked him if he was all right. All he could reply was, "I just kept winning and winning and winning." Then he handed me a big rolled up wad of money and told me to go buy beds and furniture for our new home!

We bought everything we desired, including fresh piles of sheets, pillows and comforters and moved them into the house. The kids were so grateful to finally have beds again that they laid in them for days!

## Time for a Change

One day I felt a change come over me. I realized the original reason for my request for the collections work had been fulfilled. I was juggling too many things and understood it was time to let go of this responsibility. I didn't know exactly how to do this.

I knew I didn't desire to be fired, and I didn't wish to quit or leave the company dangling without someone to provide those services for them. Plus, I still had a contract to honor.

With those thoughts in mind, I went back to my Team and called another Council Meeting to share with them what I now would love to see happen. And I also included the details about being released from that commitment while being free of the consequences of being fired or quitting.

I didn't know how my Team would be able to create what I was seeking since it seemed my request painted us into a corner... there were just not too many other options available. Yet I felt peace and absolute confidence in what the outcome would be.

I also felt assured our employees would also be fine if these jobs closed down because they only worked for me one weekend out of the month. They all had fulltime occupations with other companies in the city (in other words this was not their main source of employment for them).

Not long after I formed that preference within my soul and finished my meeting with my Team, I received a phone call from Sam, one of the head people at the cable business. He began the conversation by reminding me that the company had been sold several times. Then he informed me that the new owners had their own in-house collection department within their existing business.

This man was calling to inform me that they no longer required my services!

The line went quiet on both ends. He knew and I knew we still had a contract with one another. We both grasped the crux of the matter: the owners were responsible for coming up with an amount to pay us off. I had them by the *short hairs*. (Crudely put, but accurate!)

However, instead of feeling offended, used up, cast aside or rejected by this company, I clearly understood that this was the perfect answer to what *I* had asked for. With that realization, I immediately knew what my response would be.

So I told him, "When this conversation is finished, our contract will be completed."

"What did you say?" was his surprised reply.

"I said, when this conversation is finished our contract will be completed."

Relieved, Sam visited with me for a few moments longer. We exchanged our appreciation for each other and best wishes, and then said good-bye.

When I hung up the phone, I breathed a happy sigh. The literal desires of my heart had been met. I didn't have to be fired and I didn't have to quit plus the company also had a smooth transition in place for the departure of my services, precisely as I had requested. The job just evaporated as quickly and easily as it had materialized! And not one of my employees complained about the change. They appreciated the extra income while it lasted.

I don't know how this always-amazing Group does it. Thankfully they take care of most of the details. But I absolutely know and trust that somehow what I desire and request will transpire. I feel such gratitude for the personal attention they give me and my heart is flooded with grateful thanksgiving for our relationship. I tell them often of my appreciation for them…but better yet, I genuinely feel that appreciation for them. I also feel and see the evidence of their love and appreciation for me!

> **Note:** It is really important you stay aware of the pulse of your life situation. As you master experiences and glean all you can from them, it is important you recognize when you have completed an adventure and are ready to call in another one so you can continue learning and expanding while you are here. Be open to change and welcome it. It is when you run from it or avoid it that you begin to create misery, frustration and fear, which inevitably distracts you from swiftly moving on with your life mission.

In reflection, remember the desires of your heart are often quickly and easily brought to you. You don't even have to search for them. When a knock comes to your door, open it and have the courage to say, "Yes" to the opportunities being offered to you!

## TAKE ACTION!

Take a moment today to identify what you would love to experience. Add the details to it. Call together your Team and have a Council Meeting With them. Activate and follow through with the impressions they provide you. Don't know how to form that kind of meeting? The next chapter, "How to Create a Council Meeting," will share those details with you.

> **End Note:** I would like to take a moment to thank **Emily**, a supervisor in the cable TV business that I worked with. You were transferred before I was able to tell you of my sincere appreciation for all of your fine efforts. You were the perfect example of a bright, caring, calm, *got it together* kind of leader with a *great head on your shoulders,* while being completely free of any *ego* or postulating. You were a beautiful person inside and out. It was a pleasure working with you.

# CHAPTER SEVENTEEN

# ~ How to Create a Council Meeting ~

Perhaps you, too, would like to create your own Council Meeting but are unsure of how to accomplish this. If so, the following are directions describing how I create my meetings with my Team.

I initially ask for a Council Meeting to be formed by getting on my knees and uttering a formal prayer. I begin my supplication by respectfully recognizing my Creator by name. I refer to my Creator as *Heavenly Father* (He is the head leader of my amazing Team. I also recognize that I have a Heavenly Mother…that always has been a basic truth for me). I also ask for other members of my Team to join us and I often envision those individual members gathering in my behalf (I detailed who is on this Team in the chapter "The Team, Power and the Divine").

I then give forth thanks and appreciation for the many blessings that have been given to me already. Long ago, I learned it is very important to flood my soul with thanks, gratitude and appreciation while making this connection. This action literally expands my soul to fully unite with my Team because love and appreciation drives this Power to create!

Next, it is vital that I openly communicate the desires of my heart concerning what changes I would like to see happen in my life. During this time, I include as many details as I feel is important so my preferred goal can be fleshed out. Those details help me to recognize that objective when it comes into my life. I also ask for assistance in the formation and creation of my plan.

Then, I close my supplication by recognizing the Savior who made the Power of my living At-One-Ment with Him (and them) possible through his atonement. Finally, I say, "Amen" to indicate I agree with what we have discussed and also to formally end our conversation.

In between the beginning and the end of each of our visits, I say a lot of words like: *thee, thy, thine* and *thou.* But I learned long ago that my being able to fully connect to this loving group does not require a checklist of formalities. I am an inclusionary person and so is the Team I have personally come to know. From my experience, they just simply adore communicating with us and are definitely NOT concerned about our ability to speak to them in perfect biblical lingo. They already know us and our hearts' desires. They enjoy it when we personally remember them.

This simple way of communicating is an important part of our being able to create an amazing life. It also provides us with a joy and exhilaration at the same time—better than any feel-good drug or elixir mankind could create, except this experience has only positive benefits and zero negative side effects! That is precisely how it feels when you are connected with Them and in the flow of the Power which expands and moves you forward.

## Praying With Your Whole Soul

Most of the time, I communicate with my Team as one being speaking or having a conversation with another, in much the same manner that you would talk or visit with a close companion here on earth.

One day, I began sharing some of my stories with four girlfriends while we were taking a day trip to Mesa, Arizona. After a while, one of them stopped me and expressed confusion and consternation. She informed me that I wasn't praying the *right* way because I wasn't using the formal method and steps to which she was accustomed. She said I was just thinking and feeling what I desired throughout my day. Yet, at the same time, she admitted that she was moved by the amazing, miraculous results of my supplications, intentions and actions.

I totally understood where she was coming from. She was accustomed to praying only in the formal manner that she was taught—and that had been originally taught to me. To her, that method became the only acceptable way to contact the Divine. I reasoned that if that form of communication continued to satisfy her and provide the results she was seeking, no problem. If it isn't broken, don't fix it. Right?

I then told her what I was actually doing. I shared this personal information not because I was trying to prove that my avenue to the Divine was more desirable or acceptable: I did it because I just felt she might be interested in learning another route to get to the same goal.

Take my petite, 88-year-old Aunt Thelma for example. The majority of people I know like to take the I-10 freeway to travel from Casa Grande to Tucson. Not my Aunt Thelma. She prefers the frontage road. Sure, her method may require a little more time, but she enjoys this slower-paced route more than the rush of the highway and she still arrives at her destination.

I explained to my friend that while I might not communicate by means of the exact step-by-step formula we were both taught, I nonetheless enjoyed a deep and meaningful, personal communication with the Divine.

I told her that I do not communicate with words alone. I communicate with every word, every thought and even with my feelings. I went on to say that when I went to my Team in prayer to share my desires and be counseled about my requests, every part of my soul connected with Them. Even the cells in my body partook of this experience. Together, as united beings that were one in purpose, we would form a plan and then collectively put that plan into action.

For me, this method of praying meant ritualistic, less meaningful, rote prayers could be thrown right out the window! I say this because that is what I felt I was doing when I prayed by means of the traditional method I was originally taught. While others might do this and stay focused and communicate in a sincere manner, my own mind would begin to wander. It just didn't feel like I was as fully engaged. That approach to prayer seemed more like a checklist to tick off instead of a genuine conversation with my Team members.

However, when my entire soul is speaking to my Team and listening to their responses, it actually feels like my visits are more significant and meaningful. I don't have to wait until I can find a place to kneel to share the desires of my heart. In fact, my entire day is often drawn out in continuous prayer or meditation with these Beings.

We enjoy one another's company. We like being together. Our conversations are in the same form as I would have with my best friend. We joke and laugh with one another.

I learned I could talk with Them about anything important in my life. Even *sex*. And by the way, they have got some great, mind-blowing information on that subject. (Sorry Mom...Did you just say, "Oh gosh!"?) Anything of significance to me that I desired to understand was *A-Okay* to discuss with Them.

## Gifts of the Spirit

I could see from the expression on her face that my friend really understood what I was sharing with her. But more importantly, she also *felt* what I was feeling. Together, we experienced that contagious, warm, sweet, delightful, eternal love from the Divine.

Then she said, "I've read in the Scriptures that there were prophetesses. I believe you are one of them."

I responded, "I will not deny my amazing spiritual gifts. I do indeed have the Power to receive prophecies and to some degree I am a prophetess about those things that touch my personal life and the lives of my loved ones as well as what I am responsible for or a steward over. I embrace my truth. But this gift is not offered uniquely to me."

Then, in order to put my gift into perspective, I further explained:

"Even though there are many examples of men who were prophets, the Scriptures also say women and children were capable of receiving prophecies, visions, healings and miracles on a regular basis. In fact, according to the Scriptures, all of us are capable of having gifts of the Spirit."

In fact:

*If we are not regularly receiving and experiencing these amazing blessings it is only because we lack faith.*

Additionally:

*When we choose to activate our faith and allow it to come alive in us, we all will rapidly see an increase of blessings and miraculous situations come into our lives.*

Actually, we all at one time knew these gifts and how to use them. Most of us have simply forgotten about our ability to utilize them. But at any time we can reawaken and begin to remember once again.

This is why I am sharing this information with you. My hope and most ardent desire is that you will allow yourself to be brought back to a remembrance of your ability to purposefully use your Divine gifts. In fact, the majority of my clients begin to experience this remarkable, transforming awakening within the first hour of their training! (Remember the short stories about the student who listened to her inspired thoughts, the recovering alcoholic no longer felt like a victim, the wife who released the need for antidepressants and the business woman who stopped worrying about her mom.)

*Your gift and eternal birthright is to purposefully create whatever you desire in this world, by connecting with the Divine.*

## You Ask, They Answer

This ability to ask and receive is more perfectly created when we put a plan together so we can more precisely identify what we desire. While forming this plan be sure to include as much detail in that request as you feel is necessary. Those details will help your recognize your blessing when it comes your way. Then just reach out and receive it.

That last sentence may initially appear redundant but I have seen many people request their desires. When those blessings came their way they hesitated and did not open up to accept them!

*Remember: Don't concern yourself with how the plan will be accomplished. Your opportunities will easily and quickly come to you.*

How hard did I search to find that collection business? The person extending that work came to my home! However, *do* completely trust and believe it will be created for you. Let deep feelings of appreciation and excitement swell within you for the adventure that is *NOW* coming your way. And then, simply relax and *allow* yourself to receive what you asked for…a pretty fabulous way to live life!

## TAKE ACTION!

**Okay. It is time to GO FOR IT! FORM THAT COUNCIL MEETING! Speak to them with a deep sincere desire to completely connect with them. Take some deeps breaths and flood your soul with the sincere belief that this is happening NOW. Catch the FEELING! Release any other distractions. Enjoy the ride…it is a sweet, powerful, life-altering experience!**

# CHAPTER EIGHTEEN

# ~ *Picture This Instead* ~

I remember the moment well: I was traveling in a small commuter jet that was being rocked by thunderclaps. Bolts of lightning slashed through the dark sky spreading an electrical web into the night. But I couldn't help but smile as I watched the turbulent weather; my thoughts and feelings were immersed in a plan that was brewing. With each clap of thunder and bolt of lightning, my body felt a growing thrill of anticipation, a rush of delight as I thought of the next twelve hours.

It was Thanksgiving and a miracle was coming; in fact, I could feel it already forming!

### Removing the Wedge, Allowing the Healing

The real story began weeks earlier. My husband Ronnie and I were preparing a Thanksgiving Feast at our home for our family. This was an even more exciting and important celebration than usual because, this year, his extended family would be joining us.

It had been many years—over a decade to be exact—since we had collectively come together to celebrate a family dinner. A number of unfortunate events, decisions and choices, mixed with unresolved discordant feelings, had all come to a boiling point long ago. As a result, a huge wedge had been created between our extended family members, and that wedge split our kinship.

Thankfully, over time, most of our family began to feel a desire to change the situation. They started opening their hearts to the possibility of healing and to a reunion with one another. Little by little, they let that desire grow until they had the courage to admit a trickle of trust; that trust, in turn, created an opportunity for change.

Finally, after sufficient soul-searching, and after setting aside fear, ego and shame, different family members started reaching out to one another. To the family's great relief, these efforts were reciprocated and the process of healing began.

The autumn holidays were approaching. Various relatives suggested Thanksgiving dinner should be at our new home since most of the family had never visited us there. Ronnie and I eagerly agreed and quickly began polling everyone for their input on ideas for the event. We made a list for the menu and noted down what each individual person chose to contribute to the feast.

### Food, Glorious Food!

I could already imagine the delicious, mouth-watering dishes we would have that day. I saw myself washing, salting and peppering the insides of a giant bird, stuffing it with pieces of celery, and onion. I could see Ronnie wrestling this "tom" into the roasting pan, breast side down. I pictured myself pouring a quart of water into the roaster, covering the bird with a stick of melted butter and topping it off with more salt and pepper. (Ok, it's a Southern recipe...we like butter!)

I imagined that it was morning and the house was filled with the delicious aroma of roasted turkey with oodles of gravy for mashed potatoes made with lots of butter and half-and-half cream.

I visualized the famous stuffing with a *pone*—or for those of us not raised in the South—a *pan* of corn bread with secret ingredients. (Mmmm, good: top it with a little gravy and it's a knock out combo!) I imagined a broccoli rice casserole; so simple, yet delicious.

There were other amazing dishes I envisioned too, beginning with the appetizers and relish trays. I pictured the fruit salad with nuts shelled from the family pecan trees in Saint David, and steaming hot rolls emerging fresh from the oven. I imagined the colorful vegetable side dishes; so pleasing to the eye. I saw the fresh bunches of flowers that would bring a sweet, vibrant surprise to the table setting. I imagined the most delectable pies and Mom's chocolate Texas sheet cake with the perfect vanilla, rocky road and chocolate mint ice creams to top them off. And of course, I envisioned Uncle Ronnie whipping up his secret recipe for lemon ice box pie with its rich, scrumptious flavor; no ice cream necessary.

After I imagined all of this delectable food, my thoughts turned to the family members who would be attending. There would be over forty people present at the celebration, most of them children.

Before the rift had occurred, there had been a tradition that each adult family member would contribute a dish to this feast. After the rift, we had continued to cook, but with no family to share it, it had never felt right.

We had even tried to duplicate the dishes of some family members on our own, but they had never quite tasted the same. Plus, the presence of those dishes made us think all the more about the person who used to make them. We would invariably feel a void. It was like preparing a favorite dish with the key ingredient left out.

With the family finally coming together again, I also envisioned everyone happily interacting with one another and playing outside. Our home is designed to welcome visitors of any number, age or physical ability during any season of the year. We had wonderful play areas and gardens for children to explore and let their exuberant spirits run free.

Ronnie and I both agreed that we would pull out all the stops for this special day. We would heat up the pool and the Jacuzzi, and we would tell everyone to bring their swimsuits.

### Planning Our Miracle

While we were organizing our family celebration, several members of the family called to tell me they had been checking the weather forecast and that clouds, cold rain, lightning and thunder were predicted for Thanksgiving Day. They felt anxious and were concerned that the rainstorms would ruin the celebration.

On the other hand, my girlfriend Sue also mentioned the weather to me, but she was excited about it! She envisioned a fire in the fireplace as she cuddled up with her husband, while her children and grandchildren gathered around in front of the toasty crackling flames.

We live in the Tucson desert and it occurred to me that the desert could really use that rain!

Could I ask for sunshine for my celebration at the expense of the desires of others?

I reflected on the situation for a little while and then I formulated what I preferred to have happen. I saw a plan beginning to materialize in my mind. I received that wonderful, familiar feeling inside of me that I completely trust in.

## Picture This for Thanksgiving

Holding on to that assured awareness; I began to respond to each family call about the stormy weather, by saying:

"Every time you think about our Thanksgiving, allow yourself to clearly visualize the following scene:

"Picture it raining, thundering and lightning during the beginning of that day. Then just before ten o'clock in the morning, the rain will stop—but only in the area of our home. After the rain stops, the sun will come out and warm everything up. The children will be able to run and play outside and even enjoy swimming. All the adults will take pleasure in each other's company while watching and playing with the children.

"Then, visualize that at noon everyone will come in and enjoy our feast together. Afterwards, we will take a brief moment to put some of the food away and then we will immediately go back outside and play some more. Once we are finished playing, and everyone has dried off, and is getting ready to go home, it will start raining again." (I do so love imagining win-win, mutually uplifting scenarios!)

I also suggested to those anxious family members that they let go of their *need* to keep checking the weather forecast and let go of any concerns. They were to only picture the wonderful day to come. I told them to simply allow themselves to focus on and feel the excitement of what was going to happen.

I then said, "Picture this change already happening *now*!"

I shared with each of them my sure belief that this was an opportunity for all of us to participate in creating a real miracle.

Everyone I spoke to became engaged in the vision that I was presenting, and they all began to allow themselves to feel the excitement for the potential of that special day.

This was an important moment for me and Thanksgiving Day began to take on special meaning. I knew I was already deeply united with the source that created me. I also knew my active faith was in itself enough to provide what was required to trigger a powerful chain reaction. I realized that if the rest of the family also united with that empowering group and with one another, what would be created would be exponentially more delightful and mutually uplifting.

I realized that no better blessing could come into this family's life at this particular point in time. What else could encourage us all to weave back together as one, than to team up as a group to create the experience of a perfect day?

We had the opportunity to deliberately form this event by connecting with the Divine in order to celebrate our thankfulness that we were once again a united family.

I felt wonderful every time I focused on purposefully developing the activities of that day.

### Let the Festivities Begin!

Just before Thanksgiving Day, I was invited to go on a short trip out of town: I flew with my son to see one of my grandsons in Washington State. We visited my grandson at school, enjoyed seeing him in his classroom with his classmates and we attended a parent-teacher conference. Afterwards, my grandson flew back to Tucson with us on Thanksgiving eve so he could be part of our family holiday.

It was that evening, during our return flight, as the rocking jet neared the Tucson area, that I noticed the clouds and rain with their beautiful displays of lightning and heard the sound of rumbling claps of thunder. Now you know why I was excited. The thunderstorm reminded me of our family plan for a miracle and I was filled with feelings of thrilling anticipation about what I was going to be a part of in less than twelve hours.

All night it rained. Each time I heard the thunder I smiled and felt that tickle of Enthusiasm inside my being.

The next morning it was still raining heavily. Sometimes the downpour would taper off to a slow steady drizzle—just what the parched, thirsty desert could use!

Ronnie and I set about assembling the huge twenty-four by six foot dinner table and chairs. We moved everything out of our living room so the family could all be together in one area. We also set up two small, low tables so the little children could be more comfortable and still be near the rest of their families.

The storm continued all morning; I felt a little giddy with my building feelings of excitement.

I couldn't help but smile and laugh as we spread out white linen tablecloths and layered on deep green toppers. We arranged big pumpkins down the center of the table on beds of raffia and wove in greenery, flowers and candles to make a long centerpiece.

The turkey was falling off the bones and the mashed potatoes, gravy and rolls were already dished up and in the warming drawer, ready and waiting for the families to arrive.

Then just before ten o'clock, the rain stopped, the clouds parted around our home and the sun came out to warm up the patios! The front door swung open wide and the throng began to enter into our home. Their arms were filled with contributions for our feast.

The children burst out the back door into the play areas and gardens almost as quickly as they had come in the front door.

Two of them immediately started jumping on our trampoline and a couple more went down through the grape arbor to the room underneath to playfully tease and joke with those above them. Another couple of children began a game of tetherball; a few little ones received help taking the cover off the sand pile and started digging and sifting for hidden treasures of seashells and coins. One group formed a hide-and-go-seek game. I could hear someone counting, while others darted in and about the yard, fruit trees, bushes and gardens as they ferreted out the best hiding places.

As I watched, some of the family headed to the outside pool bathroom with swimsuits in hand. Soon, the swimming pool was filled with splashing, jumping and sliding. Those playing in the pool were arrayed in sundry life vests, floaties, noodles and goggles. Could the calls of "Marco Polo!" be far behind?

One of the bravest of the children gathered up his courage, climbed up the circular stairs to the top of the ramada and sat down in the entrance of the boulder lined slide—a slide so daunting that even grown men have been known to have second thoughts. Letting out a loud squeal (a blend of terror and delight) he victoriously entered the pool with a gigantic splash.

Soon, other thrill-seeking souls were scrambling up the stairs to join him, while others got a gush of excitement from being shot from one side of the pool to the other by the swim jet's fast current. The less adventuresome went to sit on the benches near the fireplace inside the pool's cave grotto, located just behind the waterfall.

Our home and gardens were something Ronnie and I had created along with our Teams to provide opportunities for joy and pleasure to those who lived with us or visited us. I watched all this activity and enjoyed every second of the morning and soon the noon hour arrived.

## Giving Thanks and Feeling Thankful

My husband called his family all together; the banquet was spread out before us. Our watering mouths and gnawing appetites were ready to start the feast. Ronnie gave thanks and asked for a blessing upon our bounty and the feast began! Everyone dove into the meal.

After some time had passed and our family members had settled in and gotten comfortable, I suggested we go around the table and share what we were each thankful for. The exchanges were moving and heartfelt; a few tears of gratitude and appreciation were shed. There were some very tender and happy moments. A sweet spirit had filled the room, and our souls were nourished that afternoon as well as our stomachs.

When we completed our expressions of thanks and were sufficiently stuffed, we cleared off our plates and put some of the food away. Most of us headed back outside to pick up swimming and playing where we had left off before the feast. A few even jumped back into the pool, clothes and all. Some of the men checked out the football game on the flat screen TV in the family room. Meanwhile, a couple of others picked out two cue sticks and racked up the balls for a quick game or two of pool.

Everyone kept remarking that day, as we shared our time with one another, how wonderful this celebration was and how perfect the weather had been the entire time.

Finally, the afternoon started winding down and the tryptophan in the turkey began to kick in. The little ones started showing signs of wearing out. Everyone decided it was time to come in and gather up his or her belongings to prepare for their journey back home. We said our good-byes and gave each other our final hugs and kisses.

And do you know what? Just as the families rounded up their offspring and counted heads, it started to sprinkle outside. In fact, they barely managed to make it into their vehicles before the rain started pouring down again at a steady pace!

It was astonishing to see and experience how perfectly the day had followed the plan that we—as a united family—had asked for. I marveled how every detail of our preferences was met and I expressed my heartfelt thanks to all who assisted in that miraculous creation.

Each time we had thought about our Thanksgiving plans, an immediate feeling of excitement had followed and had become attached to our desired goal, which gave our request even more Power to be created.

We had given zero attention to the weather forecasts after we had expressed our preferred plan. Hence, the opposite of what was deliberately chosen was not acknowledged and therefore was completely released from our experience.

I am continually amazed at how we are capable of lifting our lives to a more desirable place when we deliberately choose the life we prefer and invite those Divine Beings to join us in that creative process.

## Something Extraordinary

George Burns used to say, "Happiness is having a large, loving, caring, close-knit family in another city."

Most of us have or have had families and extended families in our lives. We eventually recognize that living with a family can bring us some of our greatest opportunity for growth as well as some of our greatest challenges. No one knows quite how to *get to us* or understand us like our family does. It is our family who will try, try and try yet again to get it right, when friends and acquaintances will have long since walked away.

But it is also true that even family members can sometimes use a time out from one another to go lick their wounds and get some perspective. Hopefully, they will eventually allow themselves to heal and will return to their relationships as healthier, more enlightened persons.

I am so grateful that our family chose to unite with the spirit of goodwill that Thanksgiving. We open-heartedly embraced one another while celebrating our kinship and feelings of gratitude. As a result of our actions, we drew something extraordinary into our lives that we will always remember.

Our family really did participate in creating and witnessing a miracle that day. We allowed ourselves to trust as we activated our personal faith, completely believing that this experience would happen!

Each of us is able to enjoy similar blessings. We, as individuals, can allow ourselves to trust and then activate our personal faith bringing miracles into being. We can also send our desires out to others; extending an invitation for them to join with us in this mutually uplifting adventure. Creating with others while being connected to the Divine is an exceedingly enjoyable experience!

## TAKE ACTION!

**Creating amazing miraculous situations with others is a profoundly rewarding experience that strengthens and enriches relationships. Command into your life a wonderful opportunity to do just that! Plant the seeds within the hearts of those who are coming into your life to mutually create with you. Go ahead and put a date on it!**

**Whenever you visit with one another, encourage everyone to allow those seeds to sprout and grow as you each eagerly speak in detail about the visions and feelings of what is being formed. These types of adventures are lots of fun!**

CHAPTER NINETEEN

## ~ And That Gift Is My Gift ~

I had been working as a volunteer for nine months. Although it was an unpaid position, I often found myself working long hours—from before the sun rose in the sky until well after it set at night. My responsibilities had dramatically increased during the previous couple of months to the point that I only stopped to eat, shower and sleep. Quite frankly, I was feeling the heavy weight upon my shoulders of the tasks required of me.

I glanced at the clock. It was noon and I had already put in five hours of work at our home office. Right then, I decided to unplug and downshift my gears by setting the work aside so I could spend the rest of the afternoon playing. It was time for me to let my hair down and have a little fun because everyone knows all work and no play creates burnt-out, dull, miserable people! This chilly Saturday morning in December felt like the perfect time for me to allow some carefree enjoyment and relaxation back into my life.

Thankfully, a wonderful refreshing activity had already been created for me. I was invited to go to a wedding shower that very afternoon for my girlfriend Sandee's soon-to-be-daughter-in-law, Allison.

Sandee is one of the most supportive, understanding and positively encouraging friends a person could ever have. Luckily, she lives little more than a stone's throw from our house. I looked forward to the party that day, and I also looked forward even more to the evening of the wedding because my husband and I had the honor of hosting the couple's reception in our home.

As I got ready for the afternoon shower, I glanced at the clock. The party had already started. Yet I felt certain I still had plenty of time to relax and enjoy every moment of the rest of my day. Instead of letting anxious feelings well up, I began right then to activate a conscience change. I then simply allowed that shift to flow into me.

In fact, when I start to feel stressed over not having enough time, I have made it a habit to take a deep breath and say to myself:

**"I have plenty of time and more to do whatever I desire to do today."**

I will say this a few times while taking deep breaths. I soon feel the stress completely leave me and a soothing balm of peace flow into my body. Then, I just relax my body and wait while something joyful shifts into the equation. After that, time expands to fit the situation at hand. Somehow, everything just smoothes out. It's a quantum physics kind of thing that kicks in. This shifting of time is also known as Prophet's Time (chapter 25, "Only Green Lights," provides further explanation of what this gift is and how you can activate it).

### Preparing for the Fun!

That afternoon, after I had readjusted and started to relax from all my responsibilities, I decided to indulge in some good old tender loving self-care for the occasion. I took off my Levis plus imaginary *working hardhat* and headed to the shower. While there I completely enjoyed lathering up my long hair with shampoo and exfoliating my skin with bath mitts and spicy smelling liquid soap. Then I took my time as I rinsed off in the warm, relaxing, stimulating water. Sounds rather like an oxymoron, but that is how my soul felt and I delighted in every second of that pleasurable activity. Next, I quickly dried off, smoothed on raw coconut oil and blow-dried my hair.

While getting ready, I continued to allow my attitude to shift as I slipped into my tunic sweater dress, leggings and the black knee-high leather boots Ronnie had bought me for Christmas. (I irreverently call them my *Chi Chi Mama's Boots*.)

My thoughts returned to the bridal shower. I decided that I was going to completely savor this party. Every moment I was there was going to be absolutely delightful. I was fixing to have fun with my girlies! I was going to enjoy sharing my love, appreciation and affection. I was certain I would receive those same genuine blessings from them, as well.

I thought about sampling all the scrumptious food and decided I would relish every sinfully, decant, delectable bite.

I figured that I would have already missed some of the shower games, but I didn't mind. Personally, what I enjoy the most is the time I can spend visiting and sharing heart to hearts with good friends.

When I finally arrived, the girlfriends were rounding one another up for the last game: *Bridal Bingo.* I felt that game could actually be a lot of fun. Sandee set three presents on the coffee table in the middle of the room. When she did this, I decided to play a little internal game with myself just to dial up the excitement a bit.

Because I had felt drained for weeks, I acknowledged that I had allowed myself to lose my work/life balance. Therefore, I decided to readjust my thinking and let surprises and lighthearted feelings rise up in me. I envisioned receiving one of the gifts sitting on the table. I boldly thought:

**"One of those gifts is going to be my gift!"**

Autumn, one of Sandee's twin daughters, started reading off the words. Everyone, including me, was busy marking the words off on grid paper. Each bingo sheet included words relating to a wedding...honeymoon, ring, veil, bouquet, bridesmaids, groom. The players in the room were starting to feel more excited with every spoken word. Some of us only had a couple of words left to mark off before we would be able to shout, "Bingo!"

Then something happened. There was a lull in the crossing off of the words for almost the entire group. This included me. As the words were read, some of the players jokingly asked if the right list of words were still being spoken. At this point, I was still playing my internal game. I had been feeling a continual rise of excitement within me and I could sense the time was drawing near; my last word would soon be revealed to all by the reader of the list.

Finally, someone called out "Bingo!" and the winner eagerly retrieved her gift.

I was getting so excited I could no longer keep my internal game a secret. I was clearly seeing and focusing on my final word and feeling happy anticipation about it. I could also feel that connectedness to my Team increase within me. At last, I playfully told the rest of the group about the private game I was simultaneously playing.

I briefly explained that I had allowed myself to experience a few rough patches lately. As a result, I was feeling rather overwhelmed, worn down and discouraged.

But, I explained, I chose to purposefully change my paradigm by deliberately creating more fun and joy in my life so that my soul could be refreshed and restored. I told them that I also thought I would allow myself to be pampered a bit more right now. I said, "With that in mind, I've decided that one of those gifts on the table will be my gift!"

### "You Didn't Say Bingo!"

I then surprised them by announcing that Autumn was soon going to read my winning word. I showed everyone in the room what that word was (except the reader of course). I told them how much I liked that word. In fact, at that moment, it was my favorite word in the whole world! By then, everyone in the room was also seeing, hearing and getting excited about my word, too! Little sounds of amusement and laughter rippled through the group. I could feel the awareness and intensity of their curiosity.

Another word was read from the list. Bingo!" said a girl and a gift was handed to her.

"You didn't win! You didn't get to say 'Bingo!'" some of the others pointed out to me. "And you didn't get the gift either!"

"Oh, that's all right," I said confidently, keeping my assured, excited feeling within me. "Because, there is still one gift left." I pointed to the package on the coffee table. "And that gift is my gift!"

I felt unwavering feelings of well-being knowing this truth was firmly rooted in my soul.

The reader next said, "Hawaii."

"BINGO!" I said with a big grin on my face and looked around at the surprised and amused expressions on the faces of the rest of the party members.

### The Gift Was Not the Present I Was Seeking

But the gift was not the actual present I sought. The real and valuable gift I personally desired was the spoken word, "Hawaii." For me, just experiencing that love and playful interaction with my Team was the best present I could receive. I quickly explained this to the group, declined the gift and suggested that the next person who called "Bingo" could have it instead.

As soon as the next word was announced, seven or eight people all shouted, "Bingo!" But Sandee stood up and told everyone that the last gift really was supposed to be my gift. She handed me the package. We all started laughing over the events that had unfolded before our very eyes.

Notice that earlier in my day, I recognized that I had allowed difficulties to be drawn into my life. I recognized that truth, that I was drawing experiences to me that diminished my personal joy. I also knew that I had the ability to release those experiences from my world as soon as I desired to do so and bring to me what I currently preferred instead.

### Stay the Course!

At any point in the game, I could have allowed myself to become distracted by the teasing of my friends. Two of the three presents to be given away had already been claimed by other players, so the odds of winning were low. I could have let my playful, confident feelings evaporate and allow doubt and embarrassment to take their place (especially in view of the fact that I had made a bold statement to people who knew me socially).

Instead of sliding into the activity of creating discouraging feelings, I focused only on the private game that I purposely chose to enjoy. Any other thoughts I immediately cast aside as soon as they tried to wriggle into my mind. I kept my wonderful happy feeling and ended up receiving the prize I desired.

I unwrapped the gift to find a beautiful selection of "Thank You" notes. How appropriate. I had been feeling especially thankful for the many activities that took place that Saturday afternoon.

I felt an increased vigor within my soul and my heart was light as I drove my car back down the narrow, winding mountain road to my house. I marveled at how amazing my day had turned out to be. I had experienced many things: a wonderful sisterhood of friends, light-hearted laughter, carefree playfulness, fun surprises, delicious food and Divine love. I felt grateful, blessed and restored that afternoon.

## TAKE ACTION!

**Too often, we hesitate because we are concerned about what others will think of us. As a result, we shrink back and never fully open our arms wide and embrace this life experience. Pay no heed to what others might think. Their opinions often change like the wind. Do what you feel impressed to do with your life. Unflinchingly tell others about your desires and allow those blessings to swiftly come to you.**

Allow yourself to boldly live your life. The saying, "Nothing ventured, nothing gained" has real truth within it. Start venturing out more. If you get a feeling that you would love to explore or try something, if you think something would be enjoyable, playful and uplifting to you and those around you...GO FOR IT!

# CHAPTER TWENTY

# ~ The Box in the Tall Grass ~

Last fall, my mom and I enjoyed some quality one-on-one time together. We were sitting in my living room quilting a silky pink tricot baby blanket for my former daughter-in-law's new baby.

The mom I am referring to is my new mom. I received her when I was five years old, a few years after my birth mom passed away. That autumn day, we visited while we hand-stitched our project. Every once in awhile, I stopped stitching to check on what was happening in my backyard gardens.

## The Plan for Multiplicity

I really enjoy working in gardens. I love to see what can grow from a seed. It seems like I've always had gardens in my life.

While living at our first resort home in Mexico, I would often be awakened early in the morning by a rapping at my door. I always knew who was rousting me out of bed each day…the head gardener, Juan. He would come straight to my home not long after he arrived at his job so we could design and create beautiful gardens together. We happily worked many hours side-by-side. Numerous resort guests and condo owners enjoyed the fruits of our labors.

Meanwhile, at home in Tucson, I was on my own when it came to the housecleaning and gardening. Most of the time this wasn't a problem, but sometimes I really would have appreciated some extra helping hands. I missed Juan's presence and wished he could come play with me at my home in the States every once in awhile. But I didn't have the extra funds to hire someone at that time, so instead I devised a plan. That plan was to turn my work into a game.

All right, I'll just lay my cards on the table: I prefer to create fun ways to accomplish the tasks I am undertaking in my daily life. I sometimes imagine amusing situations to get through my to-do list in and around my home.

So, I *hired* an imaginary companion to do the yard work for me. His name was *Juan*—just like the Juan in Mexico because we had had such an enjoyable time when we were together.

After that, when I worked in my gardens, it seemed like a part of my friend Juan was with me in my soul. We became one as we worked together.

When I told my husband about him, he responded, "Don't you mean Juanita?"

I told him, "No!" Then lowered my voice to sound more masculine and said with a rich Latin accent, "My body feels stronger and more able to do the work when I am Juan!"

Then we both burst into laughter because I'm only a hundred and ten pounds. In reality, I desired all the help I could muster, even if it was just imaginary extra muscle!

### Searching for Juan

One day, I realized my imaginary Juan was no longer enough. My husband had been suggesting that I spread the wealth by hiring a real person to help me at our home.

I began asking friends, neighbors and family for the names of people who were helping them in their yards. Thankfully, my daughter shared with me the name and contact number of the man that worked for her and her mother-in-law. Both women were very pleased with this man and highly recommended him to me. And do you know what his name was? It was Juan!

The very sound of that name immediately tickled me and I couldn't help but laugh out loud. I eagerly looked forward to actually meeting this real Juan in person. My wish to have someone in Tucson who was like my friend Juan in Mexico was actually coming true, right down to the exact name!

When Juan the gardener arrived at my home, he quickly introduced himself. After he walked through the yards and gardens he announced, "Mrs. Ezell, you are two people. Your husband must love you!"

Oops. Did someone clue him in about the gardener I occasionally had living inside me?

Juan was a fit, sturdy man, about my same height. He had an easygoing personality and I immediately knew I would enjoy having him work around our home.

### Juan, Juan, Juan, Juan

I could tell Juan would be a joy to work with because of the feeling I received as soon as I met him. He hadn't come alone either. He had brought a helper, too.

When I inquired what the helper's name was, he replied, "Juan."

I asked, "Juan?"

He said, "Yes. I'm Juan number one and he is Juan number two." I started laughing and I told him, "Then I am Juan number three!"

I shared with them both my story about my friend Juan in Mexico and my make-believe game that I was Juan whenever I did the yard work. Both Juans were laughing with me by the time I finished my story.

Meanwhile, on the day my mom and I were quilting, I checked the yard to see if Juan required any help or support from me. While doing so, I remembered an incident that had recently happened with him at our home, which then reminded me of something that took place in our family's yard when I was a little girl.

I decided to reminisce by sharing the stories with my mom when I returned back to quilt with her.

### Hearing the Still Small Voice

One Saturday, when I was about five-years-old, my parents decided that we were going to clean the yard together as a family. We were all helping to clear everything out so my dad could use a sickle to cut down the overgrown lawn.

While doing this activity, my dad spied a cardboard box that had blown into the far corner near the white picket fence. It was now lying in the tall green grass. He told me to run over, pick up the box and put it into the trash that we had been collecting.

As I ran to do his bidding, I heard a *Still Small Voice* whisper in my mind, "Be careful! There is a snake under the box!" I immediately froze in place.

I was afraid of two things as a child in Arizona: spiders and snakes.

I had already been introduced to creepy black widows, daddy long legs and big hairy tarantulas. I was good to go with six-limbed insects, but those eight-appendage spiders sent chills down my spine. My fear of snakes existed simply because I didn't have any experience with them. Although in the rugged Southwest, there are plenty of spine-tingling tales about sidewinders and diamondback rattlers.

So I just stood there like a frozen statue that day, fifty-five years ago: a petrified five-year-old.

"Pammy, go over and get that cardboard box," my father repeated to me for the second time. I desired to be obedient, but I felt stuck.

### Calming Comforting Guidance

Then, at that very moment, a calm yet alert feeling started to flow into me and pushed away the fear that had welled up inside. My pounding heart settled down in my chest, and its banging in my ears ceased. My fear was exchanged for courage. I started again to make my way toward the daunting object in the far corner of the yard.

Once again, I distinctly heard those words of caution, "Be careful! There is a snake under the box!"

I noted that the warning voice did not say, "Don't pick up the box!" He said, "Be careful!" I weighed this in my mind and then proceeded to carefully reach for the cardboard container. I grabbed it and jumped back at the same time, and then shouted to my parents that there was indeed a snake under the box. My father came running to my rescue with a hoe in his hands and quickly chopped up the snake into small writhing pieces.

Now, over five decades later, as we sat sewing, I asked my mom if she remembered the snake incident. She told me that she not only remembered it, she also remembered that before I picked up the container, I informed her and my father there would be a snake under the box!

This was the first time I could remember being *told* something was about to happen to me. I learned from that incident not to discount what I *heard*. This was definitely not a case of wild imagination. There was actually a snake present to prove to me that the information I had received was indeed correct.

Over the years, I have learned that the Still Small Voice I heard that day was a voice of protection, well-being and guidance from my Team. Their influence was always for my good and I could consistently trust in the counsel I received from them.

## A Persistent Thought

I then began to share with my mom an event that had taken place in my home a couple of weeks earlier.

I had been working all morning with Juan and decided to go inside and get caught up with some other work. While there, I kept getting the feeling to ask Juan if he would trim the large potted plants that had become overgrown on the patio. I kept getting the feeling that a snake would soon be hiding at the base of one of the potted plants. I had reasoned that if the plants were trimmed away, it would be easier for me to spot the snake.

Now, I have lived in this house for well over eight years and I have had many overgrown potted plants. Not once have I ever received an impression or feeling that a snake would be hiding under one of them. Yet, this specific idea persistently re-occurred to me several times that day. I finally decided to walk outside and tell Juan to trim back the plants and ask him if he'd like a soda.

As I walked out, I discovered Juan had already trimmed the plants without my even asking him to do so. When I realized this, I started to laugh quietly. That he had even thought to do so was unusual—Juan never trimmed those plants, even though he had worked at the house for over a year. He normally waited for my instructions before taking action. This was especially true when it came to cutting back something like my potted plants.

I've learned long ago that sometimes we communicate more powerfully to one another with our souls. Suffice it to say, my soul had desired for those plants to be trimmed. In response, Juan "heard" that desire and snip, snip, the job was done.

I went to the end of the covered porch. I felt constrained to go no further. I called out to Juan and asked, "Would you like to have a soda?" He said he did and I immediately went back into in the house and returned with his drink in hand. But I kept picturing and thinking about the rattlesnake that I was sure was at the base of a large potted plant.

I was in my bare feet and as I walked further on, past the covered porch toward the ramada, I felt a wave of caution wash over me.

Then, I noticed that the gate between our backyard and the wild desert was standing open. Just minutes earlier, Juan had gone into the desert to check on some things and he had apparently forgotten to close the gate when he returned. From the feeling in my body, I knew for certain that a rattlesnake had already slipped through the gate into the yard.

**Listen to your feelings. They are your perfect guides!**

I called out to Juan and pointed to the open gate. I told him I was sure a rattlesnake had come into the yard. He tried to reassure me and told me that the gate had only been open for about ten minutes. Both Juan and I had left the gate open before for longer periods of time without any problem.

But I couldn't shake off the feeling of alarm. I felt my whole body shift into a hyper-alert mode. It was as if I was filled with an electrical buzzing. I continued to walk into the ramada towards Juan who was working in the gardens just beyond.

Suddenly, I got the strong impression to look down to the right. As I glanced in that direction, in response to the now familiar prompting, I saw the last foot-long portion of a big rattlesnake as it slithered around the base of a large potted plant.

"Look! A *rattlesnake!*" I said to Juan. He looked startled and immediately ran to get a shovel to kill it. Within minutes, it was over. We both took time to relax, decompress and get our bearings.

### Responding to the Words of Inspiration

I marveled over the unfolding of these the events.

- Several times I had been *instructed* and *cautioned* by the Still Small Voice that a snake would be hiding at the base of a large potted plant.

- I had never had that feeling before, even though we previously have had rattlesnakes in our yard.

- Moreover, when I first experienced that revelation, I had felt constrained to stay within the covered porch area instead of walking out to Juan.

- Had I walked into the ramada, the snake would have struck me because we would have crossed paths as it slithered in front of me to conceal itself at the base of the pot. (I'm thankful I just followed those feelings and went back inside.)

- If I had allowed myself to get distracted for even five minutes— which I often do when I'm in multitasking mode—I would have missed seeing where the snake was going to hide in the yard.

- But, I had felt impressed to go inside the house and immediately return with the soda for Juan.

- I followed the inspiration to look down and to the right, spotting the venomous serpent.

- This timing was critical, because if we had not seen the snake when we did, we would have unknowingly shut the gate, which would have trapped the rattler inside the yard!

My mom got the creeps and shivered as I finished telling my story. I walked over to the bookcase and showed her the remains of the snake's tail, rattlers and all. The snake had been almost four feet long, though in fishing lore I'm sure it would have measured a full six feet or more!

I am thankful for that Still Small Voice.

If you don't experience this gift of knowledge, comfort and protection on a regular basis, you can always exercise your desire to have it more abundantly in your life. Send out that desire with the excitement that you feel about receiving it in your life. Then trust and be open to having it given to you.

If you recall having some of those special moments previously, remember those experiences and feel them clearly in your being.

Ask to have more of them *now* in your life:

**"More of this in my life now, please. Thank you!"**

Ask this with *feeling* not merely with words.

Meditate and ponder regularly. It doesn't require a lot of time but it does help your "vessel" or body to be better prepared to receive what you desire.

Do these things by quieting your soul and allowing yourself to *think, visualize, hear and feel* your way through your world. By doing so, you will receive more of these experiences and will grow to better recognize this gift. You will also become more confident and certain that your Team is guiding you.

These opportunities will assist you in more purposefully preparing the future you prefer.

The Team member I refer to as the Still Small Voice is also known as the *Holy Spirit* and the *Comforter* that Christ told would come to the world when he departed. This Spirit knows all things past, present and future and can reveal what you desire to understand at anytime.

That knowledge, comfort and protection is available for everyone, including you.

This support assures our safe journey as we meander our way through the tall grasses of life while confidently avoiding or sidestepping all that creeps and slithers.

## TAKE ACTION!

**This very day, allow yourself to experiment with the following**

to connect more fully to the Still Small Voice by taking the following actions:

Be attentive to your thoughts and feelings. Do not discount them. They are not your imagination gone wild. If you remain attentive, you will soon be able to dial in to what is being told to you.

Your feelings are always your unwavering guides. They will not fail you. Allow yourself to develop the ability to trust in what they are revealing to you.

Set aside all fear, doubt or negative emotion. Release those feelings. Take deep calming breaths and allow an alert awareness to take their place.

This act of reducing distractions is critically important for you to be able to hear and feel the pure information that is being revealed to you. Any negative feelings and thoughts are only distractions created by your own lack of confidence and faith in the fact that something better is available for you now.

The Team members you seek to connect with will never send you negative feelings or thoughts. Release them now and move forward.

After you have released the distracting feelings and thoughts, you will begin to feel a shift inside your soul and pure thoughts and intelligence from your Team will start to flow into you instead. That Source will also bring with it the more positive feelings you desire.

There will also come to you a knowing and confident certainty of how you should best proceed.

Receive and follow the impression you have been given with nothing wavering inside you.

Remember to give thanks for this gift when you recognize it has been presented to you.

# ~ *Reading Stories and Playing Monopoly* ~

My grandchildren Enthusiastically leapt into my bed and shouted, "Nana, please read us another chapter of the story!"

I had been caring for them at their home in Utah while my daughter was at work. They plumped and fluffed the pillows and snuggled up next to me under the down comforter.

Each day we were reading a chapter of an adventure/fantasy story: *Percy Jackson and the Olympians: the Lightning Thief* (a children's novel about a demigod teen that has superhuman Powers because his father was Poseidon).

Together, we enjoyed picturing the many twists and turns of the plot in the action-packed tale. The children and I could hardly wait for the next opportunity to read more about this young hero's exciting escapades.

My grandchildren also loved the stories I shared with them about how everyone is able to purposefully create the life he or she prefers.

### "These Stories You Tell Us Are Real!"

As I read to them that early spring morning, my grandson suddenly had an *Ah-Ha!* moment.

"Nana, the story in this book is just pretend, but the stories you tell us are real," he said with bright-eyed Enthusiasm.

"You're right," I said. "That is true. You know it is true because you are already exercising your Power and you know it really works!"

I was pleased to see he understood the difference between the fictional account of the hero's godly powers and the reality of actually being able to create daily with the Divine.

Moreover, he had experienced his Power only a few days earlier. He and his younger sister had helped to create what they desired in their seating arrangements when they flew with me to Utah.

Both of the children desired to know how to have more of those experiences, how to have *stories* of their own.

I assured them they were powerful creators and that if they looked around, they would begin recognizing the stories they had already been creating. I reminded them that they had their personal gift to shape their world. I continued to teach them about the eternal laws that they could utilize. I introduced them to these laws by teaching them through experiments and by playing games with them.

### Teaching Eternal Laws by Playing Games

My other grandchildren were also interested in learning how to effectively use this Power or energy.

One day, while three of my grandsons were spending time at my home, I decided to introduce them to some experiments and games. In the past, we enjoyed playing Monopoly together but sometimes, unpleasant feelings of contention would grow within the boys and they would bicker and tease each other.

Suddenly those feelings of annoyance would spread through everyone. I realized that they were ready for me to teach them how to feel the difference between using their potent abilities and not using them. I understood that through these *games* they could learn how to recognize when they were united with the Divine by how they felt. They would also know exactly when they pushed away their Team and their Power through their unhappy, negative feelings.

I asked them if they would like to play a game of Monopoly with me. They all excitedly exclaimed, "Yes!" and clamored off to the playroom. The boys soon had the board set up and I joined them, quickly counting out the money.

The dice was rolled. Metal game pieces were moved around. Properties were purchased. Most of us passed *Go* and *Collected $200*. Others went to *Jail*. Some landed on *Free Parking* and took the *cash* that had been collecting there. There were *houses* and *hotels* to be bought, *rent* to be paid and *Community Chest* or *Chance Cards* to be drawn.

The players took turns whooping it up on each other. They excitedly trounced their fellow team members; the losers looked crestfallen and discouraged. One pouted, another sighed with loud exasperation, while a third loudly exclaimed, "Dang it!"

At first, everyone except me was able to successfully get ahead in the game. Yet I was genuinely glad for my small victories and for theirs, as well. I enjoyed every moment of my time with them. I continued to keep my happy feelings and remained excited, savoring the fact that we were all able to be with one another that day.

Little by little, everything began to fall apart. As some of the boys started losing money and properties, they became sullen and cross. The boys who were winning started to gloat about the *wealth* they had amassed and teased about how well they were doing. Instead of feeling united as a family, each brother started focusing solely on his own performance, ignoring how his actions impacted the other players.

## Playing Games While Being Connected

Then something began to shift in the group dynamics. I started to win money and properties, but I did so quietly and continued to be supportive to all the players. In fact, I started doing so well that within a short period of time I had bought up almost all the properties and had accumulated most of the money in the game.

Now all the boys were staring at me and wondering what was going on. How was I able to so quickly effect such a huge change in my favor? I revealed to them that I was using my Powers while I played the game. I then asked them if they would like to play again, but this time with them using their own Powers.

They all excitedly agreed to another game and soon the money was redistributed and the board was readied. The game was on!

This time as we played, when someone did well, we all felt happy and excited for him. The person who was successful during their turn never gloated at the expense of someone else.

Those who lost money or property learned how to let go of their feelings of loss. They also stopped making sour, pouting faces, loud sighs and noises of frustration and anger. Instead, they genuinely began to look forward to what they preferred to receive, like *"Free Parking."* The children pictured themselves landing there and receiving the money that had accumulated.

Sometimes, they would actually count out the moves that were required in order for them to land on a specific square. Then they completely focused on reaching that exact square. They got excited about the opportunity that was coming their way. Finally, they rolled the dice and actually landed on the square they selected! We congratulated one another often as this happened and expressed feelings of real encouragement to one another.

## A Different Outcome

The boys could *feel* the difference between the first game and the second one.

When they played the first game, they could feel the discouraging responses in their bodies when they gloated, sighed, or had mild outbursts because they were pushing themselves away from their full connection to their Team and their Power.

But during the second game they purposefully directed their thoughts and feelings and released anything else that was less than what they desired. As a result, they experienced wonderful feelings of happiness that continued throughout the game.

They could actually feel their Divine connection strengthening as they purposefully maintained their preferred feelings.

For this reason, the outcome of the game was completely different. After several hours we decided that we were done playing and changed activities. When we counted up the money and properties, we each had almost exactly the same amount of *wealth*! We all felt like winners.

This phenomenon also happened with my ten-year-old nephew. Before he learned how to use his Power, my nephew would play Chinese checkers with me and was always unable to win.

After the games he felt cross and irritable with himself and those around him. Sure, I could have let him win, but he was smart enough to know if I did and he would have felt a hollow victory. Besides, that would have been a form of deceit on my part...not an activity I would prefer to participate in. Nor would that be in anyone's best interest.

Instead of falsely influencing the outcome, I shared with him how to purposefully create what he preferred by changing his focus, thoughts, words, feelings and attitude. Then I reminded him how to fully *connect*. Now he beats me every time we play, but only by one or two moves.

## A Winning Attitude in the Game of Life

These teaching moments provided my grandsons and my nephew opportunities to understand some of the great eternal laws—laws they can use throughout their lives.

The boys learned they had the choice to go through the game of life on their own or connected to their Team. They learned that going it alone is far more difficult and far less productive or enjoyable for them. Before, if they acted alone, their goals were often not met. If they were victorious, it was usually at the expense of someone else, which in turn also affected them.

Their relationships were negatively impacted. They had to use more energy for less in return. Often, they would receive no gain at all. When they played together with that negative attitude, they frequently felt spent and irritable with themselves and with each other.

When they used their Powers effectively, they simply felt better all over, as did those around them. They would receive the outcomes they purposefully chose plus what they requested came easily and quickly to them. Better yet, they enjoyed the experience as they progressed toward reaching their goal. Everyone felt uplifted and could remain openly appreciative of one another.

Those elevating feelings continued even after the games were over and everyone enjoyed feelings of renewed vigor.

A positive, encouraging attitude can do much to bring about a more uplifting world for all of us to work, play and live our game of life in as we throw our dice, make our moves, pass *Go* and collect our $200.

## TAKE ACTION!

**Purposefully form WIN-WIN opportunities for you and the people you create with. It is soooo much fun! Everyone really becomes a winner in this scenario.**

**Let go of ANY lack, jealousy, envy…adjust your feelings to what you prefer to experience. Then, HOLD ON TO THOSE GENUINE SUPPORTIVE FEELINGS! Observe how quickly everything changes for everyone's enjoyment!**

# CHAPTER TWENTY-TWO

# ~ *Valley Fever, Bells Palsy and The Still Small Voice* ~

When my oldest son, Jason, was in seventh grade, our family loved to play the game "Wink'em." The game is simple: it only requires chairs and people. The first group sits on the chairs in a circle while the second group stands behind them. One chair is left empty. The person standing behind the empty chair looks around the group and winks at one of the sitting players. The player being winked at quickly darts out of his or her chair and dashes over to sit in the empty chair.

But there is a little catch. The player darting for the new chair has to move before the person standing behind him can grab the player's shoulders and keep him pinned in the original chair.

It is a fun and lively game people of all ages can enjoy. If you don't have enough chairs, you can always play a modified version of the game by kneeling on the floor with the other players standing behind. Adolescent kids really get a kick out of this activity—especially when the girls are sitting down and boys are standing behind them, or visa versa.

Around the time Jason was in middle school, we decided to look for a family pet. One day, we came across a cute, little white puppy. He had a happy attitude, a perpetual smile on his sweet face and bright, curious, dancing brown eyes. One eye was lined black while the other was pink. When you looked at him he looked like he was winking. So we named him "Wink'em."

## A Happy, Smart Little Mutt

Wink'em turned out to be the perfect pet for our family. He grew into a medium-sized dog that was playful and patient with the active children during the day. At night, he would blissfully curl up in bed with his quiet slumbering brood. He was also a smart and endearing little mutt. Let me share this short side-story:

Shortly after Wink'em's arrival, Katrina also joined our family. Katrina was a little white Maltese that was nearly five pounds and an absolute joy.

One evening, while the family was gone, Wink'em climbed onto the antique piano and knocked off a large potted philodendron with long draping vines. During the commotion, both Wink'em and Katrina found themselves covered in potting soil.

Not long after, we returned from our family outing. As soon as we walked in the door, we saw the plant and dirt spilled all over the carpet. A dirty little fluff ball was playing in it to her heart's content. It would have been easy to blame Katrina for the entire incident except for one small detail: she simply was too small to be able to successfully jump up on the piano and pull down the plant on her own.

We wondered where the heck her partner in crime was.

Meanwhile, Wink'em had figured out he was in big trouble. So he had run from the scene of the crime and headed straight to the bathroom, where he washed the evidence off his paws in the toilet and then hid behind it. The only little flaw in this cover-up was that he forgot to flush!

t took us a while to find him. We went throughout the house, calling his name. Finally, we spied the innocent-looking culprit steadfastly hiding behind the porcelain throne. We all burst into laughter and someone pulled out the vacuum.

## Something Just Didn't Feel Right

One day, while we were building a new home and living out in the desert, this adored little family member seemed different to me. Wink'em still appeared to be doing well and enjoying life. He still had a great appetite and his Enthusiasm for living and happy-go-lucky nature was as vibrant as ever. But something just didn't feel right.

When I pondered what could be wrong with our little fellow, a feeling came over me...that feeling of being connected to the Divine. I suddenly received a strong impression or inspiration to take the dog to the vet to be tested for Valley Fever. I was *told* by the Still Small Voice that our little mutt had contracted this life-threatening illness but that it was still just in the initial stages.

Valley Fever is frequently contracted in the desert area where I live, especially if the dirt has been stirred up. This fever is caused by a fungus that lives in the soil which can get into the body and form lesions on the lungs. The fungus can penetrate into the bone and invade other vital areas of the body and really create havoc for the being it enters, sometimes even causing death.

We had recently leveled the land and dug up the soil for the footings of the new home we were building and Wink'em was right there sniffing around the dirt every day, checking out the latest progress.

I had personally contracted Valley Fever in my lungs when I was a freshman in high school. I had to have complete bed rest for three months to try and overcome the effects of the fungus. To this day, I have scars on my lungs. There wasn't any medication that could help me at the time, but since then, things have changed.

I felt comfort in knowing that if Wink'em had Valley Fever, medications had been developed that could assist his body in overcoming the disease. I also knew that if he were treated during the initial stages, before the fungus became deeply entrenched in his body, he would be able to heal quickly and continue to have a full, energetic, healthy life.

I realized my swift response would make a difference to his full recovery.

I picked up the phone and made an appointment for him that same day. When we arrived at the veterinarian's office, I was asked what the problem was. After all, Wink'em looked perfectly healthy to the eye.

I told the doctor that he was in the early stages of developing Valley Fever.

The doctor inquired if Wink'em was coughing or running a fever. I admitted he was not. However, I told the doctor I was positive that this is what was wrong with my pet and that a blood test would confirm this fact. The veterinarian did the blood test. To his surprise, it came back positive.

Wink'em was put on medication to kill the fungus and he quickly overcame the problem before it could gravely affect his health.

I was so thankful I listened to that Still Small Voice and the feeling I received when I heard it.

## Once Again Hearing that Inspired Voice

Years later, my son became a father. One day, Jason and his five-year-old son came to our home to visit with us for a few hours. We enjoyed our time together and filled our afternoon with fun activities and comfort food.

But something just felt off that day. I couldn't quite put my finger on what it was that seemed so unusual. Perhaps it was because I was so completely engrossed in enjoying the moment that I could not focus on anything else.

The following day, as I drove east on the Arizona I-10 a clear commanding thought suddenly came to me.

"Call Jason and tell him to take his son immediately to the Children's Emergency Room at the Tucson Medical Center. Have him tell the doctors to check the boy for Bell's palsy. Do this *now*!"

*Bell's palsy?* I didn't know anyone who had Bell's palsy and I didn't know what Bell's palsy was. But in my mind, I began to understand why I had felt there was something odd happening the day before. In my mind, I thought I saw the slightest, almost imperceptible beginning of one side of my grandson's face begin to change. It looked like his eye, his cheek, mouth and face were starting to droop.

Half of his face was becoming paralyzed!

I quickly reached for my cell phone. Within a moment, I was able to tell my son about the strong impression I had received.

Thankfully, Jason stopped what he was doing and immediately took his son to the hospital. While there, the doctor confirmed that the child indeed had the beginning stages of Bell's palsy.

The doctor explained that a nerve that controls a major portion of the movement of the face sometimes becomes inflamed. This nerve threads through a small hole in the skull, near the ear area. When the nerve becomes inflamed, it isn't able to function correctly because it becomes too swollen to properly fit through the canal. Therefore, it can no longer send normal signals. If the patient is not quickly diagnosed and properly treated, he or she can end up with permanent nerve damage, including paralysis on the same side of the face.

By the way, it is actually quite rare for a young child to develop this condition. In fact I now know a number of friends that have experienced this situation. Some of them were able to recover but some still have a partially paralyzed face. However, none of those individuals were children when this occurred.

Because the little fellow was immediately diagnosed and treated in the early stages of his palsy, he was able to completely heal within a week and had no lingering signs of ever having had a problem.

I'm deeply appreciative that my son trusted in the counsel I shared with him and followed through by taking swift action on what he was told. Those choices made a difference in our grandson's future well-being.

### Grateful for Guidance

I am profoundly grateful that I listened to the inspiration from that Still Small Voice within me and quickly acted upon the directions I was given about both the family dog and my grandson.

Experiences like these strengthen my courage, confidence and conviction that we are all being watched over. Because I trust in this fact, I am better able to live my life in a joyous manner, knowing that I will be given the inspired knowledge I desire at the perfect time. I'm also completely certain that I am able to hear and act on specific instructions that are given to me. This gift is available to all of us.

Notice that I felt something was *off* the day my son and grandson were visiting. Yet, the following day, I was given a second opportunity to understand the circumstances that were developing.

Our Teams are aware that distractions surround us. We sometimes experience sensory overload and simply are not able to take in any more information. Thankfully, they provide us with ample opportunity to hear their counsel and supportive suggestions. It is then up to us to follow through with their helpful insights. Those promptings can be life changing and life saving!

## TAKE ACTION!

**Stay open. Listen, trust and follow through with the impressions you receive from your Team, even if you don't initially see tangible evidence of what you have been told. Embrace your truth. Release everything else.**

# CHAPTER TWENTY-THREE

# ~ The Rice Experiment ~

"Who would like 'Sponge Bob Square Pants' for Breakfast?" I said, as I called out the kitchen door toward where my three grandsons were playing in the backyard.

"I do!" they replied in unison.

I heated up the griddle, mopped on butter, cut out squares from the center of the multigrain bread and set the bread, along with the squares I had cut out, on the griddle to toast in the butter. Then I cracked some eggs and dropped one in the center of each slice. Next, I added salt and pepper and flipped everything over to finish toasting on the other side. Then I doled everything out onto plates and handed them out.

The boys were staying with me for a week. It occurred to me as I cooked that they might also enjoy cooking up some rice so we could do the *Rice Experiment* to learn more about our Power and our ability to influence the world around us.

So, after breakfast, we boiled and partially cooled some rice and then separated it into three clean canning jars. After screwing on the lids I labeled the jars with a few words indicating what we were going to do to each jar.

I shared with my grandsons the fact that water holds a tremendous amount of information. Our thoughts, words and feelings affect our bodies, the bodies of others and also everything around us such as plants and animals. That is because of all the water we have within us. The human body contains anywhere from 55% to 78% water depending on body size, age and gender.

I then asked the boys if they believed the rice had a brain or feelings; if they believed it could think and respond to what we said or felt about it.

They quickly responded, "No!"

I told them to go to the first bottle of rice and shout at it, "You fool!" with great feeling. Next I asked them to then go to the second bottle and say kindly, "I love you!" and send out a feeling of affection. Finally, I instructed them to completely ignore the last bottle. "Don't even look at it," I said.

It was difficult for boys to rev up the feeling that equated with the words they were speaking. When they shouted, "You fool!" they would sometimes burst out laughing. So, the first jar didn't always receive the full impact of the feeling of what they were saying. They were, however, able to say with more consistent feeling, "I love you!" to the second jar, even though it was an inanimate object. They easily ignored the third jar.

Toward the end of the week, we began to notice changes in the rice. The "I love you!" rice began to turn a golden yellow and had a mellow smell. The "You fool!" rice started turning brown, and the rice we ignored began to rot by turning brown and black. It even began growing some *hairy* looking mold!

### Being Ignored is Devastating

I explained to my grandsons that our thoughts, words and feelings have a profound impact on us and upon those around us because we absorb and remember what is thought, spoken and felt. The information is literally held inside the cells of our tissues and very likely our DNA. When we judge others or ourselves harshly the words and thoughts that are formed have the ability to affect us deeply. They can even start changing our body chemistry.

Like the jar that was ignored and turned brown and black, people prefer attention, even negative attention, to being completely ignored. It is too damaging and painful to be shunned, left alone or cast out.

However, when we think, speak, act, but more importantly *feel* loving, understanding, acceptance and forgiveness toward others and ourselves our chemistry changes in a positive, healing and even miraculous way.

We can actually feel invigorated or drained of energy depending on what thoughts and feelings we allow to resonate within our being. In fact, for our own increased happiness, this is why it is vitally important that we completely forgive anyone we feel has offended us even if they never choose to change or ask for that forgiveness.

By willingly allowing this healing process to activate within us, our energy is increased and sabotaging, negative thoughts are released. When we purposefully choose to forgive others, while freely releasing hurt, bitterness and disappointment, our personal happiness can then be restored!

Plus, willingly releasing those painful feelings and distracting burdens helps us to more fully connect to the Divine.

### Responsive Elements

I walked over to the bookshelves in my family room and showed the three boys the books that a renowned researcher, Masaru

Emoto had written about the life, power and messages contained in water. I showed them what formed when water was frozen after it was infused with negative or positive information. The results were consistent, dramatic and thought-provokingly clear.

The water that was introduced to positive uplifting words when frozen formed beautiful jewel-like crystals. The water subjected to negative harsh words was not able to form a complete crystal. Often, it could not form a crystal at all but would form a blob that looked grotesque compared to the beautiful crystals formed from the positive uplifting waters.

That rice can respond in this way might seem strange. It is true that cooked rice and water don't have brains in the same way we do, but they are also created from elements and those elements do have intelligence within them; as do the very cells of our bodies. This intelligence is able to respond to influences around it. Amazingly, rice boiled in water, although no longer considered living or viable (because it can no longer sprout, grow or replicate itself), still responds to the different thoughts, words and feelings presented to it.

About a month later, I had the opportunity to begin training a ten-year-old girl in my office. She was a bright, intelligent child. There was some discord that had developed in her family and I thought she, her parents and siblings would benefit from doing the rice experiment so they could literally view some of the ways their actions were affecting the world around them, including their family members.

I knew that through this activity they would be able to see evidence of their personal positive or negative daily influence on one another.

They boiled the rice, and put it into separate jars, and put on lids.

Then I instructed them to expand the experiment into even more areas of testing. I told them to write on labels on the jars so they could clearly know which jar was to be influenced by what action. (In fact, written words alone have a vibrational influence on the rice.)

The labels said: "I love you," "YOU FOOL!" and "Ignore." In addition, there was a jar labeled "Soft Classical or Instrumental Music" without lyrics and another labeled "Heavy Metal Music." One last jar was created to sit beside the Telephone/Computer area.

The mother told me they seldom used the Telephone/Computer area. I suggested the family leave their home when they played "Heavy Metal Music." This recommendation was not to condemn this form of music because all experience, including all forms of music, can be for our good. However, Masaru Emoto's research as reported his book, *The True Power of Water,* and *The Hidden Messages in Water* has shown that *problematic* words and lyrics in any form of communication or music do have a negative impact on the water and I was not selecting the music for this family.

By the way, problematic words and lyrics can be found in any form of written material and music. Even scriptures and church hymns can have curse words in them such as damn and hell.

Look at the words to the music you listen to. If they are discouraging and demeaning or uplifting and joyful, those words do have an influence on your life.

Be aware of the thoughts you are having in your mind, the conversations you are observing and participating in with others as well as what you are reading and writing on the Internet. What you send and receive in emails, Facebook, Twitter, text messages…also have an effect on your life!

The following is the result of their experiment, as reported by the mother:

- **"I Love You"**: The rice had a white and golden yellow color; it expanded and looked fluffy.

- **"YOU FOOL"**: The rice turned grey and dark; it had shrunk down to one half the size of the bottle.

- **Soft Classical and Instrumental Music**: The rice was totally yellow without spots; it had shrunk slightly.

- **Heavy Metal Music**: The rice had black spots all through it; it was shrunken in appearance.

- **Telephone/Computer**: The rice was mostly yellow with a few spots of grey; it had also shrunk in volume.

- **Ignore**: The rice was mostly black mold. It was the worst jar and first to go; the rice had shrunk in size.

The ten-year-old girl I was training said the "YOU FOOL," "Heavy Metal Music" and "Ignore" rice all looked "Nasty!"

Her mom said they have re-thought what they were doing in their home as a result of those experiments. Since then, I have noticed some truly positive changes in this family.

I find it interesting to note that all the rice shrank in volume except for the "I love you" bottle, which expanded and became fluffy.

### Creating Your Own Rice Experiment

You, too, can try these experiments; really get into it and rev up your thoughts, words and feelings. Let go of being timid and allow yourself to fully experience what you are creating. Visually see how you, other people, animals, plants, food and the like are influenced by the things to which they are exposed.

The results of these experiments can reinforce awareness within us about why it is so important that we consciously choose how we think, speak and feel about others and ourselves. We can lift or we can discourage. This powerful knowledge has far reaching effects and can be utilized in many areas of our lives.

As an endnote, think about these straightforward examples of how we can affect everything around us. Perhaps this cause and effect is why it is actually a great idea to pray over your food so it truly can be more positively compatible and nourishing for your body!

### TAKE ACTION!

**Put together your own RICE EXPERIMENT. You already know how to do this from the instructions included in this chapter:**

- **Gather some clean glass bottles with lids and some materials to write some words on that you would like to affix on the jars that you will be playing with.**

- **Cook up some rice and let it cool. Then put it into the jars.**

- **Screw on the lids…you know how to do the rest!**

**More importantly, awaken and take command of the words that you are thinking, speaking, writing and listening to throughout your day. Words do indeed have Power. Use them wisely!**

CHAPTER TWENTY-FOUR

# ~ *The Fearful Husband and The Zen Man* ~

About a year ago, I met with a husband and wife for an introductory training session. They felt as if they were struggling with many life challenges and were seeking some relief. They didn't know if they would like to stay in the same line of work or if they should move to another place and begin a new life. The couple was in their early sixties and thought they were too old for a new employer to be interested in hiring them.

They were very worried about their finances. The couple had been together for about forty years. The husband explained that this was the first time since they were newlyweds their income had become so scarce. The stress they experienced from what they perceived as a dismal situation was manifesting itself in the husband as discouragement, depression, physical exhaustion and confusion.

They just did not know how to navigate their lives to a better place.

I asked some basic questions such as: what line of work would they enjoy creating in? If they were to relocate, where would they like to live? Each time I asked what they would like to change or purposefully prefer to create in their lifestyle, they replied that they didn't know. They were so stuck in the mud they couldn't find a way to pull themselves out.

I understood why they felt so paralyzed. Almost everyone I have trained has this exact response, so I was not surprised.

Many people know a part of themselves that seems a bit *off* or even miserable. They feel overwhelmed by their lack and discouraged by their longings for their preferred desires. Those feelings blind them to the clear and simple route that has been provided for them to get beyond their perceived roadblocks and attain their chosen goals. They are so entrenched; they no longer even know the top three things they would like to release from their lives!

Moreover, when I ask them to tell me the three things they would love to create and bring into their lives, they are equally blank! These individuals inherently know they are not as happy as they could be and they yearn to experience something better. They simply don't know where to begin.

### "I've Heard About Those Exercises Before!"

I suggested this couple put together their Road Map For Life and set it in motion by doing the simple, yet powerful activities that were taught in the chapter, "Reconnecting to Your Team," in Part I of this book.

As I began to describe the three-page exercise, the husband, in sheer frustration, exclaimed that he had already been told about these types of exercises and he *wanted* me to tell him something new.

I then shared with him that the situation he was experiencing *was* new and different from what he had experienced before. Therefore, it was imperative for him to map out a fresh plan with the details of what he preferred to create *now*.

I also pointed out that unless he applied genuine feelings and desires to open up and receive his Team into his life, his ability to rapidly create would be greatly thwarted. In fact, even if he went through the motions of these exercises without allowing himself to be deeply motivated, the words would be just that…hollow words on pieces of paper with little or no Power!

Perhaps the husband had performed similar exercises. But if he performed them stating his desires in the form of *someday,* those blessings may be well-developed and organized in a spiritual dimension and are simply waiting in his future until he commands them into the present. Perhaps that is why he didn't feel the importance of what I shared with him that day.

> **NOTE:** Sometimes it is advantageous to create portions of your world by commanding it to remain in *someday* for a season of time. Perhaps you recognize you are not ready to receive it at the moment you begin to form that goal. Maybe your desires include others and they are also preparing their part of the formation of those like desires. In an upcoming chapter, "Green Cars," I share an experience that I held in someday for a year before I commanded it into my life.

I taught this husband and wife everything that was required for them to begin rapidly creating, but they let their fears hold them in check. I could feel them slamming on the brakes of their life vehicles and putting them into park. There they sat in front of me, paralyzed and immovable. As my oldest daughter would say, this couple didn't have their *shirt in the game*—they were not actively engaged.

In their game of life, they weren't even sitting on their Team sidelines…they were still in the stadium parking lot! All because they were not willing to take the first steps to climb out of the dark hole *they* had placed *themselves* in. Heck, I'm not unsympathetic. I know what it feels like to have my shoes nailed to the ground. I've been stuck there a time or two myself before I learned I could unlace my shoes anytime, slip my feet out of them and *get going again.*

However, I also learned that I had to first set down the hammer I was holding in my right hand and the nails I was holding in my left hand before I could unlace those shoes!

Remember, we are the ones creating our individual world. No one and nothing is imposing anything upon us.

The husband was so caught up in the distracting problems of his life he could not allow himself to see that he and his wife were on the cusp of some amazing life changes that would be filled with growth and opportunity.

I felt great excitement about their situation because I could clearly see those amazing life changes rapidly being created for them. I also knew they could claim those experiences at any moment if they would just set aside their fears, doubts and discouragement, and allow themselves to receive their desires.

In fact, if they opened up to receive this shift they would feel more vital and alive than they had in years, perhaps even in their entire lives.

As they left that afternoon, I understood that they were not yet ready to make the change they dreamt of. Instead, they continued to stay paralyzed by fear and smothered by feelings of being overwhelmed. And that is all right! That is what they knew. That is what they were familiar with. And that is what they were still interested in exploring in their daily lives.

At any moment, when they finished thinking and mulling through those situations, they could allow an immediate shift in their reality. They could then quickly release this experience to move on and master other goals.

About a month later, the husband emailed me and shared that he was still going to do the exercises, perhaps that weekend. He revealed that he still had not taken the time to read the instructions for activating his life-altering experiences. I could see he was not yet motivated to take the action that would bring him relief. He was *still* sitting in the parking lot!

The husband told me he just didn't believe it was possible to make the changes we spoke about even though he had felt very inspired during our visit. He also marveled at the Enthusiasm, active faith and miracles I enjoyed daily.

I felt he was right about his not being able to make the changes he desired. None of those amazing changes could occur until he first allowed the shift within his soul to *believe* and *accept* the fact that *he had the ability* to purposefully create *exactly* what he desired to have happen in his life. So, he reaped what he sowed. He received exactly what he believed in. In other words:

***Allow yourself to perceive what you would love to conceive. Then, with all of your being believe that you can achieve that goal. It can rapidly form for you. Lastly, open up and receive your blessing.***

### What We Expect is Exactly What We Create

On the opposite side of the spectrum, a few weeks after I met the husband and wife, I received a request from a young man who asked me to assist him with some spiritual life training. He had recently made a mess of things, losing a relationship with his longtime companion, his job and his home. He had no family in town and no car. He had not slept in three days and did not know where else to turn. He felt he had hit rock bottom.

I shared with him that I, too, had once been homeless while I was in high school. I also had been without an immediate family to support me, or a job to sustain my financial responsibilities. I truly understood how he felt.

Then, I told him how he could start putting together a plan that *he* could *activate* so his personal happiness could return.

I gave the young man instructions for an exercise he could do after we had completed our phone conversation. It was the same three-page Road Map for Life exercise I had given to the "fearful husband" and his wife.

I explained, "On the first paper, write down *moments of gratitude, joy, thanksgiving or appreciation* you have experienced in your life." I gave him some simple examples—blessings of comfort that so many of us take for granted.

I could feel the words coming out of me, going into him, and deeply resonating in his soul: "A comfortable bed to rest your body, a soft pillow to lay your head, a warm blanket to snuggle under when you are cold, a hot shower, a refrigerator in which to put your food."

I shifted my attention even more purposefully to him and added, "These are blessings of comfort that mean much more to you now than they did a week ago. Do you agree?" He awakened to what I was saying to him and he answered, "Yes!"

He started looking all around and began to realize how blessed he had been, and how he had not noticed those blessings before.

I told him to easily and quickly enjoy filling up his first paper with a list of these simple blessings. He immediately began receiving the soothing balm of peace and well-being; verification that his entire soul was literally connected to the Divine. With that connection, all things were now possible for him to create and manifest.

I then told him about the other two pages of the exercise and gave him instructions on how to create them.

## Simple Solutions, Powerful Results!

I walked him through gathering up all his fears and worries and instructed him to take a deep breath. As he exhaled, he began to freely let go of those concerns. Again he gathered, again he exhaled and released. I spoke to him as he released all of his burdens in just three deep, meaningful breaths. Next, he took three profoundly nourishing breaths. As he inhaled, he allowed himself to be flooded with warm comforting feelings of relief.

He immediately united more fully with the Divine and felt feelings of acceptance, forgiveness and love flow into him. He cried tears of joy and happiness.

I cried with him as I also felt those amazing, unifying powerful feelings with him and with *Them,* even though we were speaking over a phone to one another.

## One Soul Speaking to Another Soul

I also shared with the young man a way of speaking to his former companion without using verbal words. I told him he had the Power to communicate with his soul directly to his former companion's soul. He could invite his loved one back into his life. He had the Power to show a mighty change had come over him and that he would like to share that change with his companion, restoring any pain or damage that had occurred during the past weekend.

I told him to visualize with detail this person and the other friends with whom he desired to rebuild his relationship, seeing that they were all doing well and enjoying their time together. I suggested he say, while allowing that wonderful feeling to resonate within his soul, *"More of this now in our lives, please. More of this for all of us now, thanks!"*

The man swiftly began the process of creating precisely what he preferred in his life.

### "I'm Feeling Afraid!"

After that, for a moment, he allowed himself to hesitate and become distracted from his goal.

All of a sudden, he realized he was afraid. I asked him how he felt when he thought and spoke those words. He confessed he didn't have that wonderful feeling he had had only moments before. I immediately told him to command those feelings to leave him.

I continued to instruct, "Turn that page and release the four-letter word called *fear*. Realize you are allowing the feelings this word evokes to shove you back into that dark place where you lose your vision, stumble, fall and create chaos. Just moments ago you purposefully moved yourself fully back into that zone full of light, joy and bliss. In a moment, you can be there again. Remember, you are the one in the driver's seat and you are steering your vehicle at all times. Turn around and come back to that abundant, good-feeling place *now!*"

Within a moment, he was back in the *zone,* this time more deeply and fully connected to his personal creative Powers and those Beings who created him, his wonderful feeling more intense than before. That experience further reinforced his awareness that he really was and always had been in charge of his own feelings and circumstances.

I told him, "Hold on to that wonderful *feeling*!" as he extended the invitation for his former companion to return to his life. If the invitation proved to be valuable and mutually uplifting to both their souls, their relationship would indeed be able to mend and flourish once again.

## The Zen Man

At the beginning of our conversation, my client explained to me that he was actually at the home where he and his former companion had lived. The other man still lived there but was gone at the time of our visit.

Suddenly he realized his former companion had returned to the home they had once shared and the young man began to slide back into feeling fearful. I reminded him to release those feelings and instead, continue to hold on to those great feelings he preferred. I assured the young man that if he would do this his partner would easily be able to see and feel the shift that had taken place in him. We quickly said our good-byes and hung up the phone.

When his partner walked into the room, he literally did not recognize the young man who was there to greet him because of the great change that had occurred. The young man had been transformed from a miserable wretch of a human being who had been unable to sleep for days into a person in a state of *zen.*

*Zen* was literally the word his former companion used to describe what the young man looked like that life-transforming day. The healing of their relationship had already begun.

My phone rang again. It was the young "Zen Man." He asked when he and his companion could come over and start their couple training. I suggested they come *now*! I reasoned it was the best time for making immediate life changes.

Soon they were both with me in my office. I mentored and carefully assisted them as they opened up their souls to the changes they desired.

Now the other man was also weeping tears of relief as he joined his Power with his personal Team and us. He told us that while I was instructing them, he started remembering information he had known all his life…in fact, all eternity. As I spoke to him, he began receiving answers to questions he had desired to know without even asking me the questions.

I told him that when I am mentoring and training others, I'm only reminding people of what they already know eternally and deeply within themselves. Their bodies verify the truths I speak.

At the end of the session, the two shared with me that they felt every couple should go through this kind of training. They found it was so powerfully healing.

I told the young man's companion about the three page exercises I had shared just hours earlier with the Zen Man.

I then discovered that within the first hour after our initial phone visit, Mr. Zen had already eagerly completed his three-page assignment! I noticed his attitude. He willingly and excitedly embraced the experience. It was fun for him. Any work or struggle was gone. His burdens were lifted and made light…just as his eternal Team had promised.

Now I could physically see the validation of that mighty change in him. He shared with us that he could feel a fullness of love and a well-being radiating in his entire chest, spreading throughout his whole body. It felt like ecstasy.

Your Team is always willing to lift your burdens for you when you make that request, too.

## Allowing the Blessings to Flow In

Two weeks later, the young couple came for another training session. They eagerly shared with me the wonderful news about the exciting adventures flooding into their lives. They had been given great job opportunities, and they were both beaming with hope and delight. What a profound turnaround from the initial phone call I had received only a couple of weeks before!

Unlike the husband who shut down, overwhelmed and paralyzed with feelings of fear, Mr. Zen and his companion easily and quickly allowed their creative juices to flow out upon those three pages and were already experiencing the fruits of what they desired to create!

I can clearly see how motivated individuals can create, activate and enjoy rapid changes in any aspect of their lives!

## Which One Are You?

The two couples presented in these stories were all amazing people who were absolutely worthy to receive whatever they were willing to allow into their lives at that moment. And they each ultimately created what they came to expect.

You, too, are clearly able to deeply bond with your Team, rapidly creating and living more fully the desires of your heart. How motivated and committed are you? Are you the *Fearful Husband,* hunkering down and closing off from the Divine; feeling alone while stumbling about in the darkness? Or are you the *Zen Man* who is flooded with light, joy and exhilaration while being fully engaged with the Divine? The decision is in your capable hands.

## TAKE ACTION!

**Did you complete your three-page "Road Map for Life" yet? If so, are you actively using it to create your wonderful world? If you have already reached those goals, create a fresh new roadmap.**

**One of my clients created her road map, which included moving into another home, finding a great man to marry and getting married. Amazingly, she completed everything on her list within a very short time. Then she slid into a depression. I pointed out that she had accomplished everything she desired and it was time for her to form a new "Road Map for Life" and continue on her creative journey!**

**If you haven't yet enjoyed this experience, allow yourself to do this simple quick exercise TODAY.**

# ~ Only Green Lights ~

"Everyone have their seatbelts on?" I asked my grandsons as I started up the diesel engine of our Ford Excursion. We were arranging to meet two of their uncles and some cousins at a movie theater across town that afternoon and everyone was excited.

I preferred for us to arrive in plenty of time to meet the rest of our group. There was only one little hiccup with this plan: it was a long drive for us to reach our destination and we were short on time.

I had allowed myself to become distracted with various activities including lunch, so when I finally took a moment to glance at the clock I realized we only had twenty minutes before our movie was to begin. Unless we had some help from our higher Power, we would be physically unable to make it to our intended goal in time for the show.

Having recognized this fact, I realized that this was also the perfect opportunity to teach my grandsons another way to use their Power. I shared with the boys what the situation was and asked them if they would like to learn more about purposefully creating what they preferred in their lives. They all got excited about the plan and they were definitely willing participants in allowing those ideas to unfold and become activated.

## The Power to Change Time

I told them we had the Power to adjust time (you were briefly taught that information earlier in the chapter, "And That Gift Is My Gift"). I explained that we could expand time or slow it down in the world outside of us and accelerate it in the world inside of us. We could let ourselves picture in our minds this change and then feel and allow it to actually happen by believing that this desire was really possible.

To help us allow our feelings to increase inside us we could say to ourselves, "We have all the time and more to get to the movies." We could also say, "We have all the time and more to accomplish all we desire to do today."

I explained that we could simply permit a sweet feeling to settle within us and enjoy those comforting words while trusting that they were our truth. Then we could allow a shift to come into our beings and let in the change of time we desired. Once again, that wonderful feeling in our vessel or body always would indicate to us that we were connected to our eternal source of Power.

## "We Love Green Lights!"

In reaching our preferred goal, there was also something else we could do. We could ask to have only green lights as we traveled from the far western part of the Tucson Mountains all the way to the mall on the eastside. The boys agreed that this was a great plan.

As we drove east on Speedway Boulevard, we soon approached our first signal light. It was red. No worries. We all started boldly saying in unison out loud, "We love green lights!" with great Enthusiasm and feelings of happy excitement and gleeful anticipation. Sure enough, just before we came to the intersection, the light turned green.

Our vehicle exploded with shouts of exhilarated amazement, which only fueled our desire to allow this gift to flow into us all the more abundantly. Commanding the situation so boldly would only happen if we held our attention to our belief and assured feelings that this was indeed possible and truly part of our reality. Any hesitation, doubt, wavering or any sliver of disbelief and we would have pushed ourselves away from the Divine that was now connected to us. We could all feel it.

After everyone settled down again, I shared with the boys that it was very important to give thanks and appreciation to our Team for playing with us and for answering our requests. With that, once again the vehicle was filled with joyful, heartfelt words of appreciation: "Thank you for the green lights! We love green lights! Green is our favorite color! Thank you, thank you!"

These Enthusiastic words were spoken and felt as we continued across town. As a result, we did indeed receive all green lights. There was only one light that turned yellow, but it was green when we entered the intersection and it turned yellow as we were leaving it.

We were able to get to the mall in plenty of time to join the rest of our family, buy our treats and enjoy the movie.

### The Lord's Time

When I was a young girl, I also learned about changing time. I learned that there was the Lord's Time and there was Prophet's Time. Some would explain it as Quantum Physics Time where you can even access a different dimension. Basically, it is possible to enter any portion of time, past present or future at anytime or shift time around our outside world or within our individual world.

I learned that one day in the Lord's time is like one thousand years in our time. That's how this world could be created in seven days. I also realize that according to carbon testing and other tests, it would appear that there are much older examples of life existence and matter on this earth.

But then I am reminded that this matter is able to be reshaped and reformed over and over eternally, from matter unorganized to matter organized, to matter unorganized, to matter organized.

We are not the first ones to come up with the idea of recycling!

We are experiencing a portion of the Lord's Time when we recognize how rapidly a day or even a year seems to be flying by. It is when everything on our outside world speeds up while our inside world remains the same or slows down.

During the Lord's Time you can move more rapidly through your day, for example, shorten the time it takes to heal from an illness or go on a long trip…like time-lapsed photography.

Think about it. Have you ever made those observations or even heard comments like, "Seems like it was just January first and it is already the middle of June! My how time flies!" Or, "Wow! Where did the time go? It was just 1 o'clock in the afternoon and now it is already 5 o'clock in the evening!"

Those are examples of when you are experiencing a portion of what the Lord's Time is like. Whether you have recognized these facts or not you are already using or observing these eternal laws and powers. Learn how to use them more precisely.

## Prophet's Time

Conversely, you can also experience the opposite expression of time and get more accomplished during your day when you use another aspect of Quantum Physics. This shifting of time is also known as Prophet's Time. It is just the opposite of the Lord's Time. It is when everything slows down on the outside of our world while our ability to accomplish our desires speeds up in our inside world.

Prophet's Time is not described as precisely as the Lord's Time; a thousand of our years equals one day of the Lord's Time. Prophet's Time expands to accommodate our being able to accomplish what we desire. For example a prophet in the Old Testament (Joshua 10: 12-14) was able to extend the length of a day by commanding the sun and moon to stand still so the people could be avenged.

Now I know that sounds absurd and quite impossible given the fact that we understand the laws of gravity. But these scriptures did note that what was accomplished during that time period felt as though it was two days given the scope of what the people were normally able to do.

When I use this gift, what I have noticed is that somehow we are simply able to speed up our ability to preform our desires without experiencing those rapid movements. We don't feel frenzied. It seems like we are doing things at adnormal pace and we are savoring the experience while the world around us —especially clocks and time pieces—take on a slow motion movie type of feeling.

Most of us have heard about Einstein's Theory of Relativity. Well in my reality and in the reality of those with whom I train and interact with, it is most certainly not a *theory*, it is an *eternal law* that we can quickly and easily master!

My family, friends and clients frequently tell me stories about their being able to readily experience this remarkable gift once they have been reawakened to this principle.

It was Prophet's Time that my grandsons and I were experiencing when we were able to expand our twenty minutes into the equivalent of an hour of time so we could drive to the mall across town, find a parking place, walk from the parking lot to the theatre to meet our family, stand in lines to buy the tickets and treats plus find our seats in plenty of time and extra to spare before the movie began.

That day my grandsons clearly learned that they could change time and draw to themselves the outcomes they preferred to experience by boldly asking for what they desired. They continued to believe that their request would easily and rapidly come to them. All the boys kept an excited feeling inside as they opened up and allowed their blessings to enter their world. And they learned to express sincere thanks afterwards.

## TAKE ACTION!

**You too have the ability to shift time. If you realize you feel frazzled and pinched with deadlines and overbooked in your schedule, expand your time if it would enhance your day. Allow a peaceful shift within your soul. Notice that doors are easily being opened on your behalf. Take joy in the opportunities that are constantly being prepared for your happiness and well-being and open yourself to the green lights as you drive through your adventurous life.**

**Many of us allow our minds to unconsciously slide over into using the words need and want. Remember that those words will disconnect us from being able to fully utilize our Power**

to create! Notice that the examples in the story of using this eternal law were completely free of these words.

Here are some other examples of how you can use this gift:

I have plenty of love and more to accomplish whatever I desire to do today.

You can also say:

I have plenty of support...
I have plenty of understanding...
I have plenty of strength...
(or wealth, knowledge, courage...)

# CHAPTER TWENTY-SIX

# ~ *Recognizing and Releasing Personal Fears* ~

I would not at all be surprised if science someday discovers that birds migrate because of how they feel. About thirty years ago, I envisioned this process in my mind. The water in their bodies and their DNA holds the memory of where their desired destination is—just the way the rice held the emotion to which it was exposed in the rice experiment.

The birds get excited about their journey and become connected to the source of energy that created them. Between the information stored within them and their excited feelings of anticipation, they literally just keep feeling their way to their desired goal.

There is an additional situation that happens during this feeling process. Everything has a vibration, a magnetic resonance in our world. When the birds desire a particular destination, they tune into the resonance of where they desire to be. They begin to experience a similar reverberation and magnetism emanating from their destination.

This magnetic resonance, coupled with the information stored within the water in their bodies, supports their positive feelings and draws or moves them toward their preferred goal.

If they start to slide a bit off course, or if they become momentarily distracted, they simply keep turning toward that better-feeling place within them as they adjust their course direction until they are back in their correct flight pattern.

They don't think or fret about how they will reach the end point of their journey. They do not toil or study maps for hours as they plot out their route. They don't pick apart, scrutinize or dissect the fact that they have a type of magnetic and vibrational property in their being. That would be a misuse of their precious energy and time. They just simply *trust, open up* and fully *allow* those feelings of well-being to *flow* through them.

## Creating a Game to Conquer My Fear

I once decided to experiment with the ability to feel my way toward an intended goal, much like a migrating bird. I realized that somehow I had developed an apprehension or fear about getting lost; unable to find my way to a specific destination. That fear felt quite unnerving considering I was now a mother responsible for four young, dependent little people.

Many years earlier, I set a precedent as a young child. Instead of running away from perceived fears, I deliberately chose to develop games to overcome and conquer them. I would start the *game playing* soon after I recognized I was struggling with something before it grew into a monstrous overwhelming beast of a problem.

This proactive approach to life was important to me. It also was the key to my consistently happy, adventuresome life experience.

I purposefully explored the perceived problem I chose to overcome so that concern would not become a stumbling block in my future.

Because I had developed an apprehension or fear about getting lost, I decided to take my four children on a trip to visit my cousins in Chandler, Arizona. They had recently moved there and I had no idea where their home was. All I had was a phone number.

With that goal in mind, I called my cousins early one weekend morning to see if they would be home and asked if it would be all right if we came for a visit. I shared with them my idea of overcoming my fear of getting lost and my plan of feeling my way toward their new home.

My cousins were very supportive and encouraging about my objective, so they did not mention their new address to me. They looked forward to seeing how this adventure would play out. So now, not only was I sending out my desires to find my cousins, but my cousins were also creating with me and sending out their wishes to have me locate their home as well. This united focus increased the Power for us to develop our preferred outcome.

## Moving Forward in My Adventure

I topped off our station wagon's gas tank and packed it up with food, water, my kids and the phone number for my cousins. We headed northwest on I-10 in the direction of Chandler. I held a positive, excited and assured feeling in my body and trusted that my feeling would direct me where I desired to go. I kept thinking about the fun we would have when we reached our destination and held on to the great sensation I felt inside my body.

We drove for almost two hours through the parched Arizona summer desert before we finally reached the turn off for the city of Chandler. I chose that particular exit and more purposefully started feeling my way toward the location where I felt my cousins were now living. I continued to steadily sense my way forward. I followed my impression and turned into a neighborhood that seemed like the one they lived in.

## Feeling My Way Toward My Goal

Now Chandler is a rather large and spread out city with many neighborhoods, and my cousins have lived in a variety of homes there (in other words they hadn't always lived in a particular type of home or neighborhood that might have given me a hint of where they might have moved). Nevertheless, this particular neighborhood just *felt* right to me…nothing wavered inside me.

I finally sensed it was time for me to stop and call my cousins to find out their exact location. Since I did not own a cell phone in those days, I had to find someone who would allow me into their home to use the phone. I soon found a friendly looking residence where some children were running through the water sprinklers. I reasoned that this location looked like a safe place to ask for assistance.

I knocked on the door. The parents opened it and I asked if I could use their phone. They welcomed me inside. Within a few minutes I was speaking with my cousins.

To my delight, my cousins indicated that their home was just south of where I was parked, on the next block over! I drove the car the short remaining distance and found them gathered in the front of their home, ready to greet us. It was truly an amazing experience for us all to be able to participate in.

This adventure reinforced in me that I did not have to be fearful of ever getting lost again if I just trusted in how I was feeling and then followed through with how I felt. Besides, even if I did get lost, there is always a backup plan that has been put in place for me. I can always ask for help and assistance and someone will easily and quickly provide me with the information I desire to have!

*By our feelings we will always know how to traverse our way through this life.*

### Our Feelings Are Our Perfect Guiding Compass

Our bodies help us *feel* our way through this temporal life. They are our perfect compass to point out at all times if we are headed in a direction pleasing to us or if we are meandering in a direction less enjoyable. When we unite our soul with our feelings and our Team we have the ability to experience consistent, abundant joy in this world.

It occurred to me as I later reflected over the events of the day that if I were a migrating bird flying toward a destination like a field or lake, there wouldn't be any houses to block my vision. As the crow flies, I would easily and clearly be able to see my desired target less than fifty yards in front of me!

After that experience, I readily let go of my fear of getting lost. Now I travel all over the world by myself with confidence that all is well with my journeys. I am able to enjoy every moment of my adventures because I allow myself to release any fear of getting lost. Instead, I trust steadfastly in the eternal truth that my soundly proven feelings are my perfect guiding compass. In fact, those feelings steer me through every facet of my life.

### Magnets in Fowl Size Noggins

Thirty years later, I was sitting in a plane one afternoon while flying home from a family wedding in Colorado. To help pass the time, I visited with the passenger to my right. During our conversation, the woman shared with me that she was a science teacher at one of the high schools in Tucson.

Out of curiosity, I inquired if scientists had discovered how birds migrate. She informed me that they still did not have all the details but they did discover that birds do have some small magnets that are located in their heads! Hmmm! They are getting closer to discovering all the pieces to the puzzle. I'm not sure how they can figure out how to measure the birds' feelings but somehow I am confident a way will be provided for them.

## TAKE ACTION!

**All of us at times feel like we have become lost. When this happens, take some deep breaths, quiet your soul and release any fears you may have collected. Then turn yourself to a better-feeling place and follow what you feel impressed to do. It really is that simple!**

# ~ Little White Lies ~

"Oh no, I'm going to be late!" I thought one afternoon as I drove to Vail, Arizona. I was rushing to attend my grandson's elementary school graduation ceremony. I found myself preoccupied with the thought that I was going to miss this special passage in his life.

As I traveled down the highway, I didn't notice that my body was beginning to feel stressed and tensed up. I didn't perceive this shift because I was allowing distracting thoughts to enter my mind; busily making up excuses for my tardiness.

I was searching for scenarios or reasons for my lateness that I could tell my daughter and her family. I *wanted* to justify myself and avoid the disappointed looks and feelings I projected and imagined I would receive from them when I finally did arrive late. (Noticed that I *wanted*...in other word I was disconnected from the Divine and stumbling on my own.)

On the other hand, none of the stories I envisioned seemed valid enough to explain my being late.

**Finding My Perfect Excuse!**

Then I saw an accident on the off ramp for the road to the school. Immediately, I realized that this could be the perfect excuse to explain my delay. All I had to say when I greeted my family was, "There was an accident on the off ramp." With that *truthful* statement, they would assume my delay was because of the accident and excuse me. But that excuse, because of my lack of full disclosure, would not be the truth—not the full truth anyway. I was late simply because I was late.

The accident had not impeded my ability to make the event on time. The damaged cars, fire trucks and other emergency support vehicles were already moved safely off to the side of the road.

I began to reason in an effort to convince myself that it was just a little white lie. How could that be a problem?

## Pulling Myself Back from the Slippery Slope

Suddenly, I snapped back into my *now* presence and became fully conscious of what was happening. I took swift action to stop my slide down this slippery slope. I realized I no longer felt joy inside me. I decided to immediately change my course of action.

It didn't matter if no one but me knew the details of the situation. I still understood what my intentions had been: to mislead my loved ones. I knew my truth. I clearly comprehended that *any* form of deceit would affect my ability to exercise my full potential to purposefully create my preferred world, even if it was just a seemingly innocuous little white lie.

In all honesty, simply being less than who I usually am, because of the diminished joy I was feeling, would be expressed to all with whom I came in contact. My friends and family would also know something was *off* with me. Their trust in me and their ability to rejoice in my being there would be affected because they would be able to feel that negativity emanating from me.

## Genuine or Phony?

Ever have someone approach you all freshly scrubbed and polished? Hair perfectly styled, clean pressed clothes, a smile on their face and lips forming the most politically correct words in the loveliest of tones? Despite their perfect appearance and smooth, flawless elocution, did your skin just crawl? You just could not believe anything they were saying. You knew there was something phony about them.

You may have noticed this is true of someone who is selling something or running for a political office. Now, I'm not saying these people are deceitful the way I was that graduation day. Perhaps they are just exhausted, distracted or worried and are robotically going through their canned or memorized speeches.

But you know their soul is not genuinely feeling what they are saying with their words and faces. Their soul expresses their truth to yours and the difference between what you see and hear, combined with what you feel, confirms that they are not in harmony within themselves.

## Your True Genuine Feelings Will Never Fail!

Thankfully, I listened to what I was doing and immediately decided to turn to a better-feeling place. I am in charge of the direction my life is heading. If what I am doing is not personally pleasing and satisfying to me, I can change my actions at any moment and draw personal joy back into my soul.

I quickly released the distracting thoughts I had allowed myself to experience as I exited off the highway ramp and headed toward the school. I also chose to leave the darkened avenue of deceit and purposefully turn once again to my path of light and truth.

I adjusted my soul, as I quieted my body, and spoke these words, "I have all the time I desire and more to reach my destination and enjoy seeing my grandson's graduation."

I could feel the shift that was swiftly coming into me. There was a feeling of calm, peaceful relief as my disharmony and resistance departed and my joy was quickly restored. I could also feel time being altered and an assurance that my desire was now physically my reality.

As I felt time shift, I was reminded of another eternal truth:

***When we are honorable beings, even the elements will obey our commands.***

In fact, that is the way these mighty worlds and universes were created, by Beings or Gods that were honorable. Their honor literally was the key to their being able to use their godly powers.

They did not take each stone and hand-stack them one upon another to create majestic mountains. Nor did they gather the waters, drop by drop to form the mighty seas. These Honorable Celestial Beings commanded the elements and all things pertaining to those creations were performed according to their godly designs.

That is precisely what each of us is able to do now. Create the world we prefer by allowing ourselves to more perfectly connect with our Team while we further develop into honorable beings.

***Remember, we are either creating the world we prefer, destroying our world or creating the same world over and over again.***

I felt great thanksgiving that I had willingly forsaken those thoughts and actions to deceive. Had I acted upon them, I would have damaged my integrity and also my ability to connect to my

Power to swiftly and purposefully create what I preferred. Instead, I reclaimed my honor.

I had turned and deliberately walked back into the presence of my loving Team, into their outstretched arms. They eagerly embraced me. There were no expressions from them that indicated any chastising, lecturing, disappointment, shaming or feelings that I was unworthy of their love and adoration for me.

Instead of a rebuke, there was complete acceptance and delight that I was able to grow and expand from this experience to learn what I more purposefully preferred to have in my life. I felt sincere happiness from them because my personal joy had been restored.

That is the response they have always had for me. That is the response they will always have for you.

### Just In Time!

I parked my car along the road and excitedly headed—okay, *sprinted*—toward the school auditorium. I walked inside just before the program commenced. My grandson happily waved at me from the stage. I quickly located my family standing in the back of the packed room. The program began and I enjoyed every second of it. Afterwards, we took pictures and shared hugs, words of congratulations and good wishes before we departed. It turned out to be such a sweet life experience.

From my personal example above, any form of deception, even if it is a little white lie, will reduce our personal feelings of well-being and begin closing us off from our full connection to those eternal Beings that love, adore and support us. Remain an honorable person and maintain your ability to command your world while retaining your personal joy!

## TAKE ACTION!

Look deep within, and then ask yourself, "Am I an Honorable Being?" Create adjustments depending upon your answer. Stay aware and keep empowered. Consciously choose to manifest honorable intentions and feelings that reflect a life filled with integrity. If you begin to be distracted and slide off your preferred path, allow yourself a speedy course adjustment and reclaim your balance.

# Chapter Twenty-Eight

# ~ The Prophecies, Song of Joy, Full of Prayer ~

It was hot and humid from the monsoon summer rains. Even though I knew my efforts would most likely be useless, I tried to find some relief as I moved to the family room to feel the evaporative cooler's breeze as it blew through the vent in the wall above the hall door.

Everyone in the southwest knows evaporative coolers aren't very effective once the monsoons hit the desert, but I still tried to improve my miserable situation.

I especially felt the heat this summer as I glanced in the mirror and saw my quickly expanding, round abdomen; I had just entered the eighth month of my pregnancy. Only one more month to go!

Our family had already been blessed with two sons and now we were getting ready to welcome a third child. These were the days before sonograms were available; however, I was certain this child would be a girl. In fact, I was so sure of this that I decided to design and create a beautiful white blessing gown for her. That hot, sticky day I was busily embroidering ribbons, lace and tiny pearls with silk thread on the soft, delicate fabric of the little dress.

### That's My Knight in Shining Armor?

While in junior high school I had been told by my Master Teacher or Savior, through the Still Small Voice of the Comforter, that in five years I would marry Ronnie, a boy I did't even know at the time. I also learned we would have four children close in age: two boys and two girls in that exact order.

This knowledge was revealed to me when I saw Ronnie for the first time as he came walking up the sidewalk to my family home. Ronnie and my stepsister were friends and he was picking her up so they could go to an activity together.

I knew this information was my truth because I had experienced such floods of intelligence in my mind previously. My connection to the Still Small Voice had always proven to be valuable and for my good. So I trusted completely in what was being shared with me.

For instance, during a particularly violent episode in my home when I was about seven years old, I began earnestly praying in bed one night. I asked for help and relief from my beatings and hardships. I sought out this counsel because I desired to know what I could do so my family members would accept me.

"What can I change so they will love me?" I questioned.

The response my Master Teacher shared with me, through the comforting Still Small Voice was immediate and to the point:

*"You are beloved by us. You are capable of giving and receiving love. There is nothing wrong with you. They are miserable, unhappy people...If you will be patient for a season, We will bless you with everything your heart desires, but especially a husband that loves you."*

Now my Master Teacher knew that above all else—looks, education, spirituality, health, material wealth and general well-being. I desired to be loved by my future eternal companion. My

Master Teacher and I both knew that *love* is what drives the Power to create all things. With that deeply committed love, my husband and I would have the ability to overcome all obstacles and create whatever our hearts chose to experience.

I understood that night, as I sought comfort while tearfully pleading for guidance, that I had been given a mighty blessing. That blessing was already being formed for my long-term personal happiness.

I always remembered that promise and held it close in my thoughts and heart. That information provided the comfort and the understanding I sought, helping me to bear my burdens and adversities more easily.

This knowledge also helped me to let go of many distractions, worries and concerns about why things happened in my life so I could continue forward and grow up, develop and mature. I was also able to focus my energies on my studies, designing, sewing and working at odd jobs for money to provide for my personal provisions.

Meanwhile, I became somewhat of an outsider, an excluded member of the family. I felt something change within me. I now was more of an observer of situations in my house than an active participant in the drama. This, too, was my blessing.

These observations helped me more clearly identify what I preferred to release from my life, and encouraged me to further search for more pleasing situations and traditions I could implement in their place. I soon began envisioning the wonderful life I preferred to live.

That said, when I received the *news* about the man I was to marry I was actually pretty upset. Because I had never seen a happy example of a married couple or family, I wasn't too excited about the thought of getting married at all. I felt that commitment or obligation would require way too much work and little to no joy in return!

Besides, I was only a 14-year-old girl for golly sakes! Until that moment, I had been envisioning myself going to lots of dances, dating lots of people and kissing lots of boys before I found my husband. I was certainly not prepared for this revelation, especially since I couldn't even date until I was sixteen. In other words, I was forming this opinion from the perception of a young, romantic, daydreaming teenager.

Yet somehow, when I did receive this information from the Comforter, I remembered the promise that had been revealed to me seven years earlier...that I would marry a husband who would love me.

That memory, coupled with this new information, really awakened me. I quickly became very conscious of how I conducted my life and was keenly aware of how important my choices were while I shaped my future into something I desired.

From the many years of communicating with me, I had clearly learned how to discern this Still Small *Voice* from other thoughts. Certain feelings also attend this Voice. Sometimes it came in the form of a warm burning in my chest that assured me all was well. Other times it came in a feeling of hyper alertness that awakened me to be more cognizant of my situation. It even came with an added electrical jolt rather like lightning to really drive home the point.

But by far, the greatest reassurance of this comforter was when I was filled to overflowing with the rapturous feelings of Divine love. That feeling brought me—and brings me—to tears of great appreciation for all my Team has provided so I can more fully enjoy this life experience.

However, deep appreciation was not exactly what I felt the day I was told I would marry Ronnie. He did not look like the knight in shining armor I had always pictured in my mind: a man of my faith; a missionary who had successfully completed his calling; a person who was profoundly, spiritually alive. I had imagined finding this *knight* and being able to recognize that fact when I looked into his eyes.

Instead, what I saw that day was a mix between a likeable student/wrestler/baseball player and a touch of a bad boy: someone who liked to drink, drag race, hustle pool for college money and beat people up when they provoked a fight. Plus, we definitely were *not* of the same faith. I clearly understood that this fact alone could be the source of extended family problems from the beginning of our relationship.

Not that I was without my own problems. It's not like I was the perfect catch. I came from a violent home and had been molested for years as a young child. Not to mention I had trust issues. I felt hyper-vigilant and was unable to just let my hair down and be a teenager.

You would not use the adjective *easy going* to describe me. *Intense* was a better word. I clearly understood that if I made a mistake there would be no parent to pick me up, dust me off and help me get back on my footing. I knew I didn't have the option of screwing things up.

Yet true to the prophecy, in five years we were married. Thankfully, during those five years we both grew and developed together and became a strong couple while we individually polished up some of our rougher edges. Ronnie's drinking, fighting and racing were the first things to disappear. Unfortunately, my own issues took somewhat longer for me to master.

## An Inspired Knowing

When we started our family, our children were born close together in the exact order I was promised many years earlier. Our first son was born two weeks after our first anniversary and the second came twenty months later. Then, this next baby was due twenty months after that.

My mom explained that I'd better be careful not to get my hopes up because I already had two boys. She didn't *want* my expectations dashed and felt it was her duty to inform me that this baby could also be a boy.

I then shared with her a fact that I already firmly understood. I told her without any hesitation that the child I was carrying within me would be a little girl. I went on to share that I was already making her blessing gown because I had a feeling I would not have time to make it after she was born.

I had already learned that babies come in their own due time and do not always follow a schedule. All of my children were born early, some earlier than others. My first son was born a month premature; my second son came two weeks before his due date. But they both were able to come home with me from the hospital, each free of any complications.

Our third child, a baby girl, was also born a month premature. However something felt different to me this time. In fact, after she was born and I was wheeled into the recovery room, I asked my husband to tell the doctors to watch her closely for respiratory problems. I had an inspired knowing within my soul that she was going to struggle with her lungs. Perhaps that knowing was to help prepare me for what would happen next.

Sure enough, the doctor came in and told me my newborn infant had Hyland Membrane Disease because her lungs had not been fully developed. Her legs, other extremities and her mouth were turning dusky blue.

Later, in the middle of the night, the doctors awoke me to sign papers to have her transported to a neonatal unit in another hospital in Tucson in the hope she could receive the emergency care she so desperately required.

If I could have grown wings I would have swiftly flown with her in my loving embrace to the next hospital. As it was, I signed the papers as quickly as I was able and kissed her goodbye.

The next morning, I checked out of the hospital and went home to care for my three-year-old and nineteen-month-old sons. It felt so strange coming home from the hospital with empty arms, but I maintained a certain peace that all was well with my daughter. I fully understood how serious her plight was, but I also felt completely assured that she was in the best of care and that she would be able to recover.

### The Daily Odyssey

Every day I drove over to the hospital to see my six-pound, three-ounce, eighteen-inch baby girl. My strong feelings of confidence in my baby's ability to overcome her circumstances were reinforced when I saw her situated next to one and two pound infants. Compared to them, she looked like a robust sumo wrestler!

I also began the odyssey of hauling in and out of the hospital a bulky forty-pound breast pump several times a day so I could bring her my milk. All my children had had allergies to formulas. I knew she required all the help she could get; naturally, mucus-forming formulas would not be part of that healing equation.

Physically carrying in and out a forty-pound machine several times a day proved to be quite daunting for my one-hundred-and-five-pound body!

The problem was that I had just had a baby. It was important that I received some help and rest. I was also caring for my sons at the same time as I was trying to provide the necessary nourishment for the new baby. Additionally, while at the hospital, instead of bonding with, caring for and comforting my little daughter, I was hooked up to the machine in the doctors lounge!

Finally, the hospital gave my husband permission to bring the milk to the hospital for our baby after I filled the bottles in the privacy of our home. In turn, I was able to spend time with my infant so I could cuddle her and sing and coo to her.

When we were separated she cried and was unhappy as she courageously battled to overcome her obstacles. But when I was with her she would feel calm, relaxed and assured. She was surrounded with the familiar love and comfort that could only be provided by the resonance and touch of her mother.

### Her Ordeal

Our daughter surmounted every obstacle that came her way, and they weren't small challenges. Her eyes were taped shut. The sides of her head were shaved to accommodate IVs after the veins in her umbilical cord closed off and the IVs ceased working there. She was provided food by gavages or feeding tubes in her stomach.

Air was forced into her lungs to try and get the bubblegum-like material to open up in order to provide oxygen to the recesses of her little body. The oxygen levels and force required to pump the air into her lungs continued to increase each day.

She often had to have percussion and drainage treatments: her chest was regularly pounded on over the different lobes of her lungs, and she was continuously repositioned to let the pulling powers of gravity play an assistive role. After the treatment, her nose and mouth were suctioned out to remove any loosened materiel from her lungs.

For three days her body slid further downhill. The doctors warned us there was a chance that if our daughter did recover from the lung problems, she might develop learning difficulties and become blind before the age of preschool because of the air that could pool behind her eyes.

Yet, in spite of the increasing difficulty, I still felt a perfect peace and assurance that all was going to be well with my little girl. My heart engaged in continual prayer for the welfare of our newest child. And, in spite of all of these mounting pressures and activities, I slept well each night. That, in itself, was a blessing as I physically continued to recover.

## A Crushing Weight on My Chest

Then one night I was awakened with what seemed like a crushing weight on my chest. I instantly knew my little infant was in serious trouble. I quickly called the hospital to find out what the situation was. The doctor told me the oxygen was now at 100% and the pressure to push it into her lungs was as high as the machine could go. They were standing by and watching, waiting for her lungs to blow out. When that happened, they were prepared to insert tubes into the sides of her chest to try to re-inflate her lungs; this was to be done without pain medication.

She was at a critical point in her recovery: she could either turn the corner and start getting better or the battle could press on.

I told the doctor I had to get off the phone. He questioned me and asked if I truly understood the severity of her status. I assured him that I was clearly aware of her situation and we ended our conversation.

I felt impressed to get off the phone so I could go and be comforted by my Team. I could feel them draw tenderly near to me. I was certain they were completely engaged in resolving our concerns. I knew they had been supporting me in numerous ways, including providing me with a perfect peace while I experienced this ordeal.

However, at that moment, I was no longer feeling that peace or comfort. In fact, I felt it was imperative I completely open my heart to them about what I preferred to see happen on my daughter's behalf.

Too weak and exhausted from my plight to get on my knees, I laid in my bed with tears streaming down my cheeks and sent out my heart's desire for my precious child.

I told them this little infant had valiantly weathered all that had happened thus far. I asked them to intercede on her behalf and allow her lungs to create a shift and change so she would not have to have tubes inserted into her little body. I further requested that if this were indeed possible, that the crushing feeling in my lungs would be lifted from me and that I would be allowed to receive my required rest.

As I prayed those words, a balm of well-being flooded over me and the anvil-like weight was gently removed. A soothing peace and reassurance that all was well returned to my soul. I immediately drifted off into a deep, restorative sleep.

## Song of Joy, Full of Prayer

When I awoke the following morning, I excitedly called the hospital to see how my daughter was progressing. The doctor reported with amazement that half an hour after I spoke with him on the phone, our little girl began to show signs of recovery. Her lungs did not blow out, nor did they have to insert tubes in her chest. It looked like she was now on her way to overcoming the adversity and crisis she had been grappling with.

That half an hour after my conversation with the doctor was the exact moment when I felt the relief of the Atoning Powers that lifted my burden as well as my daughter's burden from our chests.

These Divine Beings who personally know and love us really do exist; they are actual entities, not merely something imagined or written about. I am exceedingly appreciative I was able to hear and feel those supportive whispers and assurances in my soul.

After that night, our daughter quickly recovered and within a month was able to come home and join the rest of her family. While yes, she did have much to overcome in her life, her exuberant, never-give-up attitude and tenacious spirit helped her to become a powerful force of nature.

Today, this diminutive being is a bright, charismatic, take-the-tiger-by-the-tail, intelligent businesswoman with two children of her own.

On the night our daughter was born, her unabashed daddy went uncharacteristically running around the neighborhood street while exuberantly waving his arms and shouting for all to hear, "We have a girl! We have our little baby girl!"

The nurses at the hospital remarked how much joy this little girl had brought into our lives. They suggested we name her something joyful. I told them we were naming her *Carole*, like a song. Later, I learned that Carole means *song of joy.* We also gave her the middle name *Ann*, which means *full of prayer*. She was indeed our song of joy that was filled with prayer.

## TAKE ACTION!

**You do not have to suffer for long periods of time. When you feel awakened to the fact that something in your life can improve by your requesting and convening a council meeting, do so swiftly so your comfort and peace can be rapidly restored. Forgot how to form a meeting with your Team? Review the chapter, "How To Form a Council Meeting"**

# ~ *Releasing Negative Feelings* ~

One summer weekend, I discovered my grandsons were interested in learning how to release the negative feelings in their memories and bodies. I told them that their Team had the ability to instantly remove those negative sensations, sorrows or pains.

I also shared that they can individually release situations and related sensations by using a method called *Tapping* or the *Emotional Freedom Technique* (EFT) by literally tapping over specific areas of their bodies where their energy points or meridians are located, which releases old information that is held in their body. Afterwards, they can immediately draw into the newly created void what they would prefer instead.

Tapping can release Post Traumatic Stress problems. Let's face it: we sometimes feel like the walking wounded because of the life injuries we feel we have sustained. Tapping can release these triggers and also free us from the grip of addictions. Any suffering or lack we perceive, whether physical, emotional or spiritual, can be addressed and removed through Tapping.

I taught the boys how to use the long version of this method of release and also a shorter version that is so discreet others around them would not even notice when they were using it.

They had already learned that the water in the cells of their bodies held vast amounts of information. Some of that information was important for the forward motion in their lives and some was no longer necessary for their progress. I knew that Tapping would assist them in this helpful exchange of information. They quickly learned how to apply what I shared with them.

### Be Aware, Be Purpose-Filled, Be Genuine

I told the boys it was really important that they combine genuine feelings about what they preferred to have happen with a personal desire for change. Otherwise, Tapping would just become a rote activity and they would not receive the outcome they sought. I reminded them that mindless tapping and words that sounded like *blab, blab, blab* would never effectively relieve a negative situation.

However, being connected to the Divine by actively creating aware thoughts, focused vision, purpose-filled words and genuine feelings would truly assist them in receiving what they were asking for.

### Taking It Like a Man?!

About a month after my grandsons had gone back home, I had the opportunity to go and see them again during an evening baseball game. The bright floodlights were already on and the night took on a special big-league feeling as the youthful players ran out to the freshly mowed green field.

Our seven-year-old grandson who played that evening was a small fellow with lots of fire in his belly. In the past, he could become easily crestfallen and discouraged when things didn't go as he had expected, and tears of frustration often accompanied those moments.

His eleven-year-old brother was all dressed up in an umpire uniform and called the game from behind home plate. I sat in the stands with their nine-year-old brother and some of the children's friends and parents.

The time had come for the youngest brother to take his turn at bat. He came jauntily walking up to the batter's area and took a couple of swings to loosen up his arms and shoulders before he stepped into the box. He dug his feet into the dirt and readied his stance as he firmly grasped the bat. He looked a little like a bobble-head toy with his slight frame and his head encased in a huge helmet.

Despite his awkward appearance, however, once he hit the ball he could run like the wind.

The pitcher from the other team wound up and let the ball fly. Wham! The crowd gasped as the hard baseball struck the little guy! "Batter, take your base!" his older brother (and umpire) announced. The diminutive fellow bravely made it to first base without uttering a word.

The oldest brother looked up into the stands and spotted his other sibling with their friends.

"Did you see that?" he called up to them.

"See what?" responded the middle brother.

"Did you see him take that hit like a man?!"

He was right. Something was different about the first grader standing on first base. I wondered how he was doing considering he had just sustained a pretty painful blow. He seemed to be absolutely fine. This was definitely not his typical response.

The little guy made his way around the bases, scored and eventually headed back into the dugout.

I walked over to the bench soon after he had sat down. I asked him how he was doing and how he had managed to handle the hit he took with such a positive, upbeat demeanor. He turned to me and in doing so revealed a huge grin. Then he matter-of-factly replied, "Nana, I just did this!"

He held out his hand and showed me that he used one of the short versions of Tapping to relieve his discomfort so he could get his attentions back into the game and enjoy himself!

## Creating the World He Preferred

I couldn't help but chuckle with happiness for this cute little fellow. He had purposefully created the world he preferred instead of allowing a bad pitch to rain on his parade and spoil his evening. Pretty awesome!

Just to clarify, this young boy most certainly did **not** *take it like a man* in the sense most people would mean it. That response usually requires *sucking it up,* or *grinning and bearing it* while shoving down feelings and putting on a brave, false front. All of those are unhealthy ways of responding to life's situations. Actions like those deny how a person really feels and represses emotions while discounting genuine concerns that deserve to be individually addressed.

So often those responses just build up unresolved baggage that many of us drag around in our day-to-day lives.

Because this grandson used Tapping, he fully released from his body the discomfort he was feeling and drew to him what he desired instead so he could genuinely enjoy his evening.

That response is very different from *taking it like a man.*

As a result of that complete release, he was able to continue focusing on developing his skills and hitting abilities instead of being frightened, paralyzed or bailing out of the box when the ball was next pitched at him.

Today, that little nine-year-old has such a great *stick* that league scouts in Phoenix call one another to give updates on where his games are being played so they can come out and watch his progress!

It is vitally important that we release what no longer serves us. Why? Because those thoughts and feelings distract and sabotage us from being able to fully use our energies and Powers.

This ability to readily release from our soul what we no longer desire and draw into our being what we prefer is a powerful life-skill that is worth mastering.

> **IMPORTANT NOTE:** The technique for Tapping is not covered in this book. It will be taught in the upcoming book, *Preparing the Vessel*. However, you can easily look up examples of tapping videos on my website, **www.PamelaAnnEzell.com**. Look under the *Preparing the Vessel Section* for specific, powerful support, to see the locations of where you tap and to learn how to tap like a gorilla (alternate your Tapping by using two hands); it is so much more effective when you include this added information in your tapping experience!

Remember that your Tapping success is increased when you combine it with your sincere feelings as you do your series of Tapping movements. Be engaged and feel the words you are speaking! That fact is sometimes not included in the instructions you find on the internet or in other videos but it is a vital point.

When you add your feelings, you are better connected to your Team and personal Power to create!

Also, include in your Tapping session a round or two where you draw to you what you would love to create to take the place of what you have removed. This is also a powerful activity to include in your experience! Lastly add your feelings of thanksgiving and appreciation to those who created you so you can stay more fully connected to the Divine.

## TAKE ACTION!

**Identify any nagging situation that has become a distraction to you. These joy-reducing circumstances lessen your ability to feel your full connection to your Team. Allow yourself to use Tapping to reduce and/or remove your discomfort or unhappiness. Often, this is the avenue to take to get the ball rolling so you can reconnect to your Team and start floating down stream again or regain the peaceful center of your hurricane.**

# ~ *Some Clarification* ~

This is not a chapter. It is preface to the next two chapters, which require a bit of an explanation or enlightenment about their real value and purpose in this book.

A significant portion of the emphasis in these stories has to do with creating abundant financial and material wealth. I find these topics seem to distract lots of people. They often take such precedence that they draw attention away from equal or more important subjects in their lives. That's one of the reasons these stories were placed last in this book, to lessen those distractions.

## Flash Points that Distract

The changing economy and fears about money are flash points for many people. They are often filled with concern. As a result, those topics easily seep into their minds and in their conversations (notice how you feel when I mention those two subjects).

My clients' first-time visits often center on these topics. These worries seem to pop-up more than once during our sessions because the individuals I'm training have consistently focused so much of their time and attention on those two subjects. This is yet another reason these particular chapters were included in this book.

I often tell my clients, "Let's throw these thoughts and experiences out on the table and talk about ways you can rapidly bring these bounties into your life." (If that is the adventure they are interested in creating at that time.)

## Wealth and Happiness

Remember, material and financial wealth do not bring to you or take away from you feelings of happiness or well-being. Nor do they measure how successful you are. They are really just *stuff* that you can learn to manage. Besides, when you finally *kick the bucket or take the big leap* you can't take so much as a toothpick with you. Moreover, money is not the root of all evil. You, your attitude and the actions you take determine if those gifts will become a blessing or a bane.

I suggest that you place as much weight and value upon these upcoming experiences as you did the previous stories in this book. They all have merit.

## Keep Your Perspective

You can lose your confident, happy-go-lucky, *ask and receive* attitude by making these items a big deal to create; you can continue to spin your wheels. You can also use up your time and energy while you wait for them to appear. However, if you do keep them in the same perspective as your daily blessings, your ability to draw those financial and material gifts into your life will increase.

Note how quickly and easily the shifts in these stories happened. The same basic examples of Team, Power, time, energy and eternal laws plus council meetings are used as they were in the other stories.

Notice that other people were mutually forming those areas of desire at the same time. I was definitely not alone in this process and passion to create. There was an obvious multiple Team affect that dialed into place (another great reason to *become one with one another* and mutually play with the Divine).

The original desire to create in these stories did not begin with a focus on how to form vast financial or material wealth—although it is really fine to have both in your life. But using money and things as primary reasons to create often leads to disappointment.

When we put those two items as our main desires, it seems *we* often sabotage ourselves from believing we can actually quickly and easily reach those goals--especially when we mistakenly believe we are unworthy of receiving those blessings.

On the other hand, when we link them to life missions, mutually uplifting desires and other experiential adventures, financial and material wealth seem to naturally rise up with the rest of those blessings.

In the chapter "Millions of Dollars," the gist of the story deals with my desire to learn about drawing to myself only harmonious relationships in all aspects of life. So having a profoundly abundant financial experience was just one of the topics I learned about and mastered at that time.

The next chapter, "Green Cars," is a story that originated from a little *whisp* of an idea that came to my mind one day. I added some details to it so I could create more specifically what I desired and better recognize it when it appeared in my world. I was also learning about Teaming with other people and creating more *win-win* situations with them. Then I placed it out in *someday* so it could percolate and form.

In fact, during that time period, I learned lifetimes of vast life-altering information in sixteen months. That information propelled me into a new dimension and better prepared me for ushering in this portion of my life mission.

In none of these situations did I waver, worry or toil. I simply believed they would happen and kept the vision of them forming. I held on to my happy, feelings of Enthusiasm and revved them up whenever my thoughts happened to wander over to those desires. I then allowed them to flow into our world. In the meanwhile, I simply went forth, fully living my life and creating in other areas that interested me.

Finally, the two following stories are great examples of the fact that it really is all right to think **BIG** or *small*.

# CHAPTER THIRTY

# ~ *Millions of Dollars* ~

I am profoundly blest with many great and true friends. These are dear relationships that have grown firm roots through the happiest and most challenging of times and life situations. One of those endearing friends is Sue. We have been friends for well over thirty years and are now more like sisters.

I appreciate her out-of-the-box way of seeing this world and her passionate love for her family. I admire her curiosity, courage and zest for life. When deemed necessary, she also has an ability to tell it like it is to your face—always an important trait to have in a true friend.

Our conversations are usually centered on our families' activities, projects we are currently creating and future goals we are forming. Those exchanges are also liberally sprinkled with good-natured humor, lots of lighthearted laughter and a bit of playful teasing.

One day in mid-February, I was walking along the beach with Sue. As we walked together in the late afternoon our thoughts drifted over to the topic of the troubled economy and some of the concerns that were associated with it.

I clearly understood if we continued this conversation we would create more of those problems. Because I hold both of us in such high regard, I suggested we focus our attentions on a different subject if that would be all right with her. She agreed and we began exploring another topic.

I shared with Sue that I was experimenting with something very important to me. I had deliberately chosen to learn and master drawing to me only harmonious relationships in everything that touched my life. That desire also included creating what I would like to experience in my financial world. And, I was taking bold steps to form exactly what I desired in that arena.

In fact, I was actively releasing any financial discord in my life so I could purposefully experience something better. I also clearly understood that speaking about and listening to economic woes would only bring financial problems to me and anyone else that was participating in that conversation.

Since both Sue and I were such rapid creators I understood we could immediately draw to us more of what we were discussing that day.

With that clear eternal law in the forefront of my mind, I excitedly told her about something I had recently been reminded of that could rapidly draw to any of us what we preferred when it came to financial well-being.

### Releasing Distractions

The following are some of the key points we discussed that day:

The first steps to begin drawing financial harmony into our lives is to immediately turn off the news or radio and let go of reading the newspaper whenever we realize they are promoting negative, discouraging, inflammatory or contentious dialogues.

Why is it important we take such deliberate actions?

Because these sources of entertainment or information are often just distractions from the goals we would like to reach. In fact, they are a waste of our precious time and valuable energy.

It is also very important that we release any inclination to listen to or participate in conversations that are negative, gossip-ridden or judgmental. Those conversations have the ability to indoctrinate us again and again with negativity that create even more of what we prefer to eliminate from our world.

> **Note:** How do you feel during and after a negative conversation? Do you feel drained and more discouraged than you did before you began your visit? Those experiences have less than zero benefit for you and the people you are interacting with. The words you and they are speaking are not worthy of anyone's time or energy. They throw you out of the center of your peaceful, calm hurricane. Commit today to only participate in uplifting, encouraging, brainstorming-for-wonderful-possibilities type of conversations.

### Creating Our Preferences

I then went on to share what I had been teaching some of my clients. It was more information about eternal laws and the Teams we each have.

Simply put I said, "It is as easy for Them to create a button for us as it is for Them to create $100,000. It takes the same time and eternal laws as well as the same energy and Power."

Sue began to laugh and jokingly said, "OK then, how about this? How about you and I both create $100,000 and we will split it!"

Then I boldly bantered back to her playful suggestion, "Screw splitting the $100,000! How about you create $100,000 and I create $100,000 and we'll each take it home?"

We both laughed at what initially appeared as a pie-in-the-sky plan.

Now anyone that truly knows my friend knows that she is not one to put on airs. Nor is she one to be driven in the pursuit of great financial wealth. Yet, she is always blessed to see whatever she gives her attention to come into her life.

Actually, we could have united with one another and commanded that goal to form, but I knew Sue was already a powerful creator. She needed no assistance from me. This fact was obvious because of the constant happiness and abundance that surrounded her.

I was certain that she was already very connected to her team and was not in need of or desiring $100,000 in the first place. After all, it was just a whimsical little conversation at the end of a long day.

However, during our conversation something shifted inside of me. I acknowledged to Sue that initially this conversation seemed only entertaining—but I literally believed and more importantly felt the reality of those statements. In fact I was so certain of their powerful truth that I was going to go home and create that $100,000!

We soon finished our visit as we continued to enjoy the stroll in the sand while the sun set during the early balmy evening. Overall, the weekend was relaxing, enlightening and much appreciated. Sue and I, along with our husbands, enjoyed every moment of it. Shortly thereafter, we all returned to our separate homes in Tucson.

## "Send Millions Easily and Quickly Now!"

When I got home, I went to my Team and requested a meeting. I asked them to forget about the $100,000. "Send millions!" I requested. "Send millions easily and quickly now, please!"

I clearly could envision a particular financial situation I had deliberately chosen to change being strengthened by those funds cascading into the bank as my chest swelled with a familiar warm, expanding feeling of Enthusiasm. That feeling indicated to me that my request had been heard and was now being organized and granted.

I was also exceedingly excited because I understood that this shift in financial abundance would positively affect hundreds of people and their families.

Six weeks later on the last day in March, the first million arrived. At the end of April, the second million arrived!

I'm sharing these facts with you not to brag but to give an actual example of what is available to each one of us. These eternal laws are real. They actually work and those who created this world are willing to provide these same blessings to you!

When I was requesting this change in this financial situation I sent out my appeal and let go of how it was to be accomplished. I completely trusted that all concerned would be cared for.

I held on to those feelings of confidence and excitement about the situation being created. I also knew the evidence of this transformation was now being organized for us and was swiftly coming into our lives. Each time this subject came to my mind, my whole body would resound with that reaffirming amazing feeling.

Notice that this meeting with my Team was held only one time regarding this subject and my requests about my preferences concerning the changes to this financial shift were also asked only once during those conversations.

I did not beg, plead, yearn, remind, force, obsess, calculate, worry or fear while I created this request. Those actions would have moved me into a place of darkness, confusion and lack plus disbelief that the answer to my request was even possible.

Instead, I felt a certain active faith and belief, a kind of assured *knowing*, free of any wavering that the desire of my heart was heard and was rapidly being formed.

Our supportive creative Partners that assist us, as we collectively form our worlds, have perfect hearing and memory. In fact, they already know our desires before we ever utter a word to them.

Whenever you are creating your world, remember these Beings exist in sheer abundance! If you momentarily lose your verve and confidence in your ability to use your birthright to command your world, stop and regroup. Step quickly back into the light and build upon those wonderful assuring thoughts, visualizations, words and feelings that continue to more perfectly connect you to your Divine Source. That reconnection will empower you and move forward the desires of your soul.

## TAKE ACTION!

**If you are experiencing money woes, notice what you are thinking, feeling, envisioning, talking about and listening to that has to do with the subject of money. What are you posting and reading about on internet sites? Whatever you give your attention to WILL multiply. If you continually feel you have**

a lack of money and financial resources, you will continue to experience that lack.

Begin *NOW* to notice how profoundly rich you truly are and express sincere appreciation for all your blessings. *TURN OFF* negative news, radio, TV and the internet as soon as it begins to slide into discouraging topics in *ANY* of their forms. Focus on what you would *LOVE* to create in your life. Keep money in the same perspective as everything else you would enjoy receiving in your life. It will naturally flow in just like everything else you purposefully create!

# ~ *Green Cars* ~

A few of years ago I started thinking about getting a couple of *green cars.* You know the kind that I mean—cars that are environmentally friendly and energy efficient. I reasoned that *someday,* when we replaced the cars we had, I preferred to move in that direction.

At the time we had three sound vehicles to drive, which met our personal desires, and a fleet of trucks and cars that were used at our messenger service company.

I understood the technology for these new green cars could benefit from some further refining. I realized I preferred that a sufficient amount of testing be done to further develop the product before we actually purchased any of those cars.

I also thought I would love to have their prices reduced. I remembered how the first digital watches initially cost a lot of money to purchase but now they can be bought for 99 cents at any drug or dollar store. With that idea in my mind, I desired that before we made a purchase, the prices of green cars would become more reasonable.

## Someday Forming Into Now

Remember, when you ask for something to come to you in the form of *someday* it remains in your future until you call it into the present. So the purchase of any new vehicles remained in my someday until more of my specific desires could be dialed into my present world. However, if the subject came to mind, I continued to feel Enthusiastic and excited about the fact that this goal was now being organized and formed prior to it being brought into my world.

In September, I started thinking once again about green cars. I remembered the preference I had expressed previously and allowed my excitement for that attainable goal to continue building within me.

Then in January, my oldest son started doing what we called "Hot Shot" deliveries around the United States for a logistics company. He was using our Ford Excursion and on occasion one of our trailers, as well. The deliveries were starting to come in pretty rapidly and sometimes the requests overlapped one another. Soon, Ron and I started talking about purchasing more vehicles.

By mid March, I went to Ron and told him I felt it was now time to buy a new automobile or two. I shifted the *someday* into our *now*. I told him that it would be great if we bought something *green*.

I personally didn't know how we would come up with the funds for these purchases. I had given zero attention or energy to researching this subject. I had not even earmarked any monies for these vehicles. But I wasn't at all worried or concerned about how this would be accomplished.

Instead of focusing on those distractions, I simply allowed myself to feel elated about the reality of this idea now coming into our lives. In fact, I suggested to Ron that it would be fine with me if my Lexus convertible, which was already paid for, was traded in for one of the green vehicles.

I didn't feel any pangs of sorrow or sacrifice about letting go of my beautiful personal car. I just stayed revved up with my delight and anticipation about the new adventure!

I openly, without any reservations, sent those feelings out and fully expected to receive something wonderful to quickly and easily come into our lives. Two weeks later, on the first day of April, the green cars began to arrive. That evening my husband drove home in a Mercedes Benz. AMAZING!

We also began receiving Fords, Chevrolets, Toyotas, Hondas, Volkswagens... As I write, we have received forty-five vehicles and are in the process of receiving another thirty-six..

As it turns out, neither we nor the company had to pay a cent for any of those forty-five cars! The business is realizing a considerable savings by having these cars and it is also benefiting from the reduced amount of fuel that the green cars require.

### Where Did These Cars Come From?

These cars are a result of a research grant from the Department of Energy; the grantee is responsible for testing green cars on a large scale. We are some of the people chosen to test them. One of our requirements is to put one hundred and sixty thousand miles on each of those vehicles. Our employees are now driving around in brand new green cars!

I continue to feel amazement and appreciation every time I see one of those cars and remember the simple steps I took to provide my portion of this creative process: I received a thought to go green with my next vehicle. I agreed with that goal and added only two details: reduce the price and have them go through more testing. I got excited about this creative plan and reinforced those thoughts, visions and feelings every time that goal came back to my attention (which was only three times in an entire year!).

This is my Team's response to my request:

• How would you like the price to be reduced to zero?

• Would you also like to provide the avenue for the testing?

• Would you be interested in 45 cars instead of one or two?

My answer was a resounding, "Yes!" to each of those questions.

### Adding the Bells and Whistles

Not only do our Teams provide us with our exact requests, they also add the bells and whistles.

At the start, I was just picturing a few green vehicles for the little Hot Shot delivery service. I hadn't thought about it being for the entire messenger service.

What amazes me continually is the fact that we are able to create with Beings that dwell in a place of profound plenty. They are prepared to continually pour out that wealth and prosperity upon us.

### Creating With Others

I became curious about how this amazing blessing actually formed for us. So, I decided to do some research on how it all came together. I found that unbeknownst to me, at the time I was excitedly picturing and feeling my way toward allowing the green cars to come into our lives, I was actually creating with others.

Our requests were being morphed, organized and developed for us.

This is what I discovered:

- Someone had received a research grant and desired to find people to test green cars. These people had to meet specific criteria and maintain certain requirements throughout the period of the experiment.

- A woman working for the individual running the project saw our company a year before I felt that "whisp" while she was waiting for some friends. She had noticed how well-maintained our fleet was and that we had an onsite service center. She thought that *someday*, if the company they currently were working with were no longer able to preform these services, she would like to contact us to test cars for her company.

- One of the managers in our business used to test drive cars over a five state area when he lived in Nevada. He began wondering if any companies still utilized that type of service and started researching those possibilities.

- In January, my sister-in-law started seeing green cars that were being used to make deliveries in Dallas, Texas and suggested to her husband that our company should go green with our delivery cars.

- Then her husband, Ron's brother, started thinking about green cars as well. He contacted my husband and visited with him about that possibility.

All this thinking and talking about our future preferences of *someday* having green cars to drive, was being created in spirit when each individual began engaging in those thought processes.

The more we all thought about it, the more detail and perfection was designed into the plan as it was created. It didn't matter that the majority of us had never spoken to each other about our personal preferences. It didn't matter that many of us had not even met one another before.

Because I was working out of the country at the time most of this was being created, I didn't know about any of this background information until after we started receiving green cars!

What mattered was that we were each sending out our requests and those requests were being granted. They were being readied to bring us together as soon as we would allow them to come into our physical existence.

Meanwhile, our souls were communicating with one another and our Teams were coordinating with us and with the other Teams to orchestrate all the necessary details while adding some of their own. They really love creating with us. It is a lot of fun for them.

All of this swirling, creating and morphing of our united desires continued to form into a fever pitch until they were at last called into our *now* world! At that point, we were all prepared to fully receive these opportunities and we stretched out our arms to allow them in.

By the way, we're the ones who unleashed those floodgates. That's the knock and the door will be opened part of the, *"Ask and it is given, seek and you will find, knock and the door will be opened"* scripture.

Remember, the handle of the door is on our side, it is always unlocked and we are the ones who open it! Our Teams are always ready and prepared to pour out our blessings when we are ready to receive them.

## Go Ahead and Think BIG!

When people see all of these amazing cars and hear the story of how they materialized in our lives their response is, "How can I drive one of those cars?" and "We have been thinking way too small!"

Some thoughts about thinking way too small: Feeling blinded or having a micro vision view of the situations surrounding us is what we often encounter when we let go of purposefully remaining fully connected to our creative Powers. We limit our dreams and expectations. We shut ourselves down to the stretching and expanding that is truly ours to enjoy during this life experience.

Now, I clearly understand it is perfectly all right to be wealthy, yet I am definitely not driven by amassing riches and having lots of material things. I'm not even driving these cars on a daily basis. In fact, I have driven these cars less than a handful of times.

My joy comes from creating with my Team. Just knowing I am never alone and will always have my desires met brings me comfort and peace. I am keenly aware of our eternal mutual love, devotion and affection for one another. Keep remembering:

*The abundance and profound success in all we do together is just part of what naturally comes to us while we are playing with this group!*

If you would like to experience these kinds of miracles, start your process right where you are now. Start feeling appreciation for the blessings you currently have and actively use the information that is being provided for you in this book. Allow this knowledge to sprout and increase within you each day.

## Appreciate the Blessings You Now Have

Allow yourself to fully acknowledge and appreciate the many blessings you now have in your life so you can open up your soul to receive more!

I lived in a gray Studebaker Lark car during my senior year of high school. Sometimes I would stay with friends or in extended family members' homes. Even though I lived mainly out of a car, I felt at peace and very happy. While I was living in my car, I successfully worked at a five-and-dime store and was on the Honor Roll in school.

During that time, I was very appreciative and thankful for kindness of others and the life I lived. I looked forward with great anticipation to the life that was swiftly coming my way. I visualized what it would be like and felt a thrill about how blessed I was. I started living as if I was already that woman and in just over a year, I *was* her!

The point I'm sharing here is that you have the Power to freely release any resistance to any limits in your life experience and personal abilities. Choose *now* to enjoy continual daily happiness. Fully embrace your truth:

*Remember that deep, long-lasting feelings of happiness and success are not measured by the things you have acquired or the wealth you have gained. It comes from within.*

*Also: You are created by the Divine who adore you and enjoy having a personal relationship with you always.*

## TAKE ACTION!

BE BOLD!! Go ahead, be deeply appreciative of the blessings you now have. Think about creating BIG experiences in your life. It is actually fun!

Allow your most joy-filled visions and feelings to become fully engaged with those thoughts. Know that you are connecting to that loving eternal source that creates each and every wonderful experience in all of existence. Let those feelings flood your entire body until all your cells are resounding with that bliss and excitement.

Command your creations into your now world. Open to expectantly embrace your blessings. Then enjoy watching those opportunities swiftly come into your world! Fully receive, appreciate and enjoy them while also giving thanks.

# ~ *Creating Your Mindset of Miracles* ~

Family, friends and clients will often call or come to me and express their sincere thanks for the wonderful experiences they are now having in their lives. I always clarify to them that I am not the one who provided those opportunities for them. It is they who asked for and allowed themselves to receive and activate a personal relationship—an At-One-Ment—with the Divine.

I then tell them to go back and flood themselves with thanksgiving for the unified creative process they and their Team have enjoyed and encourage them to send out those grateful feelings to Those who created them.

Always remember *I will never be* the pivotal person that will cause you to fully exercise your ability to powerfully and effectively create with the Divine. Nor will any other mortal you know.

Yes, I may encourage and help assist you in your reawakening and in getting restarted in a direction you prefer as you gain experience and learn how to harmonize your life with others. But I am not the one actively going through *your* process. I'm not on that committee.

Only *you* can ultimately open up and discover your personal preferences, desires and life mission. You alone allow those satisfying eternal unions to form between you and your Team. They consistently support you while you build your confidence in being able to more effectively harness and wield that mighty Power to create.

Each of us have always had the ability to initiate and strengthen those everlasting relationships as we quiet ourselves and allow our personal faith to become activated. In the same way, I remembered and purposefully began my own first adventures here when I pondered the word *eternity*.

You don't have to search for a guru, pay lots of money, peruse volumes of books, unplug from the world, twist yourself into a pretzel or climb to the highest mountain top. Your search for your personal *Mindset of Miracles* begins right where you are now. Look with curiosity into your own soul. All your answers can be discovered there.

Best wishes on your journey!

# Part III. The Conclusion of
## *Mindset of Miracles*

Congratulations! You have completed the main portion of this book and are now in the homestretch. The last base is within your reach! Your Team is there to greet you at home plate and is applauding your progress. The rest of us are heartily cheering you on from the sidelines! You are so far ahead of the ball, you don't even have to slide!

# ~ *Wrapping It Up* ~

Okay, time to gather everything up and review the simple yet powerful information contained in these pages. Go ahead and ***throw your shirt into the game of life!*** Allow yourself to actively participate in creating exactly what you prefer.

Remember *you* are in the driver's seat of your vehicle, steering the wheel in the direction *you* choose. You are able to change your life, make course adjustments and head in a different direction at *anytime.* Here is your key…turn on your creative engine! Put it in gear and get going!

Always begin and end your day by doing something to prepare your vessel or body. ***Pondering*** and ***praying*** are examples of this. ***Tapping*** and ***meditation*** are also powerful preparations for you day and night as are ***Chinese Bed Exercises*** and ***Baguazhagn***.

If you would like to view some videos of these simple yet powerful life skills, go to my website, **www.PamelaAnnEzell.com**.

Meditate and ponder regularly. It doesn't require a lot of time but it does help your *vessel* or body be better prepared to receive what you desire. In fact, draw your day out in meditation. Before you take *any action,* prepare your vessel so you will more rapidly create what you prefer.

Also, support your body with proper food, rest and exercise.

When you first begin to feel ill, take charge and release that distracting discomfort. I personally use and highly recommend doTERRA oils. Because I use them proactively I am rarely ill. If I barely feel like I am catching something I begin using the French intensive method and within hours (sometimes minutes) I'm completely well. I highly recommend these certified pure essential oils.

Contact me on my website, email or by phone to learn more (my contact information is included at the beginning and end of this book) Look for my next book, ***Preparing The Vessel.*** to learn more valuable information about caring for your body. Also scan through my website to get an early jump on this information.

### Creating Your Road Map for Life

If you still haven't created your "**Road Map for Life**" from the chapter "Reconnecting to Your Team," read the instructions and quickly write up your three-page plan. To assist you, there are three pages included in this book right after this chapter. Have fun with this enjoyable process!

What three things would you love to release? What three things would you love to create? Put those creative ideas into action today.

### Turn Off Everything that Sabotages You

Many distractions come from the TV, radio, newspapers, gossip, emails, internet, community commentaries, negative thoughts and politics. They also can be experienced in discouraging and frustrating conversations or negative and passionate feelings. Even religious viewpoints may be distracting if they put down others outside their faith or promote creating any separation between you and your eternal brothers and sisters.

Become more aware of what you have been allowing into your daily life. Ask:

*"What am I thinking, feeling, envisioning, speaking, listening to, reading about, writing, posting and observing?"*

You will bring more of the same to you and those participating with you.

## Your Feelings Are Your Perfect Guides…Keep Turning Toward a Better Feeling Place!

From time to time throughout your day ask yourself this question, *"How am I feeling now?"*

If you recognize that you are participating in destructive, negative or discouraging situations, stop and head off in a better feeling direction!

Your thoughts, words, and feelings have *power!* So take *action.* Release lack, need and want. ***Believe*** it is possible to for you to allow these changes to take place in your life.

## Ask, Nothing Wavering, and It Will Be Given

Let any distractions of pride, fear, envy, embarrassment or ego flow quickly and easily out of you. These diversions diminish your ability to fully connect to your Team and your creative Powers. Ask your requests free of hesitation. Your Team will answer you. Open up and receive your gifts. Then give thanks.

*If you experience negative thoughts and feelings, you can turn the page. If discouraging thoughts and feelings return, TURN THE PAGE AGAIN!*

If these unhappy situations continue, use Tapping, pondering, meditation and prayer to assist you in releasing them. Focus your thoughts, feelings, energies and Powers on what *you* prefer to experience now.

Keep your goals squarely in your sights. Hold onto your playful, excited feelings and joyfully and expectantly open up to allow these blessings to enter your life. Watch them *easily and quickly come to you.* Everything else will diminish in size and ultimately leave you.

Release the trauma, fear, lack, health concerns and addictions stored in your body by employing the same supportive exercises mentioned above.

Stop running from your concerns and face them. You will soon master those opportunities for learning. Embrace change. Allow yourself to continually progress in life. **Being able to consistently progress is a worthwhile goal.**

### Create What You Prefer NOW!

Keep those carefree, trusting, and childlike feelings alive inside you. Keep it simple and fun. Allow balance. Savor your life. Be grateful, thankful and appreciative for all your blessings and look forward with great anticipation to the blessings that are swiftly coming to you now.

### Draw Only Harmonious Relationships

Identify anyone or anything with whom you disagree. Note any negative reaction you may harbor inside your soul. Release those blockages. Allow yourself to recognize traits or attributes you prefer to experience with people or situations in your life. Say to yourself, while including a genuine *feeling* and desire for this to be activated within you:

*"More of this please in my life (or our lives) now! Thank you!"*

View life from the *big picture* perspective. Believe, **believe**, ***BELIEVE*** that these shifts in your relationships are indeed possible. Get a little thrill when you think about these changes that are now beginning to take shape. Start looking for that evidence and trust that you now have the ability to create positive relationships. This is your truth. Have fun with this activity and enjoy becoming one with everyone and everything that touches your life.

### Send an Invitation from One Soul to Another

Ask others to participate with you in *mutually uplifting* activities by sending an invitation from your soul to their souls.

Our ability to more fully enjoy every aspect of our lives while *powerfully* creating is greatly influenced by this fact:

***If I am genuinely one with my fellow human beings, then I can become more one with the Divine.***

From time to time ask yourself these questions:

- **How am I feeling now?** Remember your feelings are your perfect guides.

- **Am I creating my world,** destroying my world or recreating the same world again?

- **Am I floating my boat** merrily down the stream of life because this life is but a dream?

- **Am I centered** in the peace and calm of my hurricane with clarity of mind?

Depending on your answers, take action to allow the change you desire, which will in turn improve your feelings and experiences. If you realize you have been creating the same world over and over, or are caught in an *eddy* and have a desire to stop the mounting chaos and drama, ask these questions:

*"What am I to learn from this experience? How can this experience be for my good?"*

Recall that an eddy is usually only a gentle whirlpool. You can easily paddle or swim your way out of it and head downstream again! Besides, all experiences are ultimately created for your good. And you are the one who requested the experience so you can learn and grow. Relax. Release any blockages and resistance to what you desire to learn. Allow the knowledge, skills and mastery of the situation to flow readily into you.

You have the Power to connect with your Team and create in this manner. You have, and always will have, the Power to unite with them if that is your desire. Simply follow the steps to allow that union to form. In fact, ponder this:

*It is my ETERNAL BIRTHRIGHT to connect with and create through the Source that formed me!*

### Release Four Letter Words

Quickly release all four-letter words from your life. Words such as: *work, hard, fear, help, make, dumb, pain, need, want, hate...*

Also release other words that feel like four letter words like: *try, force, rescue, sacrifice, doubt, discouragement, should, worry,* and *long suffering*...

Purposefully draw into your life uplifting, empowering, creative words such as: *enthusiasm, fun, joy, well-being, trust, faith, humor, honor, genuine, playful, happy, abundance, exhilaration, peace, hope, like,* and *love*. Even though *hope, like* and *love* are four letter words, they are definitely keepers! So, remember:

***Your words have the power and ability to command your world. Chose them wisely!***

Here are some examples of what you can think and say with those powerful words:

**I desire to receive... I prefer to create... I choose to allow... I would love to... I would like to... I feel passionate about...**

***Remember to utilize and feel the key word Enthusiasm (God inspiring within) and the action feeling that is associated with it!***

### Become an Honorable Being!

Allow yourself to search deeply within and ferret out any vestige of dishonor or deceit in your social, professional or personal life (including little white lies). Rapidly release those traits from your soul so you can quickly move forward and command your world.

***Be a being filled with integrity and honor. Then even the elements will respond to your requests!***

## MONEY MONEY MONEY!

It is perfectly all right to think **BIG** and to receive abundance as well! How would skyscrapers or intricate highways or bridges ever have been built if we pigeonholed our dreams and our financial well-being? How would we have been able to create all the technology we have today?

It is also wonderful to think *small*. Take pleasure in opening to your ability to find lost keys, the perfect parking space or all green lights as you travel across town. Besides, the truth is:

***There is plenty of money and more for everyone!***

Keep your focused beliefs, thoughts and feelings. Open bank accounts and excitedly visualize the money swiftly flowing into them. Allow them to be filled. It is how you choose to use your wealth that determines if it will be a curse or a gift for you and those who touch your life; you decide how your future will unfold.

Continue to picture everything happening *now!* If you envision your creations coming someday, they will always remain in *someday* and will not come into your reality until you command them into your *now* by your words thoughts and excited passionate *feelings!* Let go of how they will form. Just allow them to come. Think, picture, speak and feel these words:

***"No matter how BIG or small, I will embrace my dreams or preferences and allow them to come forth now!"***

Form a habit of saying to yourself when you start to feel stressed about not having enough time, help or money:

***"I have plenty of time (help, money, love, understanding…) and more to accomplish whatever I desire today."***

Meaningfully speak that sentence a few times while taking some deep breaths. Allow a profound internal shift within your body. *Feel* the stress completely leave you and a soothing balm of peace flow into your body. Next, relax your being while you observe something joyful entering into the equation. Then time (help, money…) will expand to fit the situation at hand. Somehow, everything will just smooth out.

### Your Personal Happiness

Have you known people with very little financial or physical well-being yet they continually maintained a happy grateful countenance? Or have you ever noticed someone that appeared to have every blessing and opportunity heaven and earth could provide and yet they were still unhappy?

Your truth is: no one and nothing can take away your happiness. Conversely, no one and nothing can provide you with your happiness. You are the one in charge of creating those feelings or diminishing those feelings! Not even the Divine will interfere with your ability to choose what you desire to experience.

Remember this freeing and empowering way of living:

*"I am completely in charge of my happiness or unhappiness. I can easily and quickly change the course of my life's direction at any moment."*

You have the ability to be guided and comforted by your Team, and to receive inspiration from Them. They know all things past, present and future and can reveal that knowledge to you at any time. Prepare your soul daily—morning and evening—and allow yourself to receive that information.

If you would like to remember how to experience this more abundantly in your life, try experimenting with the following:

1. **Allow yourself to deeply love, appreciate and accept everything about yourself.** Be patient and gentle with yourself and all others. Live as clean, authentic, honest, honorable, kindly, and thankful a life *as you are able*. That is sufficient.

2. **Awaken and become fully *alive*! SHOW UP FOR YOUR LIFE! Take time to ponder, meditate and pray with every cell of your body. Feel your thoughts, desires and gratitude as you send them out.**

3. **Be attentive to the thoughts and feelings you are receiving. DO NOT DISCOUNT THEM!** They are not the wild imaginings of your mind. *Listen to* and *feel* the instructions being given to you. Then **act** upon what you are inspired to do.

> Notice the warm burning in your chest, the thrill in your body. Feel the electrical charge when you connect to your Team. Your feelings are always your unwavering guides. They will not fail you. Soon you will develop the ability to trust in what is revealed to you. Feel yourself drawing near to your personal eternal support system.

4. **Your Team's reply is sometimes ushered in through the *Still Small Voice*. It is often as soft as the sound of a whisper.** Mike, a client and friend of mine, refers to them as "whisps." The more you allow yourself to trust in your Team and allow this information into your being, the more easily you will be able to recognize it.

When you first seek to hear this voice it may sound as distant as a weak radio signal but it will get stronger as *you* drive closer to the source, or as *you* dial in more precisely in to the channel. The information is always there. *You* are the one that controls your ability to hear it.

5. **Remember to always give thanks** for questions that are answered and blessings that are received. As a result of those appreciative actions, you will remain better connected to your Team and your relationship will continue to be strengthened.

Continue to focus on your goals and keep remembering these truths that have already been revealed to you:

*The source you seek to connect with sends only uplifting, positive information and support.*

In other words, if you are not feeling positive and uplifted, you are not connected to the Divine and are trying to go it alone without your supportive Team to assist you!

*Your Team resides in a place of continual abundance and is prepared to pour that bounty upon you as soon as you open the floodgates.*

Your Team is the best source of information that is specifically created for you. Start asking Them for help. They will respond to your exact request and even add some extra bells and whistles of their own!

If you become quiet and allow yourself to think, visualize, hear and feel your way through your world while connected to the Divine, you will receive more experiences as you recognize this gift. You will also become more confident and certain that your

Team is guiding you. *This comfort will always be available for you.*

## You Were Created to Experience Joy!

I can't help but chuckle when my family, friends and clients call me up and exclaim, "Pam, this is real! These Powers really do exist and work!" They also tell me how continuously happy they feel. In fact, this is the happiest time they have experienced in their lives.

I had been training a man for several months last fall. He was enjoying lots of breakthroughs in understanding, but very little progress in bringing into his physical world the desires of his heart.

Then one day I just flat out asked him:

**"Are you putting into *action* the information you are learning?"**

I went on to share with him that we can go through the motions in life. We can observe others and the amazing things they are doing. We can read, study, talk, learn, philosophize and pontificate about our desires to have miraculous experiences and adventures in our lives, but we will remain stuck in the same place until we *actively put this faith and knowledge into motion!*

Somehow, he finally just relaxed and let go of his personal struggle within his own soul and allowed himself to open up to his truth. He saw that he was worthy of receiving all the blessings and opportunities he desired. He internalized and put into action the eternal treasures he had been amassing over the last couple of months. Almost instantly, he began to see evidence of his own sweet, satisfying, miraculous experiences.

He recently updated me about his adventures and excitedly told me that he had done more in the last four months to create and live what he desired than he had previously done in the last twenty years! Soon he was joining the throng. His eyes were bright with energy and happy anticipation as he excitedly spoke to me one morning, "Pam, this is real! These Powers actually do work!"

"Yes, they are!" I replied with a smile.

Now that you have completed this book, what is next? You can be one of the many who have also experienced the tangible and real results of these simple teachings and powerful laws.

## TAKE ACTION!

**Apply what you've learned. Here's your Mindset of Miracles wrapped up with a bow:**

- **Prepare your vessel or body morning and evening (before you take any action!).**

- **Draw to you only harmonious relationships. Accept yourself. Become one with others.**

- **Create your "Road Map for Life." Write the details as they flow easily into your mind.**

- **Connect to your Team. Open up to that feeling of Enthusiasm! Listen to your whisps.**

- **Activate your Divine Powers. Release any doubt or wavering. Ask for your desires now!**

- **BELIEVE you can have these blessings in your life. Engage every cell of your body.**

- Give thanks. "More of this now, please. Thanks." Blessings are now forming in spirit.

- Think, Visualize, Listen and FEEL. Your dreams and goals are organizing and coming!

- HOLD ON TO YOUR PASIONATE FEELINGS. They drive your desires into reality!

- Open up. Look and listen for your answers. Let your blessings and miracles pour in.

- Fully receive, accept and enjoy your answers. Take hold of them when they come.

- Give thanks again! Stay open and receptive with feelings of appreciation and gratitude.

- Remember, HAVE FUN! You were created to have abundant joy in this life!

- When you have accomplished your goals, hegin again and create new adventures!

Start creating your personal
*Mindset of Miracles*
today.

# ~ Creating Your Roadmap for Life ~

Remember to *handwrite* your inspired responses on paper. Relax…let go of everything else and allow these thoughts to easily and quickly flow out onto these pages. Have fun.

**Page One:** Describe simple, happy, feel-good stuff that has brought you joy as if you were free of any concern or care in the world. Go ahead and fill up this page with what first comes to you.

Now say with genuine feeling: "More experiences like these in my life NOW Please. Thank You!" Let your feelings of Enthusiasm and appreciation grow. Those increased feelings will help you know when you are more fully connected to your Team.

**Page Two:** My Kind of People. Fill this page with the names and descriptions of the individuals who have been uplifting to you, supportive and understanding of you, or of people who have traits you admire. Some might be complete strangers who showed an unexpected kindness. Describe those traits or kindnesses.

Now say with genuine feeling: "More people and experiences like this in my life now, please. More of this in all of our lives now. Thank you!" Let your feelings of gratitude grow. These increased feelings of becoming one with everything and everyone will help you draw to you only harmonious relationships with all that touches your world!

**Page   Three::** Describe the creations and details of what you purposefully choose to create and receive in your life. It is perfectly all right to think BIG. Go ahead, be bold and even put a date on it!

Now say with genuine feeling, "Please allow this into my life now. I feel passionate about it. Thank you!" HOLD ON TO YOUR FEELINGS OF EXCITED ANTICIPATION whenever you think and envision what you desire to create in your world *NOW.* Activate every cell in your body. This is your *Truth.*

# ~ *Acknowledgements* ~

My thanks go out to all who have participated with me in creating this book. Those who top the longest list are all the individuals, family, friends, acquaintances and strangers who interacted with me as I gathered my experiences and stories while reawakening to these eternal truths.

I'm grateful for all my amazing clients. Our time together has been and continues to be a mutually uplifting and inspiring experience.

I also appreciate these individuals for their consistent friendship and support:

Jan Nelson, Sue Trader and Sandee Adragna for the many years of love, patience and honest support that we have extended to one another. These women are truly my eternal sisters in every sense of the word.

Michael Claridge, my adopted younger brother, for his time, creativity, patience, talent, computer skills and friendship.

Amber Topping, Autumn Topping, Cara LaForge, Jason Ezell, Katie Stirling, Missy Carter and Rebecca Lane for their support, candid feedback and hours of editing.

Enrique Daniel Acereto, Martha Hadley, Sandra Bernal, Tricia Chism and Rita Ward for their time in previewing the book and giving feedback along with the other individuals, whose names I do not know, that pre-read this book prior to it being released to the public.

Fern Busby Evans—my new mom, Hélène Gaudard-Castillo, Jashin and Tanya Howell, Marcia Farnsworth, Nina Joy and Bracken Cherry, The Claridge Family, the Thathi Family, Sue Fisher, and all the Trejo Girlies who encouraged, supported and believed in me.

Michael Lane for his many years of consistent friendship, photography skills and ever-ready willingness to go to lunch with Ronnie and me.

Our son, Abraham Yepez, his sweet wife Adriana and their sons who kept our home filled with love and laughter while I wrote and edited this book. They were a direct answer to our prayers during this special time and we were the answer to their prayers.

And finally, I am thankful for the inspiring love and support of the Divine—my patient, kindhearted, playful Team and the transforming Power that formed this world for our personal experience and joy. They are the first and the last that are acknowledged in this book and the reason it was created…thank you.

# ~ *About the Author* ~

Pamela Ann Ezell is a powerful inspired mentor that teaches others how to command their world with exactness and even put a date on it!

That bold statement is backed by hundreds of stories and people who have witnessed these truths. They too have learned how to activate in their daily lives the simple eternal laws that she has taught them.

From her personal experience of over sixty years, she understands how to triumph over the most crippling effects of life's challenges and then go forth to live a happy satisfying joy filled adventure.

This award winning speaker and author is also a native Tucsonan and Renaissance Woman, Entrepreneur, Artist, Published Designer, Patented Inventor, Community Leader and more. She happily lives what she teaches.

In her past professional life, she developed and ran only successful businesses. She is also one of the principals in the development of nationally and internationally known *EZ Messenger* with her husband Ron. When the economics of the country were faltering, they stayed focused on their goals and dreams, then hired 100 people.

Pamela Ann and Ron have been married for more than forty years. They are the parents of four and have adopted numerous children into their hearts and family. They also enjoy their many grandchildren at their home in beautiful Arizona.

This nurturing woman is a gifted, compassionate, leader, consultant and friend. Those who have trained with her and grown to know her have also called her a Mother, Elder, Healer, Doña, Master, and Prophetess.

She knows that you too can receive this gift of prophecy for your personal and family life and for that which you are a steward over, such as your livelihood, professional life and community relationships.

In fact, if you are not having visions, revelations, healings and miraculous experiences on a regular basis, it is simply because you have not allowed yourself to activate your faith and connect to those who created you while applying these simple powerful eternal laws!

# ~ *Submit Your Story* ~

Come join this happy gathering of awakened people. Learn how to command your world by connecting to those who created you. Experiment with these eternal laws. Go ahead and take action. Enjoy the remarkable results of your deliberate creations. Then submit your stories. Pamela may even put them into one of her books! Also, look forward to reading these upcoming books:

## *Mini Miracles*
Short Stories of How Normal Ordinary People Are Living
Extraordinary Miraculous Lives

## *Mindset of Miracles for Everyone*
Inspirational Stories That Teach
How To Command Your Everyday World

## *Preparing the Vessel*
How to Heal and Prepare Your Body to Connect With The
Divine and Command Your World With Exactness

Contact her today at:

www.PamelaAnnEzell.com or **PamelaAnn@ezlightning.com.**
Like the *Pamela Ann Ezell* Facebook page,
Or Pamela Ann Ezell (@PamelaAnnEzell) on Twitter.
(520) 333-6015

Share your experiences with others and spread this good news!

Made in the USA
San Bernardino, CA
07 October 2013